The Other
A.Y. Jackson

The Other A.Y. Jackson

A MEMOIR

O.J. Firestone

McCLELLAND AND STEWART

The Canadian Publishers
McClelland and Stewart Limited
25 Hollinger Road
Toronto, Ontario M4B 3G2

0-7710-3148-3

Printed and bound in Canada
by John Deyell Company

CONTENTS

To Margaret

PREFACE

A. Y. Jackson was to become a kind of folk-hero during his lifetime. Many people knew him in the role of painter, and many more learned to admire his work. But few really got to know the man himself — creative, tenacious, and genial. This book is about that Jackson.

I had been struck by a passage in a review by Michael Ballantyne of *A. Y.'s Canada* in November 1968: "There are regrets in everyone's life, but looking at *A. Y.'s Canada* one of the things I know I will regret is never knowing Mr. Jackson and, more importantly, never having had the chance to roam through at least a small part of Canada with him."[1]

I realized then how lucky I had been to know Alec well. Most Canadians had not had that good fortune; one way of thanking Alec was to share with others my recollections about him over a twenty-year period.

I don't know anyone who fully understood Alec. His was a complex personality. There was a great deal more to him than could be gleaned from the non-personal conversations he preferred, but I got some insight into the personality that he hid so well behind the placid and friendly exterior.

After his move to Manotick in 1955 and to Ottawa in 1962, I learned much about Alec Jackson the man and A. Y. Jackson the artist. He had two personalities — one an outgoing, selfless, and modest man to whom most people responded warmly, the other the dedicated artist determined to achieve creative fulfilment whatever the cost, fiercely loyal to Canada, and scornful of small-minded people unable to see beyond their noses and share the wider horizons that were part of his life's vision. Even when he felt scornful, however, he rarely antagonized people or lost his temper. His good sense of humour and his chuckle softened the impact of many a critical remark.

I learned more about his art in those years (what he considered quality and what not), about his remarkable perseverance in meeting his own high standards even when it took him months to realize what he wanted to achieve, and about his desire not to leave paintings he considered mediocre to posterity.

He taught me more about the history of Canadian art in the last half-century than I learned from any other artist or from art catalogues, books, and critical reviews or from visiting retrospective exhibitions. He was a walking encyclopaedia, particularly about art during the interwar period, and he usually elaborated his stories with references to his own experience.

7

He was hesitant to say anything except the best about his fellow artists, and only as we became close friends would he on occasion comment that a colleague was "not particularly good" or was "still trying." In earlier years, though, he had been quite scornful of academic painters who insisted on remaining behind the times.

We shared many happy times, including celebrating some of his birthdays in our home. One of our amusing experiences was our visit to Alec's sister Kay in Rawden in the Quebec Laurentians — we got thoroughly lost.

We also had sad experiences together. When Alec had what was at first diagnosed as a stroke in April 1968 his life hung in the balance for days; he pulled through but was never the same afterward. I don't remember ever arguing with Alec, but I did get annoyed at him on occasion when for example, he wouldn't dress warmly enough on cold, blustery days and when he refused to consult a doctor even though he lay shivering with flu in his studio-apartment at 192 MacLaren Street. He avoided consulting a doctor whenever he could because he felt he was basically a healthy person who could shake off illnesses fairly quickly; this he did, most of the time.

I learned about his way of life, his thoughts and homespun philosophy, his attitude toward religion, and about his loneliness (which he never openly admitted). For all his easygoing manners and friendliness, he was a proud man for whom self-sufficiency was a virtue. He did not want anyone to feel sorry for him because he was unmarried, because he cooked his own meals, or because he bore illness alone. (He was sometimes comforted by his niece Naomi and in his later years was attended by his physician and friend Dr. Robert Starrs.)

Other than art, we discussed economics, politics, international affairs, and everyday occurrences. We talked about people, about history, the theatre and so on. He had a refreshingly open mind on economics in general — though on personal economics he could be quite stubborn. In politics he was a conservative and had little patience with politicians who made promises they did not keep; in international affairs, he had warm feelings for the British, admiration for the Americans, and many doubts about the French. One of the few times I saw Alec upset was in 1967 after Charles de Gaulle's shout of "Vive le Québec libre!"

He was disappointed that the United Nations was not doing a better job in narrowing the gap between the have and have-not nations or achieving a greater rapport between Western and Communist countries in those pre-détente days. Alec had a soft spot for the Russian people while maintaining a healthy scepticism about some of their leaders. During the 1960s he was quite friendly with Ivan Shpedko, the Soviet ambassador in Ottawa.

Alec could sometimes be persuaded to pursue a particular course — I urged his contribution to the debate about the Canadian flag, for example — but he was set in his ways and often would not listen. "I'll think about it," he would say, and in most instances that meant no. He responded to my questions in a kind and understanding way. He listened patiently to my discourses about economics and showed particular interest when I tried to establish a parallel between the world of art and the world of economics.

There was a certain formality he and I maintained even as our friendship grew. Although he addressed my wife, Isobel,* by her first name during the first eight years, he referred to me as Mr. Firestone. I in turn addressed him as Mr. Jackson. Most of his friends called him A.Y. or Alex. Early in 1962, he began to call me Jack and I would refer to him as Alec, the way my wife had been doing, and to simplify this narrative I use that name in stories of all the years I knew him.

For the past 10 years people from a number of fields have urged me to write down my experiences with Canadian artists. I demurred. It is one thing to write books on economics, the profession I have practised for thirty-five years; it is quite another to write about Canadian artists and their works. How could I write about a hobby and about friends, I asked myself, when the results would be compared with the professional work done by art historians and biographers much better equipped to deal with Canadian art than I?

Trained as a social scientist and humanist, I consider artists especially gifted people who contribute to the cultural enrichment of a nation and to the quality of life of its people. This is a different perspective than that of art historians and critics; they are more concerned with what the artist produces than in what motivates him, though some interpret what the artist meant and what motivation fed his creativity. Furthermore, these professionals can look objectively at art movements and their participants — they are trained to set things in a broader historical perspective. My impressions are personal, sporadic, and based on a limited period of experience.

I faced two problems — my recollections and my understanding of Alec as man and as artist.

When I had had a particularly interesting discussion with an artist, I would scribble some headings and file them with the correspondence between that artist and me. I did not keep a diary. When I was every so often called upon to make some remarks, such as at a birthday par-

---

*My wife, Isobel, acted as a gracious hostess on the many occasions when we entertained Alec at our house. Circumstances changed, and, after Alec passed away, we parted company.

ty, I would write out my comments and keep these notes. On a few occasions, with an artist's consent, I took down interviews verbatim. Some artists wrote their opinions on their own work to me, and I kept their letters. Sometimes an artist would give me notes about a fellow artist, as Arthur Lismer did when we talked about Alec. I also had four original tapes: two are of interviews with Alec in which I asked him to comment on his paintings in my collection — gifted to the Ontario Heritage Foundation in 1972 — and two record the proceedings of Alec's eighty-third and eighty-fifth birthday celebrations.

A good part of what I have to say is based on recollections, and the trouble with memory is that one forgets. Memories may not include the full story or may have been modified by the passage of time; they may not record exactly what was said or what was meant. And they are not very flexible: either one remembers or one does not.

In the narrative that follows, I have put in quotes some of Alec's comments, but frequently I do not recall the exact words he used. When I know we had discussed a subject but remember neither the words nor the gist of Alec's remarks, I have quoted from Alec's own writings or from those of his friends in the Group of Seven a passage reflecting the spirit of what Alec was trying to convey to me.

I would be the first to admit that Alec might have attached some other meaning than my interpretation to some of the things he said. There is, furthermore, a natural tendency to remember happy events better than sad ones. One sometimes remembers only what one wants to remember or forgets essentials and remembers only trivia. Memory can play tricks.

As a case in point, here are accounts by two people about the same topic, each of which may lead the reader to two different conclusions.

Alec told me that when he arrived in Toronto from Montreal after Lawren Harris had finished the Studio Building in 1914, he and Tom Thomson moved into the first studio together. They shared the monthly rent of $22. The event was also recorded in a magazine article[2] and in a book. Alec's niece Naomi repeated this version when she wrote in 1967 that "A.Y. had been the first occupant of the first studio in it [25 Severn Street] to be finished — #1, on the ground, which he shared with Tom Thomson for a brief but glorious period before World War I broke in upon that famous friendship."[3]

But in 1954, the same year that Alec's article appeared in *Mayfair* magazine, Lawren Harris wrote a brief essay for the catalogue of the Vancouver Art Gallery exhibition of the Group of Seven. Harris wrote: "We asked him [Tom Thomson] to occupy a studio, but because of his camping habits and his shy, retiring nature, a brand new studio did not appeal to him. Behind the studio building was an old broken-down shack. We made this habitable, put down a new floor, made the roof and walls watertight, built in a studio window, put in a stove, and Tom moved in. All of his well-known canvases were painted in it and it was his home until he died."[4] No reference here to Alec sharing a studio with Tom Thomson.

As it turned out, both narratives were correct — but one was more complete than the other. Alec explained thus: "After struggling along alone for a while after I left, he [Tom Thomson] had not been able to keep up the $22 rent and had moved into a wooden shack at the back. He fixed it up shipshape, lived there rent-free, and it was there that he painted all of his famous works."[5]

My second problem concerns some of the interpretations I offer about A.Y. Jackson. I have purposely refrained from including my views about the quality and meaning of his paintings, though I am a great admirer of his work. On occasion, I report comments Alec himself made about one or the other of his works and I have tried to set these in perspective.

As the years went by Alec and I developed a particularly close friendship. It was a meeting of the spirit — the artist and the social scientist. We had one thing in particular in common: we cared about people. Alec cared about the land and the people who make up Canada. I cared about society, the problems people face in making a living and improving the quality of life.

Still concerned about the limitations of recollection and of initial impression, I started to research and write. I often found corroboration in his writings or remarks to others of the things Alec had said to me. I have tried not to repeat what is available in other published material, but I have quoted extracts that appeared pertinent.

We had talked about certain subjects many times over. The question of Alec's drawings ("notes," as he called them) — what they meant to him and how he used them — must have come up a dozen times. His attitudes toward abstract art and his feelings about not having married and not having had a family were discussed on several occasions. I have in some chapters combined my recollections from a number of different conversations into one sequence. Except for these composite chapters, the story follows in chronological order.

The concluding parts of the book were particularly difficult to write. They deal with Alec's serious illness and his last six years. I saw little of him during this period, and I cannot tell what anguish Alec may have felt or judge whether he led a serene life in his declining years, as some people claim. But I do know the views he expressed before he became ill in 1968. I am inclined to think that his last few years, involving some physical and mental incapacity, were indeed trying for this proud and once-independent man. What I write is limited to the impressions I gathered on the few occasions I saw Alec in those years. Where these comments differ from the reports of others, I have included those opinions as well, to the extent that they were expressed to me.

I faced some difficulty in understanding fully the nature, motivation, and philosophy of this great artist because it was hard to be objective. I was confronted with the same dilemma that Alec's niece Naomi Jackson Groves now faces in writing his biography. She was very fond of her uncle, and personal feelings will inevitably influence biographical writings in spite of authors' efforts. My presentation of the A.Y. Jackson personality reflects my own feelings, my own impressions. The interpretation, while as objective as I can make it, is based on subjective reaction. I have tried, in writing about my friend, to be as objective as possible; still, my feelings of closeness to him make it difficult for me to offer a dispassionate account. This task of critical review is left to professional art historians and biographers whose analytical skill and specialized knowledge equip them better than I to do justice to a leading figure in Canada's cultural evolution. What I leave written is a memoir of my recollections about Alec. Though he would not necessarily have agreed with some of the detail (we had differing views on a number of issues), I think Alec would have approved in principle of my recording some of our mutual experiences and feelings.

Margaret Kennedy helped me greatly in commenting on the text and in typing the manuscript. Janet Craig did a superb job as editor. The staff of McClelland & Stewart has taken a genuine interest in enhancing the quality of the book, as did Camilla Newman, who did additional editing. Many individuals responded generously in providing information and material. To all those who contributed go my sincere thanks.

O.J.F.

The Other
A.Y. Jackson

CHAPTER 1
Two Brief Encounters

My first meeting with Alec Jackson in Toronto late in 1954 was casual. I recall telling him I was working for the Canadian government (at that time, as economic adviser to Minister of Trade and Commerce C.D. Howe), that I had developed a great interest in Canadian art, and that I was slowly building up a collection. Relying mainly on the very few books on Canadian art history that existed at that time,* I had read what I could find about him, and had also seen his retrospective exhibition at the National Gallery of Canada in December 1953.

Most of what I had read, I told him, had not mentioned much about the artist as a person. He replied that he could help me there, for *Mayfair*[6] magazine had recently published an article about his life and work in which the interviewer had quoted him at length. Alec volunteered to send me a copy. I asked him to autograph it, and he promised he would. He kept his promise, and I still have the copy, battered and torn with the passage of time and use, with Alec's signature on the front cover.

I also asked him whether I could visit him at the Studio Building at 25 Severn Street the next time I was in Toronto. He said he was not sure whether that would be practical. He had been happy in the Studio Building but things were not now working out very well; he was thinking of moving. One possibility was the town of Manotick, south of Ottawa, where one of his nieces was living. We agreed to meet again, either in Toronto or in Manotick.

The following spring I learned from John K. B. Robertston, who owned an Ottawa commercial art gallery then located at 103 Queen Street, that Alec was building a studio and living quarters in Manotick, and from Robertson I got the phone number of Alec's niece Constance Hamilton. She told me the building had been completed and that Alec had recently moved in. Alec himself came to the phone and we arranged a date for a visit. I was also told how to find the place.

---

*They were F. B. Housser, *A Canadian Art Movement: The Story of the "Group of Seven"*, Macmillan, Toronto, 1926; A.H. Robson, *Canadian Landscape Painters*, Ryerson Press, Toronto, 1932; William Colgate, *Canadian Art, Its Origin and Development*, Ryerson Press, Toronto, 1943; Marius Barbeau, *Painters of Quebec*, Ryerson Press, Toronto, 1946; D.W. Buchanan, *The Growth of Canadian Painting*, Collins, Toronto, 1950; and Graham McInnes, *Canadian Art*, Macmillan, Toronto, 1950.

The Hamilton house was just off the main highway. I parked my car and walked the 150 yards up the hill to the house, where Alec's niece Constance met me. She pointed out the studio, another fifty yards up the hill, including a few steps that had been cut into the incline. Alec, working on a canvas, had left the front door open — he was hard of hearing, he said, and the bell was not loud enough. Sometimes he did not even hear the knocker he had installed.

As I had walked into his studio I noticed how cluttered the place was, and that the furniture had seen better days. Alec must have sensed it, for he remarked that it would take a little while to make the place more comfortable. During the seven years he stayed in his Manotick studio-home, however, I saw little change except that it became more cluttered.

I thanked Alec for the copy of *Mayfair* and asked how he felt about receiving all this publicity in what was described as "Canada's Smartest Magazine."

"I wasn't too smart," he replied. "If I had been, an interview like that would have appeared sooner."

"Why didn't it?" I inquired.

"Nobody asked me," he said.

He mentioned that the article had brought him so much publicity he was beginning to feel embarrassed,* but it had had one positive effect. His sketches and paintings were beginning to sell like hotcakes, and he was pleased about that.

I remarked that as helpful as I had found the article in *Mayfair* and his recollections in an article in *Canadian Art*,[7] I thought that more had remained unsaid than said. Also, I suspected that art critics of earlier years, whose reviews I had read had not really understood what Jackson and the Group of Seven had been trying to do or to say. He agreed, and observed that a few of them knew more about French, British, and American art than they knew about Canadian art and Canadian artists. "Some are just ignorant," he added.

But the situation was changing. The public had become more interested in the work of the Group, and Alec mentioned how successful his Toronto exhibition in 1953 and the Group of Seven Vancouver exhibition in 1954 had been. As people became more aware, reviewers responded, and in due course there would be more books on the Group, he said. "If I can find the time, perhaps I'll write a book myself." (He did, and it was published in 1958.)

He wanted to know more about what I did and about my family. How had I become interested in Canadian art? I explained that after I

---

*Alec repeated that remark when he published *A Painter's Country, the Autobiography of A. Y. Jackson* in 1958, p. 155.

finished my studies at McGill in 1942, I started to work for the Canadian government as an economist. I had modest means and could not afford to buy paintings, so visits to the National Gallery of Canada had to suffice. Two paintings there impressed me greatly. One was *The Red Maple*, which he had done in Algonquin Park in 1914, and the other was Clarence Gagnon's *Village in the Laurentian Mountains*. I took such a liking to these two paintings that I bought prints of them and had them framed for my bachelor quarters, deciding then and there that I wanted to know more about Canadian art and Canadian artists. I also hoped to replace the prints with paintings when I had more money.

In 1947, I married a woman who felt as I did about art, and we soon started to collect Canadian works. Although I read as many books on the subject as I could find, I tried to supplement what I learned by talking to artists. I had been doing this for a number of years and planned to continue. Would Alec be prepared to see me from time to time? Could he occasionally come to our home for a meal, just a family dinner or lunch? He said he would. When I asked him whether I could buy some of his works, he said that it might be difficult, with all the demand for his paintings, but that he would see what he could do.

He remarked that the two prints that had prompted my interest in Canadian art were taken from two paintings that in their time were quite bold, although, meanwhile, tastes had been shifting. Clarence Gagnon had been a friend of his, he said, and the two had painted together in the twenties at Baie-St-Paul and other places in Quebec.

Then he wanted to know what had attracted me to *The Red Maple*. I told him I used to visit Algonquin Park regularly and that the landscape in *The Red Maple* struck a familiar chord. I mentioned also that I had once had a visitor from London who had seen the print and inquired whether the colours truly reflected the Canadian landscape. I assured him that they did, but he thought they were just the artist's imagination. Alec chuckled. "As you know, the colours are there," he said "but it takes an artist to bring them to life." We talked about Algonquin Park, how large it was, about its thousand lakes, forests, swamps, and trails — some hardly passable. Wasn't he lonely, I asked, when he went on sketching trips on his own?

"I had company at times," he replied, "but I didn't mind going alone. Nature is my friend. You aren't lonely with a friend."

This remark, reiterated several times through the years as our own friendship grew, opened a new vision for me. I realized I was talking to a man who had deep roots in the country he loved so dearly, and felt much could be learned about the link between nature and the artist — a bond that turned out to be stronger in Alec's case than the bonds most people form with other people.

17

He accompanied me to the door of the studio and apologized for not continuing with me down to where my car was parked. He was anxious to get back to his easel, where an uncompleted canvas was beckoning him like Circe enticing Odysseus and his sailors in the old tale.

What led to these encounters was the collection of Canadian art I was building. One principle of collecting included meeting each artist and learning more about him or her — from the source, so to speak. I also relied on the artists to help me select one or more of their works that they considered to be of quality and to have some historical meaning that reflected their creative lives. My collection has some special aspects: about ninety per cent of the works have been purchased from the artist or a member of his or her family; for some artists, I have a work for each year or for most years of their productive lives; and I have sometimes been able to match canvases with the oil or watercolour sketches from which they were painted.

My job as a government official in the early years and later as a member of the Royal Commission on Health Services took me from coast to coast and gave me the opportunity to visit artists after my day's work was done. More recently, as a professor at the University of Ottawa, I have travelled less but still enough to meet new artists and keep in touch with friends and acquaintances in the art world.

In 1970 my wife and I made a gift to the Crown through the Ontario Heritage Foundation of 120 drawings by twenty leading Canadian artists. These are on permanent loan to the University of Ottawa and are exhibited in the Main Library.

In 1972 we gave the bulk of our collection, more than eleven hundred pieces, to the Crown under the same auspices — 649 works by the Group of Seven (of which 262 are by A. Y. Jackson, 61 oils, 2 watercolours, an original silk screen, and 198 drawings). Most of this collection is displayed in our home, which we also donated to the Crown in 1972. Since that time I have acted as a voluntary curator. One of the highlights of a visit is the Jackson Room, which contains works by Jackson and pieces of memorabilia that he gave us.

Early on in our acquaintance, Isobel began to address Alec by his first name, and he called her Isobel. For years, I continued to address him as "Mr. Jackson" and he would refer to me as "Mr. Firestone." My reason for not calling Alec by his first name for several years was in part my way of showing the high regard I had for him as one of Canada's greatest living painters; besides, I felt that friendship meant more than calling a person by his first name. It involved a genuine liking and caring for the other person, accepting him (or her) with all his idiosyncrasies and quirks, strong points and weak points, in happy and sad circumstances alike. Like all people, Alec had some short-comings. He had strong ego-feelings, notwithstanding utterances to the contrary; he occasionally lost his temper; and he was at times ready to say yes and then to change his mind. But these traits did not detract from the quality of his personality — they made him all the more human and likeable.

There was another important consideration. I wanted to avoid a conflict of interest. Alec was an artist, I was an art collector. I was concerned that if we became good friends early on, Alec might feel an inclination to sell us some of his works even though there was an increasing and strong demand for his paintings from others. He had many obligations.

Whatever my mental reservations, Alec became quite interested in our art collection and was pleased that a special room was devoted to the showing of his art. He liked to take people up to the Jackson Room when he was visiting us and tell them about his work. And because he endorsed our approach of putting together a collection that included works from as many years of the artist's productive life as possible, he helped us fill some of the gaps in our Jackson collection. Where a painting or sketch was not available, he would find us a drawing. As a result, the collection that we turned over to the Crown included Jackson works from the years 1908 to 1910, 1913, 1918, and 1921 through 1968, or a total of fifty-four of sixty-one productive years.

While I had originally met Alec because of my interest in collecting art, he became over the years a dear and close friend, admired by our children and adored by my wife. He and I developed a strong empathy — with Alec sometimes reading my mind as I read his, and both of us breaking into laughter when this happened. If there is such a thing, it was a friendship without strain.

CHAPTER 2
A Life
of Uphill Struggle

The man I met working in his own studio in Manotick was clearly untroubled by want. In fact, during the rest of his productive life he lived in a seller's market and built up a considerable estate. But for sixty years before I knew him, Alec Jackson had had a rough time, with few smooth places to lighten the burden of making an adequate living.

He first knew poverty as a child in Montreal in a family deserted by his father, as his mother tried to raise six children on her own. Then followed the poverty of exploitation, after he started work at the age of twelve in 1894. At the beginning, Alec probably earned less than two dollars a week as an office boy at the British Engraving Company, a lithography company.* After six years with this firm, at the age of eighteen, Alec was earning six dollars a week. Only in 1905, at the age of twenty-three, when he got another job at a photo-engraving company, was he earning twenty-five dollars a week.

Yet Alec managed to put aside some money. After helping out at home, he had saved over five years the princely sum of one hundred dollars — enough to take him, with his brother Harry and another commercial artist, to Europe. They crossed the Atlantic as deck hands on a cattle boat, looking after several hundred head of cattle. They were promised five shillings each for the two weeks' work; they never were paid. Alec and Harry visited London, Paris, Brussels, Antwerp, and Rotterdam, until the money ran out and Alec returned to Montreal, broke. Back in the engraving business, he saw his job evaporate with a printers' strike in 1906.

Alec then went to Chicago, where his father and uncle lived. His father was not doing well in business, and Alec did not seek any help from him, only sharing an occasional evening meal. He took a job with a firm of commercial designers. The pay was much better than in Montreal and the hours less arduous, and he was left with time to study in the evenings at the Chicago Art Institute.

---

*Alec himself did not mention any figure, but A. J. Casson indicated that at the age of sixteen he worked a nine-hour day and was paid two dollars a week by a commercial engraving firm in Hamilton in 1914. Frank Carmichael worked at Grip Ltd., designers and engravers, in Toronto for $2.50 a week in 1911.[9]

By the spring of 1907, Alec had saved fifteen hundred dollars, enough to go to Paris to study at the Académie Julian.[10] It was possible in those days to live comfortably in France on six hundred dollars a year, including money for touring.[11] He stayed in France for two and a half years and did quite a bit of travelling in Europe. After he returned to Canada, just before Christmas in 1909, he tried to sell some of his works but had no luck, so he gave some of these paintings to his family and kept a few himself.

In 1910, Alec took another job in Montreal doing commercial art work with a photo-engraving company. He worked there for a year, but he also took on part-time work in the evenings designing cigar labels to save enough to return to Europe. By the early fall of 1911 he had been able to save another thousand dollars, making it possible for him to go to France and then on to Italy.[12] He returned to Montreal early in 1913, bringing back "a lot of canvases" that he was unable to sell; "they were around my studio for years," he wrote later.[13] Apparently, few people liked the work Alec did in Europe — his paintings showed the influence of the French impressionists and were regarded as "too modern" by conservative Canadian collectors.

Beginning in 1913, Jackson's life entered a new phase. That year, at the age of twenty-nine, he sold his first major canvas, *The Edge of the Maple Wood*, painted in Sweetsburg, Quebec, in 1910. The buyer was Lawren Harris, who had independent means, and the price was two hundred dollars. (Harris sold this painting to the National Gallery of Canada for about the same amount in 1937.) The only other income Alec received was from the sale of six Venetian sketches, sold at a "little picture show" in Toronto.[14] This money helped finance his visit to Toronto to meet a number of artists who were to become his friends and who later on would join together to form the Group of Seven.

In the fall of 1913, Alec met Dr. James M. MacCallum, a friend of Lawren Harris's. MacCallum liked Alec's work.* When Alec explained that he was thinking of moving to the United States because there seemed little hope of making a living in Canada as a painter, MacCallum made Alec what he later described as a "surprising proposition": "If I would take a studio in the building he and Harris were having erected, he would guarantee my expenses for a year." Alec agreed, and that money saw him through the year 1914.[15]

In August of that year, the First World War broke out. Alec enlisted in the army in mid-1915 as a private, saw overseas service,

---

*Dr. MacCallum subsequently purchased a total of eleven paintings from Alec, five canvases and six sketches done between 1910 and 1921. These paintings were donated to the National Gallery of Canada in 1943 and were exhibited all together for the first time in January and February of 1969.

and in June 1916 was wounded by a bullet in the shoulder while fighting at Maple Copse in Flanders. The shrapnel wound healed nicely and in 1917 he was given an opportunity to paint again. He was made a lieutenant and a member of the Canadian War Records Office under Lord Beaverbrook.

The base pay of a lieutenant in 1917 was two dollars a day, plus a field allowance of sixty cents. In cash, Alec's income was approaching a thousand dollars a year, but considering the allowances for food and lodging and the other privileges accorded an officer, his gross income was probably the equivalent of two thousand dollars. This was the largest amount of money he had ever earned, and he was not to earn such a sum again from painting until after the outbreak of the Second World War, more than twenty years later. For a period of two years the feeling of poverty and insecurity that thus far had been the hallmark of most of his life was beginning to recede. Things seemed to be working out fine, and he stayed with the War Records Office until mid-1919.

Having saved some money made it easier for him to take up his life as a professional painter again. He returned to Toronto to the Studio Building at 25 Severn Street.* In August 1919, Alec and his other painter friends were discussing the possibility of an art exhibition of what was to become known as the Group of Seven, an exhibition at the Art Museum of Toronto from May 7 to 27, 1920. Alec's main sale at this exhibition was to the National Gallery of Canada, which acquired his 1913 painting, *Night, Georgian Bay*, for two hundred dollars. The National Gallery now had the largest collection of A. Y. Jackson canvases (outside the holdings of the artist and his family), for a total of three. The other two works were *Sand Dunes at Cucq* (Brittany), 1912, acquired in 1913, and *The Red Maple*, 1914, acquired the same year. Most of Alec's canvases were offered for sale for between two hundred and three hundred dollars, but there were few takers. *The Freddy Channel*, painted in 1920, was sold for two hundred dollars to P. Hilborn and ended up in the collection of Charles Band.

Between 1920 and 1925 Alec's earnings from paintings were less than six hundred dollars a year. His wartime savings had dwindled, and he was facing difficult times. In the fall of 1924, he found it necessary to take a job as a part-time instructor at the Ontario College of Art. But teaching, he observed, put an end to his "free way of life" as an artist. Alec had already established a set pattern:

---

*In 1914, the original occupants of the Studio Building were, in the order of studio numbers: Jackson and Tom Thomson, Lawren Harris, Arthur Heming, J. W. Beatty, A. Curtis Williamson, and J. E. H. MacDonald.

Every March I was accustomed to go to lower Quebec and sketch until the snow was gone. In the summer I went to Georgian Bay; in October I travelled somewhere up north to paint the autumn colour. The rest of the year I worked in my studio painting up my sketches. Had I remained teaching, this routine, very necessary for a painter, would have been destroyed; so after a year I resigned from the College.[16]

Alec did not say how much he earned a month, but he added (and one can hear the sigh): "I did miss the monthly cheque, though."[17]

The National Gallery of Canada was his best customer during the twenties, he claimed. This was true for the first half of the twenties but not so during the second half, when most of Alec's income from painting came from other sources. In the early twenties, the National Gallery acquired five of Alec's canvases: the first Georgian Bay painting in 1920, *A Quebec Village* and *Early Spring, Georgian Bay* in 1921, *Morning after Sleet* in 1922,* and *November* in 1924. The canvases sold in the two- to three-hundred-dollar range. Total income from these five canvases would have been less than fifteen hundred dollars, or less than three hundred dollars a year, so the National Gallery purchases appear to have represented nearly half of Alec's annual income during the first half of the twenties.

At this time, several small Ontario towns began to buy Alec's works. For example, Kitchener in 1921 bought *Cacouna, the Winter Road*, done that year, and Sarnia bought *Maples, Early Spring*, probably in 1922, which was painted in Emileville, Quebec, in 1915.[18] Geneva Jackson, Alec's aunt, was endeavouring to develop interest in art in Kitchener in the twenties. A group of Kitchener ladies bought nine paintings of the Group of Seven, including Alec's work.[19]

Alec also began to sell some of his sketches. When he brought back a number of these panels from his painting trips, he divided them into two lots — those from which he would make canvases and the others which he would sell to a buyer, if a buyer could be found. If somebody wanted to buy one of the sketches that he needed to paint a canvas, he put the potential purchaser's name on the back of the panel. He let the sketch go to the buyer when the canvas was completed. All during the twenties, the selling price for sketches was thirty-five dollars.[20]

In the second half of that decade, the National Gallery acquired only one of Alec's paintings, *Early Spring, Quebec,* in 1926. Other sales were picking up, however. Vincent Massey bought *Northern*

---

*This painting, which had previously won the Jessie Dow Prize of two hundred dollars, was sold to the National Gallery for three hundred dollars.

23

Lake, done in 1928.* *North Shore, Baffin Island*, painted in the same year, was bought by the East York (Ontario) Board of Education in 1929. Other sales were to Hart House at the University of Toronto, H. S. Southam, Dr. Frederick Banting, and a few collectors in Montreal. Alec's income was rising, but he spoke of his yearly earnings of about a thousand dollars as "certainly not enough to support a wife and raise a family." His early poverty continued to influence his outlook.[21]

Alec noted that during the twenties the National Gallery spent, on average, about two thousand dollars on works by each member of the Group of Seven, for which Eric Brown, its director, was soundly criticized. It appears, however, that the amount Alec received was less than the average.**[22] In terms of numbers, Jackson sold more paintings during the twenties to the National Gallery (a total of six) than did the other members of the group: Lawren Harris, J. E. H. Mac-Donald, and Arthur Lismer sold three each, Fred Varley and Franz Johnston two each. But most of the canvases of these artists were larger than Alec's and fetched higher prices. The first work by Frank Carmichael was not acquired by the National Gallery until 1931. Interestingly enough, the Art Gallery of Toronto, where most of the Group of Seven exhibitions were held in the twenties, acquired its first A. Y. Jackson canvas in 1926. Entitled *Barns* and painted the same year, it was a gift from a donor, and it was the gallery's only acquisition of Alec's work during the twenties.

As negative reaction to the work of the Group of Seven subsided and after the favourable publicity the artists received at the showing at the British Empire Exhibitions at Wembley in 1924 and 1925, new Group shows were organized. Of these, the fourth exhibition, from January 9 to February 2, 1925, at the Art Gallery of Toronto was the most successful. The enthusiastic comments that appeared in the press at that time have been summarized by Dennis Reid:

> The popular press responded with an unprecedented enthusiasm. The Group's struggle to gain acceptance of their view of Canada and Canadian art was now news, and, as reflected in the articles which appeared in the newspapers, a matter of some fascination to the broad reading public. Each of the Toronto papers sent reporters — not critics — to cover the show, and although the stories ranged in response from incredulity to sentimental patriotism, the consensus was that there was phenomenal public interest in it.[23]

---

*The date of sale is uncertain, but it is listed as about 1930. The painting is part of the Vincent Massey bequest to the National Gallery of Canada (1968).

**I could not find any indication that Alec had checked the two thousand dollar figure with the staff of the National Gallery, and his estimate may be on the high side.

Alec told me that he thought Fred Housser's book, published in 1926, also helped to make the Group of Seven "respectable."[24]

One would think that with all that favourable publicity income from sales of paintings by the members of the group would have risen significantly in the late twenties, but that did not happen. Alec observed that as a professional artist he was not yet earning as much as a bricklayer did. In 1927, a bricklayer in Toronto earned one dollar twenty-five cents an hour and worked forty-four hours a week if fully employed.[25] On the basis of sixteen hundred hours a year (allowing for some layoffs, particularly in winter), he would have earned two thousand dollars during the whole year. Alec, on the other hand, earned about half that amount from his paintings. The bricklayer would have had an income of sixteen hundred dollars in 1920 based on an hourly rate of one dollar;[26] the same year, Alec's earnings from painting appear to have been less than half of that.

Alec mentioned to me, as he did to many others (and noted in his book),[27] that the Group had been exposed to "severe" criticism in its early days. These statements seem to imply that this criticism had an adverse effect on sales to the public. This may have been true to some extent, but my impression as I listened to Alec was that the Canadian public was just not ready to spend money on the works of "newcomers" on the Canadian art scene.*

Dennis Reid stressed the public's indifference to the Group of Seven in these terms: "In later years, it has been generally remembered that the Group was severely attacked in the press as a result of this first exhibition. This is absolutely false, although judging from the number and the locations of the reviews that appeared, it would almost seem that the artists were the victims of the very evil they most feared: 'indifference'."[28]

Similar lack of understanding was encountered in the rest of the decade and the struggle for survival of the Group of Seven, and of Alec in particular, continued during the latter part of the twenties. Alec had to find some non-painting source of income. The pickings were lean, with a little money coming in from doing some illustrations for *Chez Nous* by A. Rivard** and from royalties for his book *The Far North*.***

Alec referred me to the A. H. Robson book published in 1932

---

*On questioning, Alec admitted that public indifference was a factor.

**Published by McClelland and Stewart in 1924. Alec stated that there was a difference of opinion as to whether the illustrations did justice to the book. But as it turned out, *Chez Nous* became a real success, with many of the drawings reproduced in the *New York Tribune*. See *A Painter's Country*, p. 54.

***Published by Rous and Mann, Toronto, 1927.

which explains aptly why Jackson paintings did not sell well in the late twenties, even after the Group of Seven had received a great deal of favourable publicity. Robson wrote: "If Jackson's canvases have not yet attained popularity with the picture-buying public it is, perhaps, because of his search for the significant in his subject matter, and his absolute indifference to the picturesque or pretty."[29] The public was not yet ready to accept the artist whom Robson described as "a consistent and brillant painter" who "has the ability to grasp the salient features of a landscape, and with a directness approaching genius, subtly accent the significant lines, and impart to them a quality of rhythm that frequently echoes through the canvas like a theme in a musical composition."

By 1930, the reputation of the Group of Seven was well established in Canada as an indigenous school of landscape artists painting Canada as it was seen through Canadian eyes. In December 1931 the Group held its last exhibition at the Art Gallery of Toronto, and by 1933 it had disbanded, with several of its members joining an expanded organization known as the Canadian Group of Painters,* which included a number of younger painters influenced by the Group.

With Alec's works now well known, the stage was set for sales to pick up, giving Alec opportunity to make an adequate living as a professional painter[30] rather than relying, as most of his artist friends did, on teaching or working with commercial firms. But this was not how it worked out. The Great Depression had struck Canada with a fury; mass unemployment, severe declines in incomes, crop failures, a dramatic drop in the price of wheat, protest marches, and soup kitchens were symptomatic of Canadian economic and social conditions during most of the thirties.

One of Alec's canvases, The "Beothic" at the Bache Post, Ellesmere Island, painted about 1928 following his trip to the Arctic in 1927, was bought by the Minister of the Interior, who donated it to the National Gallery in 1930. This was the only Jackson canvas the National Gallery obtained in the thirties until it purchased The Edge of the Maple Wood, in 1937. But this purchase did not mean any income for Alec because the canvas was acquired from Lawren Harris, who had bought it 1913. Thus, in effect, the National Gallery did not buy any works from Alec between 1927 and 1938. The Art Gallery of Toronto purchased its first Jackson canvas, Winter, Charlevoix County, directly from Alec in 1933; it then had two of Alec's works. It is a near-miracle

---

*The first exhibition of this organization took place at the Art Gallery of Toronto in November 1933 and included twenty-seven members and twenty-five invited contributors.

26

that Alec managed to survive as a professional painter when all he could sell during the thirties to a major public art gallery was one painting. Alec told me about some well-to-do Toronto families who invited him to Sunday lunch — roast beef and Yorkshire pudding and all the trimmings. At times, this was the only good meal he had during the week.

A price list of Alec's works shown at a one-man exhibition at the W. Scott and Sons Gallery in Montreal from November 16 to 30, 1935, indicates that fifteen years after the first exhibition of the Group of Seven in Toronto Alec did not expect to realize any more from his paintings than he had in 1920. At the 1920 exhibition the average price of a canvas was close to three hundred dollars; at the 1935 exhibition, there were twenty-nine canvases, with twenty-seven for sale at prices ranging from $150 to $600, and the average again close to $300. Ten sketches, priced at $40 and $50 each, were also for sale.

There was however, this big difference: Alec and the Group of Seven were unknowns in 1920 — and they were highly respected and widely acclaimed landscape painters in 1935. Alec was now among the leading artists in Canada, better known in Montreal than any other member of the Group of Seven. His hope was that the quality of workmanship and low prices would encourage institutions and collectors to buy his works. Quality there was, but satisfactory sales remained an elusive phantom. Nevertheless, the press was puzzled by why a renowned Canadian painter continued to keep prices of his works so low. Following a one-man show at the J. Merritt Malloney Gallery in Toronto in February and March 1934, in which thirty-two major canvases and a number of sketches were displayed, a reporter concluded his article on the exhibition by saying: "Despite his acclaim as a great artist, A. Y. Jackson has stuck to his reasonable prices."[31]

The economic situation began to change with the outbreak of the Second World War in September 1939. Jobs became more plentiful, incomes were higher, and limitations on supplies did not affect works of art. On the contrary, there continued to be an excess of good Canadian paintings available because the public was still hesitant about buying Canadian art. Alec's sales to the two large public galleries picked up, with the National Gallery making its largest purchases in 1939, one major canvas, *Terre Sauvage*, plus twelve sketches. In the following year, the Art Gallery of Toronto brought three of Alec's sketches and received one large canvas, *Springtime in Picardy*, as a gift from a donor. A foundation had been laid for comprehensive collections of Alec's work by these two galleries, and some of his paintings were also sold to smaller galleries and to Hart House at the University of Toronto.

Alec's prices were still low, fifty to sixty dollars for sketches and up to three hundred dollars for canvases, and this affected his total earnings. He continued to receive wide publicity, however, which was not without impact on his sales. Two events in particular helped spread the word among people who had not heard of Alec's works: the publicity that followed his award of an honorary LL.D. at the Centenary Convocation of Queen's University in 1941 and the testimonial dinner given for him at the Art Gallery of Toronto in January 1942. Effective, too, was the free distribution of seventeen thousand reproductions of paintings by leading Canadian painters to military personnel serving overseas. These included many prints of Alec's works. Reproductions were also sold to the general public, and the National Gallery continued this practice after the war ended, familiarizing many Canadians with the works of the Group of Seven in particular, but gradually extending the range of choice. Alec was a member of the advisory committee, together with A. J. Casson and Harry McCurry, that guided the National Gallery in its reproduction program in the early years of the war.

An exhibition in May 1944 illustrates how things improved for Alec in the later years of the war. Twenty-five of his paintings were shown at the Fine Art Galleries of Eaton's College Street store in Toronto, including a number of works he had done while on assignment to paint along the Alaska highway. A Toronto paper reported: "Very nearly all of the pictures... have been marked 'reserved'... for individual collectors."[32]

Annual earnings during the war years probably varied between five thousand and ten thousand dollars. It was during this period that Alec was able for the first time to earn more than he had as a war artist toward the end of the First World War and in the immediate post-war period.

Alec's sales improved materially after the war. Donald Buchanan observed in 1946 that his "compositions are much in demand and this assurance of economic security has enabled him to become a traveller, a seeker of new scenes, more especially of those on the pioneer or wilderness fringe of Canada."[33]

In the same year, the Dominion Gallery of Montreal had a successful Jackson show, almost a sell-out of Alec's works on exhibit. The gallery owner subsequently endeavoured to persuade Alec "to withdraw all paintings he had on loan and to finish all those which were left in his studio" over a period of two years and offer them for sale at an exhibition to be held at the same gallery. At that showing, from April 24 to May 8, 1948, thirty-four of Alec's canvases went on sale with prices on request, thirty of his sketches (10½ by 13½ inches) at eighty-five dollars each, and thirty smaller sketches (8½ by 10½ inches) at seventy-five dollars. Assuming that Alec's *net* take per sketch varied between fifty and sixty dollars, and that the canvases brought three hundred to three hundred fifty dollars, his total income from that exhibition must have approached fifteen thousand dollars, because almost all the works were sold. The canvases, which included earlier as well as more recent works, would have been equivalent to more than Alec's annual output, but the number of sketches was only about two-thirds of what Alec usually turned out in a year. A figure of about fifteen thousand dollars a year appears to be a reasonable estimate of his earnings for the first half of the decade, with further improvements indicated in the second half. Alec was by now in his middle sixties.

There were some additional sources of income at this time. Alec taught at the Banff School of Fine Arts from 1943 to 1947 and in 1949, and he also did some work for the National Gallery of Canada. In 1952 he and Frances Loring were engaged in an educational project in the Peace River district of Alberta.[34] Alec also accepted a few commissions, such as paintings of the Rocky Mountains for Canadian National Railways and of a cityscape for the Seagram's Exhibition depicting the cities of Canada.

Prices of his works changed little during this period: sixty dollars for a sketch of recent vintage, occasionally one hundred dollars for an older one; three hundred to four hundred dollars for a medium-sized canvas, with five hundred to seven hundred fifty dollars for large canvases. It was at this time that Alec was able to start building up his savings so that he could construct his own studio in 1955. I have also heard stories that he was buying securities and making money in the stock market. I believe these stories may be somewhat exaggerated, for Alec was not a businessman and not particularly interested in investment economics. Yet he did receive financial advice from a firm of investment dealers who had a branch in Ottawa. He also occasionally got tips from some of his business friends in Toronto and a few mining men whom he met on his northern sketching trips.

On several occasions, when Alec lived in Ottawa, we talked about investing in equities. I explained to Alec that people who gave tips to invest in mining stocks or other junior securities usually had ulterior motives, and that this constituted speculation, not investment. I remarked that Alec did not seem to be the gambling type; he just chuckled. I also mentioned that investment in senior securities was a possibility but that it required careful management by experienced investment analysts. As a member of an advisory committee, I knew something about the University of Ottawa Pension Fund, which was administered by a major Canadian trust company. Even with all its expertise, the trust company was not doing much better with investment in equities — about half the fund — than with returns on fixed-income securities. And, I added, things might become much worse if there were a major break in the stock market or if Canada experienced a period of rapid inflation accompanied by protracted lacklustre market performance.

Alec replied that he *had* made some money with stock investments. I asked him whether he cared to mention the occasions when he lost money. He said, "You don't lose money if you don't sell your stock at a loss." When I tried to explain some basics of investment economics, including the principle of maximizing returns from alternative investment opportunities, Alec lost interest quickly. Therefore I made the general point that he could not afford to waste a lot of time studying the financial pages every day and that playing the stock market was a task for experts, not amateurs. He nodded as if he concurred, but he kept buying and selling securities. Sometimes he appeared to throw caution to the winds. I found this surprising in a man with conservative inclinations and sound instincts, two basic ingredients of his character.

I would not deny that Alec may have made some money with his equity investments, but I gathered the distinct impression that over the longer term he too did not do as well with them as he did with his earnings from fixed-income securities. Moreover, the most significant source of his rising savings remained income from the sale of paintings, demand for which in his later years exceeded supply.

Alec said he painted about fifteen to eighteen canvases a year. This was true for the larger pieces, but if some smaller works were included, the number was probably nearer twenty-five a year, and sometimes more. In a good year, he might also be left with over one hundred sketches after destroying those he rejected; how many over a hundred would be hard to say. For example, when Alec returned from his trip to Baffin Island in 1965, he said in an interview with Dennis Foley that during that two-month period he did "100-odd sketches," from which he planned to "complete 20 to 25 canvases."[35] The figures for the number of canvases in this case are about right, but the number of sketches may be a little on the high side.

On a good day of an outing trip, Alec would usually paint two sketches. The figure given to the reporter suggests an average of three sketches a day or better, which would be a remarkable achievement for a man of eighty-three. But we do have evidence that when Alec was really in the mood, he could do up to four sketches a day. On this occasion, one hundred sketches may be correct,[36] and the figure he gave me of an average of some one hundred sketches a year (after sorting) may be on the low side.

When we were celebrating Alec's eighty-third birthday, I was able to report to our guests that during the period our friend was active as a professional painter (close to sixty years), he had painted about five thousand sketches and had destroyed close to one thousand, so that there remained in the possession of galleries, institutions, dealers, and private collections something more than four thousand sketches. Alec also estimated that the number of canvases that survived after he had weeded out those not up to standard numbered about one thousand.* I checked all these figures with Alec before mentioning them, and he also read over and corrected the notes I was using. Since he painted for another two and a half years after that birthday party, it appears that the numbers given here are probably on the conservative side. No wonder, then, that some of Alec's colleagues in the Group of Seven called him the most productive member of their small circle.

After the article about him appeared in *Mayfair* in 1954, a good many people who had never heard of Alec considered it fashionable to own a Jackson painting. A run started on his inventory, the accumulation of works from several decades. Within five years, every single piece that Alec owned and that was available for sale was gone. The walls were bare. The cupboards were empty. Alec had given many works to his family and some to institutions. There was nothing left except what Alec was currently painting — and that was not sufficient to meet the growing demand for his works. The period from 1955 to 1960 therefore set new records of earnings for Alec because it included many sales of old works as well as new output. Annual income in those years was possibly in the range of thirty to forty thousand dollars.

In the sixties, until his serious illness in April 1968, Alec's earned income consisted almost solely of sales of new paintings. That income would have dropped from the levels prevailing in the late fifties if it had not been for two factors. First, he finally gave in and raised his prices somewhat and, second, a new source of income developed — the sale of drawings, or "notes" as he called them (he had previously considered these drawings of little artistic or commercial value). Some of these fetched between two hundred and three hundred dollars each. There was also income from his books and some lectures. Royalties came from *The Far North, Banting as an Artist*, and *A Painter's*

---

*When Alec gave me these figures, he mentioned that he might have been underestimating his output in earlier statements. (See, for example, his statement in a 1959 interview in which he mentioned that he might have done "more than 2,000 outdoor sketches" and "about 600 oil paintings on canvas and thrown about 100 in the fire."[37])

Country. He also illustrated another book, *The St. Lawrence,* by Henry Beston, one of the "Rivers of America" series. These sources helped to keep Alec's earnings close to the record levels they had reached a few years earlier.

In 1960, Alec volunteered the information to an interviewer that with paintings, lectures, and his books, he made a "good living" but that he was "not in the wealthy class."[38] When he made that statement he had had only five or six really good years of earned income, but he probably tripled his savings in the next eight years.

A few years later, Alec was becoming more aware of his accumulating wealth. On one occasion after he had moved to Ottawa in 1962, he was walking with his niece Naomi downtown. As they passed the office of the Canada Permanent Trust, Alec remarked with a smile, "They are holding a pot of gold of mine. I am now in the process of filling a second one." Still, there was no change in his lifestyle.

Alec always lived very frugally. He did not own a car, he rarely bought new clothes, and spent little on entertainment (he was usually in demand to be entertained by other people). When he went on sketching trips with other artists, he spent little if anything on travel. Accommodation and living expenses were modest. His main outlays were on paint supplies and the unavoidable income tax. (Alec looked at this as expenses, not as a charge on income.) He always bought good-quality canvases, paints, and brushes. He did try to reduce the cost of his plywood panels by buying them in bulk. On one occasion, he bought two hundred good-quality panels from a sawmill at Eganville. At other times he would purchase fifty or a hundred plywood panels from another sawmill in Grenville, all cut to his size, 10½ by 13½ inches. The high quality of the materials means Alec's works can be expected to last for centuries.

The comparatively high income levels between 1955 and 1968 enabled Alec to build up what for him were sizeable savings, looked after mainly by Canada Permanent Trust. After he recovered from his near-fatal illness in the spring of 1968 and was unable to earn any more from painting (although his investment income continued), the savings helped him through the following six years of impaired health.

The figures I have mentioned for Alec's earnings in the two decades before 1968 were not his only source of income. As his savings accumulated, there were also increasing amounts of interest and dividends coming in each year. All this investment income, less income tax, was plowed back into savings, and so the cumulative effect of income on income saved began to come into play. The overall results for total savings approached rather substantial amounts. They may have reached a range between $300,000 and $400,000. For a man who was called "poor Alex" by his friends for many years, this must have seemed a fortune he had never dreamt of possessing.

After Alec moved to Kleinburg in 1968, he needed practical nurses round the clock, an expensive proposition. Even so there was substantial income after tax from his accumulated savings to look after a good part of the nursing care and some of his small personal expenses in those last years. When he died in April 1974 he left a considerable estate, which was distributed among a dozen or so heirs and also covered a number of small bequests.

These figures of earnings and savings are guesses of mine. I did not consult the family about the amount of accumulated savings when he became seriously ill in 1968 or about the size of his estate when he died. This, I felt, was a personal matter, of concern to the family only. I am using my estimates solely for the purpose of illustrating a point: that Alec was a poor man for the first sixty years of his life but that he lived long enough to receive material rewards as well as public recognition as a great artist, described by Vincent Massey as a "lengendary figure in the Canadian scene."[39]

His attitudes toward life and purpose had a strong bearing on his ability to survive poverty and economic depression. He was determined to be an artist, in spite of the difficulty of making a living. Rugged individualism made him strive harder than some of his contemporaries to be independent; many others relied on teaching or commercial art to make a living until their later years. Self-discipline kept him to a frugal lifestyle and regular habits of work, which, with his natural good health, made him very productive over a long life. And he cared little for money as an end in itself. Instead, he was more concerned to see and interpret as much of his country as possible and make his paintings available to institutions and people of moderate means by keeping his prices low. That was one of Alec's ways of showing he cared for people.

CHAPTER 3

From Toronto to Manotick to Ottawa

By 1954, his life at 25 Severn Street in Toronto had become a bore to Alec. After Lawren Harris sold the Studio building, the new owner established rules and regulations irksome to artists accustomed to the kind of freedom usually associated with the bohemian life. The last straw came when Alec was informed he would have to wear felt shoes in his studio and stretch his canvases in the basement.[40]

Meanwhile, two reasonably priced building lots had become available in Manotick, near the home of Alec's niece Constance (Ton to her friends). Alec's friend Maurice Haycock volunteered to have plans made for a combined house and studio, to engage a contractor, and oversee construction of the building. Alec arranged with Ton to have his dinner with her family every day. He would also buy her a car in exchange for drives to places he wanted to go.

Alec's departure from Toronto was the final step in a long series of events going back as far as 1936, when he began to be unhappy at the Studio Building. Many of his friends, including Lismer and Harris, had already left or were leaving Toronto. He wrote to his friend Anne Savage about moving to Montreal, and she tried to help him make up his mind in a letter written on May 11, 1936: "You want a change, and why not have it? . . . Do what you feel is right from the point of view of your work and, as you say, facts have to be faced, there is a field of interest here and Montreal has gone on a long time since you left it . . . The step wouldn't be irrevocable; you could try it out and it might do us all good."[41] Nevertheless, Alec stayed on in Toronto until 1955.

When word got around that Alec was moving from Toronto to Manotick, his friends and admirers were assailed with nostalgic regret. Many felt the move signalled the end of an important phase in the artistic development of Canada — but Alec did not agree. In moving to a small place in Ontario but continuing to travel and paint all across the country, he was emphasizing his belief in Canadianism. He was moving away from the parochialism that was still a dominant social force in Toronto in the 1950s. More than ever, he wanted to stress his love for Canada in its natural beauty and as a nation, a subject we discussed subsequently on several occasions.

One newspaper described the farewell to Alec this way: "Jackson's last days at his Toronto studio were filled with parties in his honour and leavetaking from a host of friends who associated him and the Studio Building, with its famous 'shack,' as inseparable landmarks on the art scene. There was a feeling, too, that here was the breaking of the last link, the closing of a door on the first great important movement in Canadian art."[42]

But there was more to the move than this. Alec was by then seventy-two years old, and he felt that the time for more reflection, and perhaps the writing of an autobiography, had come. His own words on leaving Toronto were: "I'm drawing into myself, but not drawing into my shell."[43] It was a typical A.Y. utterance. He wanted more time to do what he needed to do, but he was remaining the outgoing Alec who enjoyed people.

Alec's new home was designed by M. G. Nixon, formerly an architect with the Department of Verterans' Affairs, and was ready for Alec to move into by April 1955. Situated on a hill above the highway, the place had an unobstructed view of the Rideau River and the wooded areas that grace the embankment.

The building consisted of two connected structures built into the hillside. As the visitor came up the hill from the highway, he came to a two-storey white stucco house on the left with a storey-and-a-half studio attached on the right. There was a front entrance to the house, and a side entrance to the studio fronted on Highcroft Drive. A dirt road linked house and highway. The floor area of the whole structure was about a thousand square feet.

Alec sometimes left the front door, with its weird-looking metal knocker, open for visitors. I learned later that there was a bell system connecting the Hamilton house with Alec's studio so that Ton could let Alec know he was wanted on the telephone or that meals were ready.

The tiny entrance hall had "A.Y.J." inlaid in the tile flooring, and to the left was a small L-shaped room, painted blue. At the back of it was what looked to be a walk-in closet, and on the right, in the corner, was the single bed where Alec usually slept. Across from the bed was the sink where Alec cleaned his paint brushes.

A steep set of stairs led up to the second floor. Upstairs on the left was a middle-sized bedroom, painted green, with two beds which were rarely used; this was a visitors' room, but Alec had few overnight guests, his sister Kay being an exception. A bathroom was next to it, and across was a kitchen, painted blue, with built-in cupboards, an old-fashioned refrigerator (on which Alec painted his initials, in blue, at some later date), a small table, and a couple of chairs. Two closets opening on the landing upstairs provided additional storage space — of which Alec could never have enough.

On the ground floor to the right of the stairs was the studio, the walls of pastel shade. It was a room twenty-four by fifteen feet with a high ceiling, large windows about eleven feet high along the whole north side, and a door to the outside opposite the entrance, which Alec kept locked. Inside the entrance on the left there was a fireplace finished in Roman brick, which Alec enjoyed using on cold days. Next was a long chest-high bookcase, extending to the end of the room. It was filled with books, pamphlets, and magazines. (Alec's library reportedly contained about three hundred books, but Alec had never counted them and so could not verify this figure.) On the mantelpiece and on top of the bookcase was a great assortment of relics, bric-à-brac, and souvenirs, among them an old miniature sailing vessel, some small Eskimo sculptures, a Haida Indian mask, and a few carvings. Alec was like a squirrel: he would collect things only to discard them when the clutter became overwhelming. On the walls were several paintings by other artists and some bright posters which gave the studio a cheery, bohemian atmosphere.

The studio was sparsely furnished. There was a couch, and above it, placed criss-cross on the wall, a pair of snowshoes. There was also a desk, a lampstand, a few wooden chairs, a stool, a bench, and a piece of furniture that I grew particularly fond of — Alec's dark-wooded French-Canadian rocking-chair. When I sat down to chat with Alec, I would always gravitate to the rocking-chair, and he would pull up another chair. It was not until *A Painter's Country* appeared that I realized how fond he was of the rocker, a hundred years old and once owned by Grandpère Tremblay of St-Hilarion, one of Alec's favourite painting places in Quebec.* When I offered to change seats, Alec would not hear of it. He was always courteous when he was not in a grouchy mood, and he was in a happy frame of mind most of the time I knew him.

The central features of the studio were two easels, one larger than the other (Alec preferred to use the large one, but sometimes there were unfinished canvases on both easels). Lying about were canvases and panels, most of them unused, a few finished or nearly finished leaning against the wall. Fairly large quantities of paint supplies were in evidence, and there was plentiful artificial lighting overhead.

I mentioned earlier the large windows that gave the studio adequate daylight. Alec did not believe in having a cleaning woman look after his place, but every two or three months, Ton insisted on getting

---

*On page 60 he wrote: "One of my favorite possessions is the rocking chair of old Grandpère Tremblay. I am sitting in it now as I write these words."[44]

somebody to clean up the house and studio. Alec concurred reluctantly, but he made one proviso: the big windows in the studio were not to be touched. It was one of Alec's idiosyncrasies, which he felt did not require any explanation. Arthur Lismer noticed this, and he teased Alec about it. After one of the Lismer visits one of his cartoons was seen in the dust on one of the windows, with the words: "I fight to see no one cleans the windows."*

I noticed other scribbles of Lismer's on another window — apparently, every time he visited Alec in Manotick he would leave a little memento. On one occasion when he was there with Lawren Harris and his son, he was teasing Alec for living in the country. He called him a farmer. Then, holding a drink in one hand, he pulled out his felt pen and drew four little pigs on the window (Lismer was ambidextrous). A photograph commemorating the occasion was taken (Lismer is on the left; Harris on the far right).

While Alec lived at Manotick, I sometimes watched him at work. I knew that he painted his canvases from oil sketches that he had done in the field from nature. But in due course I also saw him do some small canvases from his drawings, his "notes." Alec could do a canvas in two or three days, depending on the size and the type of painting. Some would take two or three weeks, some, months. When Alec was

---

*This cartoon was also observed by I. Norman Smith, who described it in an article in the *Ottawa Journal.*

not satisfied with a painting, he would set it aside, to return to it sometimes months later.

When out in the country, he painted fairly quickly, taking about an hour and a half a sketch. When he returned to the place where he was staying, frequently late in the afternoon, he would put some finishing touches on the sketch then or in the evening, and that might take another half hour. In total, the average sketch took about two hours to finish. When Alec was satisfied with a sketch, he signed it. If he was not quite sure, he put off signing and considered adding more finishing touches at a later time; if he was not satisfied with it, he might destroy it. Sometimes Alec would date sketches. When I got to know him, I always insisted that, in addition to the date, he note the name of the place where he had done the sketch. Alec would write this down on the back of the panel, and he continued this practice in later years.

Alec preferred to be alone when he painted, but often when I had come to drive him somewhere I waited while he finished a little work. When he was working on a medium-sized canvas, he would put it on the easel and attach the sketch just above the canvas. The easel was about Alec's height. It had an extension and could accommodate large canvases, although Alec painted these infrequently in his later years. When he did paint a large canvas, the sketch would be propped up at the side.

Before starting to paint the canvas, Alec prepared the sketch. He took white thread and attached it to the panel in a horizontal and vertical pattern to divide the space into about two-inch squares. He then painted on the much larger canvas the areas of each little square of the sketch. He was interpreting what was on the panel, and he was creating a new composition with a quality of meaning of its own, frequently brightening the colour scheme and adding features that were not apparent on the sketch but in his opinion would enhance the artistic quality of the work.

Over the years, Alec got used to my asking occasional simple-minded questions. The first time I saw him use one of the panels criss-crossed with white threads, I inquired whether this technique were not confining to an artist. On the contrary, Alec replied — he liked the freedom a larger canvas gave him while still allowing him to remain true to the landscape he'd seen in its natural beauty when painting the sketch.

When Alec painted, he held his brush with his right hand curled into a fist around it. This grip looked contorted, but it did not seem to have any adverse effect on the way he painted. It was said that Alec held the brush, using his thumb in this way, as the result of an arthritic condition, and I accepted the explanation as everyone else did. But

Dr. Robert Starrs said Alec had never had arthritis: the brush technique was a habit Alec had acquired and reflected the intensity with which he approached painting. As Dr. Starrs put it, Alec had "most supple hands and fingers."

In the early days in Manotick I noticed that Alec used his left hand to hold a palette on which he had spread the colours he required for a canvas. His thumb inserted in the opening, he usually gripped four different brushes — one in his right hand and three in his left (see below).* Alec had his own painting style. In the late fifties, he gave up using the palette, for by then he found it easier to hold only the brush he was using and leave the paint and other brushes nearby.

The first five years in his Manotick studio-home were happy ones for Alec. He liked being in the country in a small and friendly community. The hilltop location moved him to look beyond where the eye could see to the far distances. The closeness of the river was inspiring to one who admired the endlessness of its flow.

But in time his sentiments changed. Alec had expected that moving

*Alec gave us this photograph of himself at work on November 29, 1964. It was taken in the fifties by the National Film Board in his Manotick studio.

to a small place far away from Toronto would allow him more time for his work, but this was not the way things worked out. He was now well known, and the world would beat a path to his door no matter where he lived. He wrote to Anne Savage on November 7, 1958: "Settling down to rural bliss in Manotick is not as simple as it seems. They shove me into the limelight."[45] Alec never admitted to himself that he rather liked the limelight and that all the lectures and press interviews could not help but keep his name before the Canadian public.

Transportation had become difficult for him. The bus service between Manotick and Ottawa was reduced to a single bus in the morning going to Ottawa and returning to Manotick in the late afternoon. It took Alec a whole day to buy paint supplies instead of an hour. He would wander around the city with little to do but wait for the bus. When he went out of town on sketching trips or visits it was difficult to make connections (he preferred to travel by bus). In an interview, Alec told a reporter that he "felt isolated in Manotick" and that it was too difficult to get to Ottawa, Toronto, and Montreal.[46] If he was invited to dinner in the city, it meant a long journey each way for friends who drove to get him and brought him home.

Moreover, his arrangements with his niece had not quite worked out as planned. Ton was busy raising three children and looking after a husband who was not well. She could not drive Alec around whenever he wanted to go. There were also occasional differences about mealtimes and privacy and the little squabbles that occur in the best of families. Alec had a way of bringing family disputes to an end that amused Ton. He would look at her and say, "All right, let's have a fight." A few arguments later, he would say loudly, "That's enough. Let's have a drink and make up." Invariably, Ton would laugh and after some liquid refreshment friendly relations were quickly restored. As a non-parent, Alec had a more effective way of dealing with the younger generation than most parents in coping with their adult children. Ton's children adored "Uncle Alec." Still, the business of everyday living had to be considered.

The time had come for Alec to make a change. A move to Ottawa became feasible in 1962 when he learned that George Loranger was leaving for Toronto and that his apartment at 192 MacLaren Street would be available.

I never asked Alec what it cost him to buy the two lots and to construct the building in Manotick, but a reasonable estimate would be less than fifteen thousand dollars. When Alec sold the place to Hubert Rogers in 1966, he mentioned to me that he sold it for about what it had cost him to build eleven years earlier. "I wanted an artist to have the place and I knew that artists have to struggle for their money," he remarked. Later, when I consulted Rogers, he confirmed my estimated figure. I have heard higher estimates from other sources, but I am inclined to accept the Rogers explanation.

It was not easy to find either a tenant or a buyer for the studio-home in Manotick. Alec eventually managed to rent the place to a civil servant, who stayed there until 1966. In 1964, Alec was approached by Hubert Rogers, a Canadian portrait painter originally from Prince Edward Island who had studied and lived in the United States. Rogers was looking for a studio, and Alec rented the Manotick studio to him for forty dollars a month, with the civil servant continuing to occupy the house. When the latter left in 1966, Rogers purchased the whole property from Alec.

In the year he bought the place, Rogers painted a portrait of Alec in the Manotick studio. There were six sittings of about two hours each. Alec, who by that time was eighty-four years old, would fall asleep during the sessions. Rogers saw in Alec a man of great dignity with most sensitive hands. The portrait is interpretative in nature, and it reminded me of Graham Sutherland's painting of Churchill, painted with less feeling but with greater compassion than Sutherland seemed to have felt for Churchill. (This painting was subsequently destroyed on order of Lady Churchill.) Rogers's way was to paint the sitter as he saw him. When asked what he was seeing as he painted Alec, he replied; "A. Y. had a flash of pure cobalt blue in his eyes as if he had spent a lifetime looking at great distances, which he had, in painting the North. He was a kindly, warm-hearted genius. Other artists saw him as a character and caricatured him, but I portrayed the man."

Alec began the move from Manotick to Ottawa after his eightieth birthday party at our house on May 5, 1962. It took him most of a month to complete transferring all his belongings in three cars to the new location. He had help from his two doctor friends, Bob Starrs and Fred Jeffries, their wives, Rita and Winnifred (Winnie), and Ralph Burton.

The apartment needed thorough cleaning and since Alec said nothing about hiring a cleaning woman, his friends rallied round and cleaned it themselves to make it habitable again. Everybody was very good-natured about helping, and Alec agreed to throw a party at the new place sometime after the move was completed.

The building he was moving into was known locally as the old Fred Booth House. Booth, who belonged to one of the well-established and prosperous "old" families of Ottawa, had made his money in lumber and raised his family in what was at that time a good centre-town location. The house was on the south side of MacLaren near the corner of Elgin Street. A block away was St. John's Anglican Church, at

41

the corner of Somerset and Elgin. Shopping, laundry facilities, a barber, restaurants, and a bank were just around the corner; the National Gallery of Canada and an art supply firm on Bank Street were within a ten-minute walk.

The location suited Alec perfectly and he continued to live there until his illness in 1968. From a painter's viewpoint, the apartment itself was not as satisfactory as the studio in Manotick: neither the space nor the lighting was as good. Nevertheless, Alec considered the Ottawa place "manageable." It also gave him a feeling of greater freedom and flexibility, and that was important to him.

The three-storey building was faced with red brick, and what was called at the turn-of-the-century a stately residence had been converted into several apartments. Alec's place, where he lived and painted for six years, was to the left on the ground floor.

The visitor came right into what Alec used as a living room. There was a large window on the opposite side and a spacious opening on the left leading to the room Alec used as his studio. To the right was a fireplace and another wide arch leading to a room that could have been used as either a dining room or a bedroom but which I called the "clutter room." It had a very large table in the centre. To the left of that room a glass door led to an unheated sunroom that Alec used for storage. The whole side of the sunroom was made up of windows, but in winter Alec had to keep the door to it closed. In summer, the apartment could become unbearably hot. The two small windows that could be opened were to the left of the sunroom. Alec had to take a stool to open these windows, and he found it quite a nuisance. Frequently he preferred to put up with the heat rather than struggle with the windows.

Alec's "clutter" was of two types, that which he sometimes used and that for which he had little or no use. Some of the clutter of the second type was kept in the sunroom, along with a second refrigerator, used to store his ginger ale. On the right side of the clutter room was a narrow hall leading to a small bedroom, which Alec largely used for storage, a tiny kitchen, and a bathroom. The main rooms were of good size and had high ceilings with an ornamental finish. The wood panelling of the walls, darkened with the passage of time, still reflected the elegance of elite living in bygone days.

The room used as the studio had two windows on the street side, both with stained glass upper panes. Alec sometimes drew the blinds on the left window, relying on the sunlight coming from the right window. He slept on a small bed just inside the entrance to the room and kept his clothes in and on top of a high ornamental cupboard which he also sometimes used to hide sketches from nosy visitors. He had set

up the large easel he used for most of his painting in front of the left window, and there was also a spare easel. Although the overhead electric lighting was adequate, there must have been little natural light on grey days. The space available to work in was a good deal less than in the Manotick studio, but I seldom heard Alec complain about the shortcomings.

One day in January 1968, Alec had a date to take Betty Kirk out for lunch. She asked him whether she could snap a picture of him painting. Since Alec was already dressed to go out, he took off his jacket, placed a finished painting on the easel, and took some brushes in his right hand. The scene is a posed one, for Alec didn't have on his painting pants and open shirt (he is wearing a white shirt and tie). He is also holding a cigarette in his left hand — something I never saw him do when he was concentrating on a painting. As the photograph above shows, there is a reproduction of one of Alec's paintings on the wall between the two shuttered windows. It was one of the only two indications of Alec's works in the apartment (the other was in the kitchen), because the painting on the easel had been pre-sold.

The living room had a couch, several chairs (including my favourite rocker), two tables, one of them quite small, bookcases, and lamps. There were three ornate fireplaces, two with gas grates, one to burn wood. Alec liked the cheerfulness of a crackling wood fire and did not use the gas grates. There were also radiators from a central heating system. The place could get quite hot in winter, and Alec sometimes had to open the door to the sunroom to bring the temperature down.

The crowded kitchen had an open shelf where Alec kept plates, cups, cutlery, and other kitchen utensils and supplies. His teapot stood on the top of the two-shelf construction, still within easy reach. After Alec had sold all his paintings, he used to prop up a print of one of them on the top shelf in the kitchen, just behind the teapot. It was one way to remind himself of his earlier work.

There was also a stove with the oven door off its hinges. As Alec never bothered to get it repaired, the oven was never used. He heated his food on the top elements, and he felt that he was doing all right. When his friend Betty Kirk visited him, she would shake her head, but since Alec seemed to be quite happy with a partially functioning stove, she accepted his attitude as one of his quaint habits.

I had the opportunity to get to know Alec's living habits somewhat better after he moved to Ottawa. They were ingrained, acquired in a long life as a bachelor, and he varied them only for what he considered good reasons. He made his own breakfast, usually an egg, toast, marmalade, and coffee, sometimes cereal, which he was used to from his camping trips. He would listen to the eight o'clock radio news and then do some chores. By about eight-thirty he would be ready to start painting in his studio. He usually worked about six hours a day, with a break for a light lunch, which he prepared himself. When he was working intently on a canvas he hardly noticed the passage of time and had little need for nourishment. A wife would have had great difficulty getting him to have lunch at a regular hour.

He went out in the late afternoon to shop, do chores, or get a newspaper and cigarettes. If he had visitors, he preferred them to come late in the afternoon when the fading daylight made painting difficult. He was invited out to dinner by friends most evenings. Sometimes he prepared his own dinner or, when he was getting a little tired of his own cooking, he would go to a restaurant nearby. Unless he was out, he would be in bed by eleven o'clock. In his studio, the work week was six days. At other times, all during the year except the cold weather in winter and in June, when he considered the landscape "too green," he went on sketching trips.

The years on MacLaren Street produced all kinds of stories about Alec. When he returned from one of his early spring trips, he looked

44

for hiding places for his sketches. He put one behind a radiator. The weather turned cold, and the janitor put the heat back on in the building. When Alec found the panel some weeks later, it was badly warped. In consternation, he phoned Ralph Burton and inquired whether his friend could help him. Burton glued the warped panel to a new panel and put it into a press. In due course the sketch was flattened, and one of the many people wanting to buy Alec's sketches was made happy.

He did not have a very technical mind. On one occasion he complained to Burton that the refrigerator was not working; when Burton checked, he found that Alec had neglected to plug the cord into the socket.

The large table in the clutter room was the main depository for Alec's mail and over several years the mail accumulated to a height of several inches, spread over a large surface. Late in 1963, on one of my visits to his studio, I asked Alec whether he answered his mail. He said he sometimes did. I picked up one letter from the pile. It was more than a year old, and I mentioned the name of the writer to Alec. "Oh, she wanted a painting," he said, adding, "it's no use answering a letter that old."

"If you aren't going to write to her, why don't you throw away the letter?" I asked.

"I'll get around to it," he replied, and I put the letter back on the table. But as time went on, the pile of unanswered correspondence got higher and higher.

Alec gave two parties while he lived at 192 MacLaren Street — his "moving in" party late in 1962 and another early in 1965. He left most of the arrangements to his friends Doctors Starrs and Jeffries and their wives. A party meant new rounds of clean-ups and removal of clutter. Between sixty and seventy people were invited to the party on December 18, 1962, for drinks and food. Alec undertook to look after the liquor, and his friends arranged and paid for the food, which was supplied by a caterer, together with glassware, plates, and other party paraphernalia.

When the place was cleaned up, it looked quite respectable. Since Alec did not own a single one of his own paintings, his friends rallied round and lent him for that evening a number of paintings he had done in years gone by. Alec remarked on a later occasion, with a smile, "I could have sold the whole bunch several times over."

In order to keep costs down, the two doctors offered to tend the bar at the first party, and Alec was happy to accept the suggestion. With two other friends to help them, they looked after the guests while Alec, as the genial host, made the rounds, welcoming guests, showing them around, and joining in the cheerful laughter. When my wife and I left the party, which went on rather late, we agreed that this was the first time we had seen two doctors serving as bartenders and that Alec had indeed some loyal friends.

The second party on February 19, 1965, was called for 5:30 to 8:30 p.m., but it lasted much longer. Alec engaged two waiters for this occasion, and as a result there was less wear and tear on Alec and his close friends. Dr. Starrs was worried that Alec might get mixed up on ordering the liquor or that when the supplies arrived he would hide them and forget where he had put them. In fact, Alec bought only a few bottles at a time and did mislay them. But the arrangements all worked out well except for the food. Dr. Starrs had asked for prices from two caterers, and he placed the order with the caterer who had quoted the lower price. When he arrived at Alec's place on the day of the party, he discovered that both caterers had delivered the order for food and equipment. In the end, the caterer who had not been asked to supply things agreed to leave the order there at half-price. It turned out to be such a happy and late party that the double quantity of food was all consumed, along with most of the drinks.

Alec grew quite flushed during this party. Although he seemed to be enjoying the company, the strain began to show. He was eighty-two years old, and it was to be the last party he gave. It was easier on him to go to a party than to give one.

The house where he lived so happily in Ottawa was subsequently sold and the new owner tore it down. The commercial complex already on the corner of Elgin Street was extended along MacLaren Street. There are now stores on the site where Alec's studio used to be, and there is no indication that one of Canada's greatest painters lived and worked there for six years — not even a plaque. Some would call this progress; others weep for heritage lost.

CHAPTER 4
Alec's Social Life

A family lunch was the occasion for Alec's first visit to our home. The year was 1955, and we lived at that time at 243 Springfield Road in Rockcliffe Park. Our daughters Brenda and Cathy, aged seven and six, and our son, Bruce, aged four, were with us.

I picked Alec up at Manotick just before noon and we were back at about 12:30. He had a drink and then we sat down to lunch. Our children were shy at first, but his friendly personality and easy-going manner won them over. When he looked at some of the works of art we had collected, he mumbled encouragingly, "A good beginning." He inquired about the two reprints that had started me collecting Canadian art, his *The Red Maple* and Gagnon's *Village in the Laurentian Mountains*. I said I had given them away when I was able to replace them with paintings by himself and Gagnon.

When we invited Alec the next time, my wife suggested that we should take him to a restaurant, and we did. The noisy restaurant proved a poor background because of Alec's deafness, and we decided that in the future we would always invite him to come to our home, as we did over the next thirteen years.

Most of the time the meals were with the family. Sometimes the other guests were visitors from different parts of Canada and from abroad — artists, actors, educators, government officials, politicians, diplomats, newspapermen, professional people, and businessmen. Alec enjoyed meeting new people as well as old friends and acquaintances. He had a fund of stories, which he was always happy to share. His smile and good humour were infectious. My wife used to call him the "belle of the ball." He was amused by this, but he never told us why he chuckled. I thought it might have had something to do with the name of our house, "Belmanor," or with Isobel's endearment suggesting that he was the honoured guest in our house.

Before a meal, Alec usually had two ryes with ice and ginger ale (later changed to water when it was found that he had a mild diabetic condition). He would have two glasses of white or red wine with lunch or dinner. He was a moderate smoker, occasionally having a cigarette after the meal. Isobel would offer him a cigarette before we ate, but he would always turn it down. He said he smoked about eight cigarettes a day but none while painting outdoors.

When we first knew Alec, the family consisted of my wife and me, three children, and a live-in maid. It was the arrival of our fourth child, Peter, that decided us to build a new home. We were running out of space, given the expansion in our art collection as well as our family. When we ran out of wall space, we had started to place paintings against windowpanes. Then we stored a number of them in the attic bedroom our maid occupied. We had to keep some of our sculptures in the garage, leaving the car outside. When the basement began to fill up with works of art, a move became imperative.

The new house, five blocks away at 375 Minto Place, was considerably larger. It had three stories with eight thousand square feet of space, high ceilings, and a special lighting, humidifier, and airflow system to accommodate works of art. We moved in on August 15, 1960.

Since Alec did not drive, I would pick him up when he joined us for a meal and chat and take him home afterward. During the seven years he lived in Manotick, I made the trip three or four times a year. It took forty-five minutes each way in winter and a little less when the snow and ice had departed. Alec used to be apologetic about this, but when he saw how genuinely happy we all were about his visits, he accepted the arrangement as a fact of life.

When he moved to Ottawa, Alec had an extra-loud bell installed so that he could hear the telephone ringing. To visitors it sounded like an alarm bell, and it needed getting used to.

On the other hand, he found that the doorbell rang too softly for him to hear. So we worked out a system — I would throw little stones at the front window of his studio, where his easel stood, until he came to the window and waved. In winter, snow covered the little stones, so I used a stick (kept in the station wagon) to knock at Alec's windows. When these knocking systems failed, as they occasionally did, I would phone him from a neighbour's, and soon Alec would open his door, looking apologetic. Once when neither knocking or phoning helped, I phoned Isobel to say that we would be late for lunch, then sat down on the outside steps and waited. Twenty minutes later a jaunty Alec, striding quickly, turned the corner from Elgin to MacLaren. He had gone to the store around the corner to buy a newspaper and had run into the minister of St. John's Church. They had had a "brief" chat. "What did you talk about?" I asked. "I told him that last Sunday's sermon was very good," he replied.

Going to church was a new habit that Alec acquired in Ottawa. In the seven years he lived in Manotick, he almost never went to church, except to the midnight services at Christmas with the Hamiltons and their children. But St. John's Anglican Church in Ottawa was only a block from where he lived. When we invited Alec for Sunday lunch, I parked the car in the side lane of his building and walked to the church to meet him. He always talked to a few people as he was leaving the church and shook hands.

Invariably I would ask, "How was the sermon today?" Invariably he would answer, "It was a very good sermon." The only variation he ever made was to replace "good" with "fine." I suspected that Alec, being hard of hearing, had really heard very little of what the minister had said, but we did not discuss the texts of the sermons.

Alec was an excellent guest. He liked good food, good drink (within reason), and good company. Isobel would say to him, "It's a pleasure to feed you." On one occasion, he replied, "It is a double pleasure if the company is good." When he noticed her pleased expression, he added, "I feel at home here."

Alec often told tales, drawing on his experiences of over half a century. In his lifetime Canadian art had gone through three stages: neglect and disapproval, neutrality and curiosity, and finally growing interest and active support. Besides talking about his life as an artist during those years, he was ready to discuss topics of current interest — politics, economics, social questions, and international relations. Alec was a cheerful conversationalist, looking where possible on the positive side and using quick repartee or a humorous remark to make his point.

When the occasion presented itself, Alec delighted in holding court. On March 20, 1966, we asked him to come to a buffet supper we were giving for the Stratford Festival Company, which was performing in Ottawa. The invited guests included the actors and actresses, the administrative personnel, and the support staff. Supper was served on the main floor and the lower level. Afterwards, everybody congregated on the main floor until I asked some of our guests whether they wanted to hear some of Alec's stories about art and artists in his lifetime. Our guest of honour and perhaps a dozen people went downstairs. After about an hour, some of the people drifted upstairs, telling others that Alec had been fascinating them with his tales (not an easy accomplishment, because actors can readily detect when somebody is putting on a show). Another group went downstairs, and later a third group joined them. For over four hours Alec responded warmly to all their questions and repeated his stories for the various groups.

By that time the audience seemed exhausted, but Alec was still going strong, with pink cheeks, a sparkle in his eye, and a half-empty wine glass in his hand. I was concerned that his health would not stand the strain, but that night he was not prepared to go to bed early. When I brought him back to his apartment, it was nearly 4 a.m. I asked, "Aren't you tired?"

"Not me," Alec replied. "I had a great time. They were a fine bunch of people, and they were really keen to hear more about Canadian art and Canadian artists. They were telling me how hard it was to make a living as an actor. Well, I told them I'm not sure who is worse off in Canada, a young painter or a young actor."

I called Alec late that afternoon to ask how he felt. He said he was okay and he had gotten up early, as usual. "How can I feel tired when I've had so much fun?" he asked.

"Well, I admire your vitality, because I'm tired," I replied.

"Nothing to it," he said, "if you lead a simple life and if you like people."

When I meet any of the Stratford group after all these years, they still speak with great fondness of that night when Alec held court like royalty.

Alec's niece Naomi also commented on her uncle's love of parties. When she was teaching at McMaster University and Alec was living in Toronto, she called him one day to ask how he was. He mentioned to her "that he had been out seven times for dinner in the past week and what a good thing it was that there were only seven days in the week."[47] Although Alec accepted invitations to dinner quite frequently when he lived in Ottawa, the pace of his social life apparently slackened somewhat from the Toronto days.

As the years passed, we noticed a little change in Alec. His memory sometimes slipped. He might forget things he had done the day or the week before, though he remembered clearly what had happened twenty-five or fifty years earlier. He also began to fall asleep briefly from time to time, usually after a meal. When he had finished his dessert, and while his coffee was being served, he would lean back contentedly and lead the subject under discussion to a situation or an incident that had occurred in his life some years ago. Then, suddenly, he would close his eyes and be asleep. He made little noises like a soft whistle.

Our children, who had heard Alec's stories many times, would excuse themselves. Isobel and I would converse quietly. Ten or fifteen minutes later, Alec would open his eyes and ask abashedly, "Have I been asleep?" We assured him it had been only for a few minutes. And then, amazingly, Alec would resume telling us the story, starting exactly where he had left off when he had fallen asleep. How he did this we never knew, but the feat became a continuing source of amusement to us in which Alec joined good-naturedly.

When Alec was living in Ottawa, he came to our house about once a month if he was in town and sometimes more often. In addition, Isobel and I would pick him up and take him to National Gallery openings, exhibitions at commercial galleries, and diplomatic receptions. Sometimes we took trips away from Ottawa. Between times, I would drop in on him, always making an appointment for a time that would not interfere with his work or other visitors. A number of people were frequent visitors. The person closest to Alec was his niece Naomi, for whom he had warm feelings and who cared for her uncle. He also saw a great deal of Betty Kirk. The other friends who saw most of Alec were his two doctor friends, Bob Starrs and Fred Jeffries (the latter a part-time artist), and his painter friends Maurice Haycock and Ralph Burton. The doctors and their wives not only helped Alec move into his apartment but also often invited him to their homes. Haycock, who was a geologist by profession, shared Alec's love of the North. Burton, a former high school art teacher, had been a student of Alec's at the Banff School of Fine Arts after the war. Both men often went on sketching trips with Alec, and his artistic influence was not without its effect on the work of both.

Alec appreciated Haycock's help in getting the studio in Manotick started, and I got the distinct impression that if it had not been for Haycock, the Manotick house would never have been built. Haycock, in turn, had a high regard for Alec. In one instance his esteem took a unique form in paying homage to one of Canada's great. In 1968, Haycock had a 9 by 12 inch bronze plaque engraved, and he deposited it in a cairn (about six feet square at the base and nearly six feet high) at Alexandra Fort, near Bache Peninsula — about seven hundred miles from the North Pole — where Alec had done his most northerly painting on his trip to the eastern Arctic in 1927. Haycock also put into the cairn an iron pipe containing a few photographs, a drawing of the *Beothic*, the supply ship on which Alec had travelled to Bache Peninsula, and an account of building the cairn.[48] Haycock told Alec about the cairn after he recovered somewhat from his severe illness, and he was pleased. It was a truly great tribute to an artist who loved the North.

Alec liked Burton's gentle nature, and Burton could not do enough for Alec, in spite of his independent nature, when they went on a sketching trip together. On one trip in the spring of 1960, Burton did a study of Alec in his hotel room in Calabogie, Ontario (see page 52). As he did later when Hubert Rogers painted his portrait, Alec fell asleep during the sitting.

Outside Ottawa, Alec regularly visited his friends the Putnams in Grenville, Quebec. When he went there in spring and fall to sketch, Mrs. Putnam (Joyce) looked after his lodging and food. Her husband, Munro ("Putty"), a forest engineer with the Canadian International Paper Company, worked in Hawkesbury. Being a diabetic himself, he

R.W. Burton, *Study of A. Y. Jackson*
Spring, 1960.   Oil on panel, 13½″ x 10½″

had great sympathy for Alec. Putty generally liked to accompany Alec on his sketching trips when he was in Grenville.

When Alec was in his eighty-fourth year, Bruce Moss did a photo-story on one of Alec's outings to sketch on the bank of the Rouge River, about sixty miles east of Ottawa. Putty was with Alec on this occasion. Sitting on his small camp stool and moving very little, Alec concentrated on his sketch to portray the coming of spring with snow still on the ground. He worked intently, disregarding the cold wind that was blowing across the river and the stiffening of his body. An hour and a half later, the sketch completed, Alec called for Putty; he helped Alec to his feet with a heave-ho and steadied him until feeling returned to his limbs. Both men laughed as the tension eased.[49]

Alec's sketching trips took him away intermittently for four or five months a year, but then he always returned to his studio to paint up his canvases, like a homing pigeon returning to its nest. It was during this period that we saw him, his visits being one of the great joys of our lives. The last time he came to our house was Saturday, April 13, 1968. A week later he collapsed, never to recover his old vigour and independence.

CHAPTER 5

Alec's
Eightieth Birthday Party

Alec's eightieth birthday was October 3, 1962. In the fall of 1961, I approached him — would he like to celebrate his birthday at our home? If so, would he like to name the guests to be invited? Would a group of about fifty people from Ottawa, Toronto, Montreal, and elsewhere at a dinner party be acceptable? Alec replied that in principle the answer was yes, and that he would think about it and let us know definitely.

When I saw him next in his studio in Manotick, he mentioned that he wanted to go ahead with the party, but he had two problems. The first was that he was likely to be on a sketching trip on October 3. Could we celebrate his birthday early, in May 1962? He liked parties and he enjoyed being with friends, but his first priority was painting. "You are eighty when you say you are eighty, as far as we are concerned," I replied, and we therefore agreed that we would celebrate, in Ottawa, on Saturday, May 5. I added, "Anyway, you'll probably have a second party in Toronto when you get back from your sketching trip." We both thought that was a good joke.

As it turned out, I underestimated the possibilities: Alec celebrated his eightieth birthday three times. The first party was with us in May in Ottawa. The second was on his birthday at Clear Lake, where he had been painting, when Robert and Rita Starrs gave him a small dinner party at their cottage, at which Maurice Haycock was also present. There was a third party in Toronto later in October.

Alec's second problem was his guest list, which was getting out of hand. He said he hadn't realized how many relatives and friends he had. Instead of fifty people there might be a hundred or more. I told him that whatever number he suggested was fine with us, that instead of one dinner, perhaps we could have two, plus a reception and other get-togethers over a period of two days. We eventually agreed on festivities to last two days and two nights – or at least a good part of each night. In the long run, about 250 people (including some who came to two or three of the occasions) helped celebrate Alec's eightieth birthday in Ottawa.

Over the next several months we discussed the arrangements. As the guest list grew longer and longer we discarded the idea of a personal note to each invitee and agreed on a printed invitation. Together we decided on the wording, and I asked Alec whether we should use the C.M.G., R.C.A., and LL.D after his name. He said it would do no harm.

We discussed the speakers at the main occasion and Alec's response; we decided who should be invited to the two dinners and who to the reception; we chose the caterer, the liquid refreshments, the menu. Alec seemed to get as much fun out of the planning as he did out of the actual events. I asked one favour: no publicity. It was to be a private party. Alec agreed.

To ease the transportation problem, we suggested that Alec might stay with us on the nights of May 4 and 5. He thought that a first-rate idea, because he was in the throes of arranging the move to Ottawa, although he was still living in Manotick. Moreover, many of his friends were coming from out of town, and he wanted to see them during the days as well as in the evenings.

He was amazed at the response we got — most of the people on his guest list were coming. He was particularly pleased by the large contingent of his artist friends. Of the five other surviving members of the Group of Seven, the three who were well enough to travel were coming. They were A. J. Casson, with his wife, Margaret; Edwin Holgate, with his wife, Frances; and Arthur Lismer. Ill-health kept Lawren Harris and Fred Varley from attending. Other artists who came to the party were Peter Haworth and his wife, Bobs Cogill; George Pepper and his wife, Kathleen Daly; Charles Comfort with his wife, Louise; Carl Schaefer with his wife, Lillian; Henri Masson with his wife, Germaine; Wilf Ogilvie with his wife, Sheelah; Anne Savage; Isabel McLaughlin; and Ralph Burton with his wife, Lovedy. Most members of the Jackson family came, and many close friends.

The festivities began May 4, when I brought Alec back from Manotick in the morning. After lunch and a walk in Rockcliffe Park, we greeted arriving guests from out of town in the garden. Most of them were Alec's artist friends, and they had years of news to catch up on. The dinner guests began to arrive at six o'clock. The party this first evening was very informal, a chance for Alec and his friends to reminisce and tell stories. At eleven o'clock Alec had a nightcap and went off to bed.

Next morning, he was up at seven, and we breakfasted together. Arthur Lismer arrived at ten o'clock. Alec was in a happy mood. He suggested to Lismer and myself that we go for a walk before lunch, and accordingly we set out. Most of the conversation was serious, but there was also much good-natured ribbing between Alec and Lismer.

As we started, the first thrust came from Alec. "Isn't it a good thing there's so much fresh air here in Rockcliffe Park? We won't be bothered by your smelly pipe, Arthur," Alec teased, referring to Lismer's several attempts to light a pipe during a gust of wind.

"Well," Lismer replied, "smoking a pipe is certainly healthier than those junky cigarettes you're using."

"I'll be eighty years old soon, and those cigarettes haven't hurt me. I'm not so sure whether it's smoking that shortens your life expectancy or the wear and tear that comes from being married."

"Now Alec," Lismer admonished, "a good wife can be a blessing. She will have dinner ready for you, and she will bring you your slippers when you are tired."

"Arthur," Alec observed, looking amused, "when did your wife last bring you your slippers?"

"I can't remember," was the response. "But I can tell you, a well-cooked meal at home beats anything you can get in a restaurant."

"Looking at your skinny frame, Arthur, home-cooked meals don't seem to have done much for you. Look at the results of my own cooking, or eating out at restaurants or at friends' places," Alec chuckled, stroking his rotund midriff.

"The trouble with you, Alec," Lismer retorted, "is that you're always claiming results that have no logic to them. You're fat not because of where you eat but because you eat too much or you eat the wrong type of food. Your drinking adds to your weight, too. Look what you missed by not having a wife."

Then Lismer burst out laughing. "What's so funny?" I asked.

"Oh, I just remembered how baffled Alec looked at a Vancouver showing of his Arctic paintings, I believe it was in 1932, when he was told about the remark a teenager who looked at his paintings made. The youngster turned to his father and said, 'If we want to know how the Arctic really looks, we better use a camera. We'd never know it from Mr. Jackson's paintings.' "*

"Well, some people didn't think that your landscapes were so hot either — they called them 'distortions of nature,' " Alec observed. "Anyway, you realize that all this is your fault, you and the other art educators. If you did a better job of teaching youngsters what art is really all about, you'd make the artists' job easier in communicating with people."

By this time, I thought I should intervene. "Arthur, we're celebrating Alec's eightieth birthday today. Haven't you anything nice to say about him?"

---

*Both Alec and Lismer used to repeat versions of this story. It appeared in print in "Artists' Sketches," an article by J. A. Radford in the *Vancouver Sun*, December 10, 1932.

"Yes, I have," Lismer replied. "Alec paints better than I do, he paints more, he travels more, and he is more popular. But he's not as funny as I am. If you come right down to it, Alec has no sense of humour. He hides it well with his modest little remarks and his chuckle, so people think he's funny. But I know better."

"Who, besides yourself, says *you* are funny?" Alec retorted.

"Now that *is* funny," Lismer broke in and we all laughed. "Talking about being funny, do you remember your 'favourite' art critic, Hector Charlesworth? He referred to you as the painter who did 'Georgian Bay cartoons.'[50] Charlesworth was an ass. *You* couldn't do a cartoon if somebody put a pin in your behind. But if you really wanted to do cartoons, Alec, and you asked nicely, I could teach you."

"But Arthur," Alec shot back, "you're having trouble teaching youngsters. What could you do with an old coot like myself? Besides, Arthur, you say I have no sense of humour, but your sense of humour can be quite cutting. Do you remember the cartoon you did of me, calling me 'Alexander the Great,' after the National Film Board did a film showing me at work? But I didn't mind it because I know better how you really feel."

"Well," Lismer replied, "the film made you look rather pompous. You *are* a little pompous, you know, but not as much as the film showed."

The conversation changed to talk of other artists and Alec's travel plans. Listening to these two men who had a genuine affection for each other, I had the feeling that I was observing two old friends in a "battle" of words. When they realized the bout had ended in a draw, they were content. It was a matter of matching wits, for the fun of it. The comradeship, not the winning of an argument, mattered.

We returned to lunch. In the late afternoon Alec's artists friends and other guests began to arrive. Alec took many of them to the Jackson Room, and Lismer guided parties to the Lismer Room. A three-hour reception for about a hundred and fifty followed, with guests at this affair a combination from Alec's list and our Ottawa friends from the government, diplomatic, and academic communities. When nine o'clock, the hour for serving the buffet supper had come, many of them had not left, although we had expected a group of only sixty guests. In the end, all of this larger group stayed on for supper. Fortunately, there was ample food and wine and a well-trained catering staff.

It was past eleven o'clock when we were ready for the speeches. Among telegrams and letters from those who were not able to be there was one from artist Joe Plaskett: he was sorry that there had had to be a choice between his father's ninetieth birthday and Alec's eightieth, and that his father had priority. With tongue in cheek, but also with a feeling of reverence, Plaskett wrote that he had been "forced to retreat" to Paris "since you have pre-empted the whole of Canada as your artistic territory." He added how much he admired Alec's work, "the subtlety and truth of your vision, and the pure felicity of your brush."

Alec's pink complexion did not permit me to tell whether he blushed or not when he heard this praise from one of the younger generation of artists, who had frequently been quite critical of their older colleagues. But I saw his eyes glow with pride as the artists and other friends present at the gathering broke into lengthy applause after hearing Plaskett's comments which, for Alec's sake, I had read slowly and loudly.

That done, I introduced the three speakers. All three and their wives were good friends of ours, and one of them had known Alec all his professional life. The other two, one a staunch Liberal and the other a dedicated Conservative, had met Alec more recently. They had great admiration for what he was trying to do in interpreting Canada to Canadians and in making them proud of their land.

Maurice Lamontagne, the first speaker, had been the leading French-speaking economist in Canada in the fifties. At the time of Alec's eightieth birthday party, he was economic adviser to Lester B. Pearson, then Leader of the Opposition. In the election of April 1963 he was elected a Member of Parliament and became a member of the government as President of the Privy Council. It was while he was holding this position that he was involved in ensuring that Alec's design for a Canadian flag received consideration from both the Government and a House of Commons special committee.

Allister Grosart had been a newspaperman and a public relations consultant, and had had a great deal to do with the election of John G. Diefenbaker as leader of the Progressive Conservative Party in 1956 and the winning of the 1957 and 1958 federal elections. Grosart became National Director of the party in 1957 and a member of the Senate in 1963. He was a very literate person — he liked Shakespeare's plays in their pure form, and could match his knowledge of Shakespeare with any professor of English Literature in Canada.

Charles Comfort, the third speaker, was a muralist and painter (landscape, portrait, and non-objective works). He taught at the Ontario College of Art from 1934 to 1938 and at the University of Toronto from 1938 to 1960. He had also had a stint as a war artist from 1943 to 1946. In 1960 he moved to Ottawa to become director of the National Gallery of Canada. He was well known and recognized internationally as a scholar and an art academic.

After my introductory remarks on our guest of honour's vigour of spirit and body, the three speakers arose in turn (two of them afterward gave me the texts of their speeches, and I made notes on Lamontagne's improvised remarks). Maurice Lamontagne addressed the gathering first in French and later in English. He said he had tested Alec before supper and had found him fluent in French — not just the French spoken by city people but also the "joual" spoken by farmers in the backwoods of Quebec.

Lamontagne referred to Alec's career first as a Quebec painter, then as an Ontario painter, and in the end as a truly Canadian painter acclaimed by the whole country. Even after he left Montreal in 1913 for the "greener pastures" of Toronto, Alec continued to have a soft spot for Quebec during the twenties and thirties and in more recent times. Such villages and small towns as Rivière-du-Loup, Baie-St-Paul, St-Hilarion near Les Eboulements, St-Fidèle near La Malbaie, St-Tite-des-Caps on Cap Tourmente all had become famous because their churches, their farms, and their barns had been painted by Alec. Alec had also painted the snow of Quebec with great feeling; it looked somehow different from the snow in other parts of the country — more blue, more windblown. He had many friends among Quebec painters, and got along particularly well with Clarence Gagnon. He felt at home with the farm folk of Quebec and their children.

But more important than Alec's personal warmth and fine painting, Lamontagne said, was his love for the land, a Canada worth working for and fighting for. He thought he could inspire people through his art to believe in a greater Canada, and became a beacon of light to Canadians from all walks of life, from all parts of the country and every cultural background.

Allister Grosart spoke next, representing "those hundreds of Canadians who once bought a Jackson that they couldn't afford but wouldn't give ... up for ten times their money back — or, indeed, for anything but a bigger and better Jackson." He referred to early reaction to the Group of Seven: "One critic said the Canadian landscape would never be the same again. Another critic said the government should outlaw the group because their realism would discourage people from coming to Canada, and sabotage immigration policy. Well, the landscape is still much the same ... and a few millions of immigrants have come to Canada undismayed by your landscapes." He spoke of Jackson as one of the founders of a truly Canadian school of painting and concluded by saying: "It was only the other day that I found out that the "Y" [in A. Y. Jackson] stood for Young, and I can think of nothing more appropriate to the occasion than to say that it was a very prophetic parent who looked forward across the years to allow me to refer to you today as one whose middle name is *Young*. May you long remain, as you are today, Young in mind and spirit, and in continuing enthusiasm for all things cultural and Canadian."

The final speaker was Charles Comfort, speaking with a great sense of propriety and a feeling for the historical occasion of honouring a great Canadian artist. Comfort in his talk mentioned a number of reasons for the affection and veneration in which Alec was held — his place as a creator of a "passionate consciousness of independent Canadian sovereignty," his contribution to Canadian cultural identity in painting, his inherent gentleness, his thoughtfulness: "Many ... as the season provides will have received from him possibly a fringed orchid or a luna moth, or possibly some moccasin flowers. Or he may have told [them] the tale of Billy France, the game warden, burning the poachers' boats, or tales of Tyson Lake, Iron Bridge, Nellie Lake, Biscotassing, or MacGregor Bay." He characterized Alec as "naturally and attractively gregarious. He meets a child with the same affable outgoing frankness and dignity as he would receive a Royal Prince. But gentleness and affability must never be mistaken for weakness. 'A. Y.' does not suffer fools gladly. Neither will he compromise or subordinate points of view which he regards as fundamental truths. He has always a word of encouragement for the talented young man or woman. But, whether their work be realistic or non-objective, he employs only one criterion for evaluation: it must be good."

Alec was lauded as "a man who has always found the sources of his inspiration in the country itself. A man who knows this country from St-Tite-des-Caps to the Skeena, from the Niagara Peninsula to Ellesmere Island. A man with a song in his heart, with the vocabulary of a poet and the energy and vision of an explorer. *Père Raquette*, who has snowshoed, paddled, and camped his way across this land, literally from sea to sea ... the man who has given us the rugged, colourful portrait of our land, who has shown us what it looks like and what it feels like to him ... for every sketch he paints is charged with his own profound emotional reaction to the subject of his interest."

Alec had chosen a seat near the piano where the speakers were standing, and his hand was frequently cupped to his ear; the speakers spoke a little louder than usual to oblige him. He now joined in the applause. When he rose to reply, he started off rather well. He was in good humour, his cheeks flushed from food, drink, the shower of compliments, the warm affection of family and friends, and the happy atmosphere that pervaded the occasion. Leaning against the piano, he thanked the speakers for their gracious remarks and the host and hostess for helping bring a lot of people dear to him together for that memorable occasion. He spoke one or two sentences in French to show that he was still in practice.

Alec's remarks had one main point: if you believe in something strongly enough, as he and the other members of the Group of Seven had, you should be undeterred by criticism, ignorance, and difficulties. You should do what you believe in, and sooner or later "right" will win out.

Unfortunately, to illustrate his point he got side-tracked into telling stories about the early days of the Group of Seven. As the clock neared and then passed midnight, it was clear that Alec was feeling the wear and tear of having talked almost continuously to dozens of people during the waking hours of the last two days. After going on for about thirty-five minutes, stopping only to catch his breath, Alec suddenly said: "I guess I'm talking too much. That's all. Thank you." There was a moment of silence when he suddenly stopped, then warm and sustained applause.

The waitresses brought in a large appropriately inscribed birthday cake with one burning candle. Alec dutifully blew out the candle; "Happy Birthday, Dear Alec" and "For He's a Jolly Good Fellow" were sung. Alec cut the first slice of the cake, with a little help from one of the waitresses, and champagne glasses were raised as the din of good companionship continued. Gradually, the crowd began to thin, and by about 3 a.m. the diehards were saying good-night-and-thank-you.

After the last guests were gone, Alec chatted with us before going to bed. Appropriately, his bed was made up in the Jackson Room. Although I should have known better, I encouraged Alec to sleep in in the morning. He smiled and said nothing.

About 8 a.m. I heard a noise in the kitchen — and went to investigate. There was Alec, fully dressed and looking as fresh as if he had had a long rest. He had gotten up early as usual. Everyone else in the house was asleep, so I made breakfast for the two of us, and we carried on what was, for an early Sunday morning, a remarkably philosophical discussion.

Marius Barbeau had asked Alec to drop in, and he also hoped to see a few of his Toronto friends who were staying over in Ottawa and say hello to Naomi and her husband. It was to be another busy day. I drove him to Barbeau's place, wondering how he could get along with so little sleep and be as vigorous as he appeared.

We received many phone calls and letters thanking us for the party. One of our friends, the counsellor of the Yugoslav Embassy, paid us a compliment by likening Alec's birthday party to a Serbian wedding. In earlier days, a wedding in the villages was a period of celebration

Meadowlark Ont
May 16th 1962

Dear Donald,

I am staying in Meadowlark. All my honeymoon in Ottawa, George Langen...

...

Very sincerely

Albert Jackson

lasting several hilarious days. Naomi Jackson Groves, as A. Y.'s eldest niece and on behalf of the Jacksons generally, wrote that the party had made him very happy, and "after all those hours of excitement, he came in the next day fresh as a daisy and pleased as Punch." Henrietta Banting, the widow of Dr. Frederick Banting, whom Alec had inspired to become a painter, remarked how happy her husband would have been to share in paying Alec this tribute. Anne Savage, of whom Alec was particularly fond, was pleased that the party "brought so many artists together who hadn't met for years. . . . It was a grand tribute to Alex — that is the kind of appreciation so few receive and what they value most." Mary Jackman (she and her husband Henry were long-standing friends of Alec's) observed that one of Alec's gifts was "his ability to continue to make new friends, both young and old. (I was touched with your children's interest in and affection for him.)" And so the letters went, the main theme being true affection for Alec.

A few weeks later a letter from Alec arrived. It was one of the most moving letters my wife ever received. Alec wrote of the celebration of his eightieth birthday as a "thrilling party" and "an event to be ever remembered." The letter, in his hand, is reproduced on page 61.

Alec's move to 192 MacLaren Street in Ottawa was completed later in May. When I visited him in his new studio shortly afterward, he returned to talk about the birthday party, particularly how pleased he was by the spontaneous way in which people from different backgrounds had blended into a homogeneous community, like an extended family willing to share a day (or days) of happiness with him. He chuckled, using understatement for emphasis, "Some party!"

Then, still smiling, he looked me straight in the eye and said, "Don't you think, Jack, it's time you called me Alex or A.Y., as my friends do?"*

"I shall be happy, Alec," I replied.

He chuckled again. "Alec is fine. That's what my grandnieces call me, 'Uncle Alec.'" And we shook hands.

In later days, he would accompany me to the foyer door of his building. On this occasion, he took his keys — the foyer door was always locked — and we walked together out of the building. He remained standing on the front veranda as I went to my car.

He looked serious and wistful as I said good-bye, and he watched me getting into the car. I waved to him as I drove away. He waved back. And so a long-standing acquaintance turned into a warm friendship.

---

*In earlier years some of his friends also called him Jackie.

CHAPTER 6

Sketching
at Kingsmere Lake

In June, 1963, Alec was in an in-between period. He had come back from a sketching excursion, and he had another trip planned. He was restless. The days were sunny and warm. The colour of the landscape was bright green, the kind I knew Alec didn't like.

Moreover, he was in a quandary. He had promised somebody a sketch, but there were none left. When Alec told me his difficulty, I offered to take him on a one-day sketching trip to Kingsmere Lake, about half an hour's drive up into the Gatineau country. Just past the MacKenzie King estate, fronting on the lake, was a place belonging to a friend of mine that Isobel and I and our children had used for many years. Alec agreed, and we set a date.

Picnic lunch in hand, I picked Alec up at nine-thirty on a fine June morning. He had his sketch box, paints, brushes, and sketchbooks neatly packed, and painting stool ready. The day was warm with bright sunshine; there was little wind, hardly a ripple on the water — a pleasant day for a picnic, but not a landscape particularly appealing to Alec. His restlessness must have been even greater than his aversion to the green of the scenery and the unruffled blue of the lake.

At our destination there was a steep drop to the shoreline. I gave Alec a hand as he slowly and carefully made his way down the narrow path. At eighty he was still lively in spirit but was beginning to slow down physically.

Alec surveyed the scenery and laid out all his painting things. After about ten minutes, he settled down on his little stool, with palette, brushes, and a paint knife ready. The paint had previously been placed on the lower panel of his sketch box. Another panel, 10½ by 13½ inches, was placed in an upright slanting position to receive the first brush strokes of the man who was going to look at nature and then compose a painting as a composer orchestrates a new music score. For Alec was not averse to rearranging nature's given forms, shapes, and colours if he felt that doing so would produce an artistically more meaningful whole.

"Very green, very green," Alec muttered to himself as he surveyed the scene, the calm lake, the shoreline on the other side, the tree nearby, the bright sunshine.

I observed Alec's eyes taking on that faraway look as he searched for things only he could see, enveloping himself with a protective umbrella of relentless concentration. His glances moved from his immediate surroundings to the farther distance, then up to the sky, very blue with a few wisps of cloud. He shrugged his shoulders and I heard a little sigh, as if he wanted to say that he had seen more interesting landscapes. Then there were the first few brush strokes on the panel, starting with an outline, then the selection of a few specifics. In this case, it was the tree nearby first, then the distant shore, then some more of the foreground. Next the lake water was indicated and a neutral sky. Then came the work on some of the details, painted unhurriedly with a firm hand and loving care — looking, painting, looking and painting again.

Alec's head moved little, but his eyes darted back and forth; a frown appeared, a few more brush strokes, the frown disappeared. The face was intent, the eyes were piercing, trying to see what others do not see, the mind and his creative instincts working with his eyes, the hand obeying instructions, as brush stroke after brush stroke gradually created the composition that Alec wanted to attain. It was his interpretation of nature, simplified to reflect its essential features. But it was more than that. It was his vision that made the unseeable seeable, that brought agelessness and unfounded space to life.

Suddenly he stopped. He looked as if he were searching for something. He mumbled and I couldn't hear. He wiped his brushes with some paper. Then he turned to me: "The water is so calm. A little wind would help." These were the first words he spoke after about three-quarters of an hour of concentrated painting. I nodded and said little, for I knew he didn't like conversation while he worked. I got up and said that I was going for a little walk. He nodded and turned to painting again without saying a word. The concentration and single-mindedness of the man fascinated me, and I thought about it as I strolled along the narrow road circling part of the lake.

What I was observing, I concluded, was a strong will at work, an urge to create, a determination to achieve a purpose, a searching spirit trying to catch the unseen, and a superhuman effort to forge a closer link between man and nature. As I looked back at Alec from up the road, he seemed a lonely, solitary figure, slightly bent, hardly moving in the stillness of the summer morning. But in fact he was not lonely.

Alec was tackling a challenge: the chasm between vision and reality. If he came too close to vision, he would be approaching non-figurative art. If he came too close to reality, he would reproduce nature, not interpret it. Could he bridge the gulf? Could he combine vision and reality without wrecking the boat on the reefs of, for him, meaningless abstractionism or mediocre realism? This was a task that required great ingenuity and deep insight.

As I walked along, thinking over what I had seen, I realized that Alec painted with so much joyous zest and dedicated intensity because he possessed these qualities. I remembered reading that at the age of twenty-four he had discovered that painting a landscape could involve the drama of an adventure story. Judging from his intensity at eighty, he still exuded the excitement felt in his youth blended with the wisdom and feeling that come from experience. Later, I looked up the quote. It read: "I got a glimpse of how the story of the land could be told with a deep feeling, with all the drama of an adventure story."[51]

I theorized: what was happening was a fusion between man and nature. The artist in the man became absorbed in its beauty, as he searched to unravel its mystery. And nature, like a light-footed elf, seemed to beckon him to come closer, only to appear more elusive the closer he approached

When I returned from my walk, I asked Alec, "Did you catch that light-footed elf?" He looked at me, startled. I explained the thoughts that had been going through my mind.

Alec chuckled and said, "You don't catch an elf; you just borrow a little of his magic. As it happened, the 'green' today was not as bad as I thought." He had achieved what he set out to do. He painted a little while longer, then he stopped. "It's almost finished. I'll do the rest at the studio," he remarked. Again, he cleaned his brushes carefully, closed his sketch box, and washed his hands in the lake.

I wished I had a camera with me to catch the intensity with which Alec tackled his sketch, but I didn't. Some three years later, however, Betty Kirk caught that same concentration when she photographed Alec at Notre Dame de la Salette (see page 66).

We sat down for lunch — sandwiches, an apple, and some coffee from a thermos. Alec was sitting on a bench in front of my friend's little changing cabin, and he leaned back contentedly. For once, he did not feel sleepy. He was feeling happy, and for over three hours we talked about many matters. Meanwhile the lake became livelier. Three children came out to swim nearby, and a sailboat appeared in the distance. In the course of the afternoon Alec took a little time off to make three drawings which he gave to me, one of the shore of Kingsmere Lake, the second a drawing of me, and the third a drawing of himself.

I inquired of Alec what made him concentrate on the Canadian landscape. He replied that he felt close to the soil himself and believed that he could spread happiness if he succeeded in communicating that

At Notre Dame de la Salette

nearness in his paintings of Canada. He had once been quoted in a way that confirms my recollections of our talk: "I have gone into places where people had never seen anything beautiful before, and tried to find beauty.... We haven't got any old architecture in Canada, any old churches, old cathedrals. Most of our towns are just horrible. But we do have some scenery.. . . . If my painting has made Canadians appreciate the beauty of their own country more than they used to, then that's my message."[52]

He admitted that on occasion he would paint or draw leaves, plants, shrubs, single trees, and flowers. He rarely did a still life. Yet Alec's severest critic, Hector Charlesworth, once observed that Alec could do a still life with great feeling. "His flower piece *Gentians*, exhibited at the O.S.A. last year [1923] was one of the most delicate and beautiful achievements in still life that has been seen in recent years."[53]

We talked about field sketches painted from nature. Alec estimated that each one took an hour and a half, on the average, and he remarked that when he took much longer to do a sketch, it was likely to be laboured and not turn out as well as one done spontaneously. His canvases were painted in the studio, usually with one sketch as the source, but sometimes combining features from two sketches, or one sketch and a drawing, or a drawing alone.

When I asked him whether there were differences in quality between sketches and canvases, he said that it depended on circumstances. If a canvas was painted shortly after the sketch had been made, either one might be of better quality. The canvas might be better because it was possible to plan carefully and improve weaknesses in the original sketch. On the other hand, the sketch could be better because it might reflect more accurately the mood and the feelings of the artist when he painted it and the spirit that moved him to do what he did.

Alec explained to me that the canvas is really a new painting. The original sketch may be the source of inspiration, but the new canvas has to pass a merit test of its own. I observed that Alec would frequently brighten the combination of colours in the canvas so that it had a less sombre appearance than the original sketch, quite apart from changes in the substance of the landscape.

A canvas might be inferior to a sketch for other reasons. In his later years, people frequently brought Alec old sketches and asked him to do canvases for them. He sometimes obliged, but invariably the sketch was superior to the canvas that followed. A canvas was also likely to be less satisfactory than a sketch if he elaborated a simple scene too much. He tried to avoid this, but it happened often enough for him to say that "many a sketch" was "a finer thing than the canvas it gave birth to."[54] Alec referred me to what Harris had said about how the members of the Group of Seven were using sketches, and I looked it up. Harris said:

Each one of us painted hundreds of sketches. The whole series of each of these represented a long communion with nature and a continuous endeavour to paint the different parts of the country according to what a scene or subject dictated. This endeavour inevitably invokes an inner vision, which is the only way an artist can respond to the dictates of a scene or subject in terms of its spirit, which alone can give a painting any enduring life. This is the creative interplay between the artist's observation and his developing inner life of aesthetic and spiritual response.[55]

I was aware that Alec set himself high standards of performance.

Sometimes it would take him weeks or months to achieve what he considered a satisfactory canvas. We have in our collection a large canvas, *Pickerel Weed, Split Rock Island, Georgian Bay*, that took several weeks just to reach the near-completion stage. One thing was still missing. Alec could not get the pickerel weed in the foreground right. He tried several times. The last time he worked on it, I watched him paint. Alec seemed puzzled at his inability to paint pickerel weed "just right." He had done it before in a sketch painted at Georgian Bay in the thirties (acquired by the National Gallery of Canada in 1939).

Suddenly he put down his brushes and said, "I'll do some sketches or drawings of pickerel weed on my summer trip and complete the canvas in the fall." And he did. All in all, it took him nine months to finish the painting reproduced below. He was a patient man where enduring quality was at stake.

I asked Alec when he had changed his sketch panels from the smaller 8½ by 10½ inch size to a 10½ by 13½ inch size. He thought it must have been in the mid-thirties, but for a time he continued to use both sizes, and he still did the occasional smaller sketch as late as the sixties.

Because I was interested in this aspect of Alec's work, I subsequently checked. The earliest sketch in the 10½ by 13½ inch size I

Pickerel Weed, Split Rock Island, Georgian Bay

could find confirmed Alec's recollection; it was done in 1934.* It was entitled *Massey Home, Port Hope*, and was offered for sale for eighty-five dollars at an exhibition at a Montreal gallery in 1948. We have in our collection one of Alec's smaller sketches, *Indian Church at Brantford, Ontario*, done in 1963.

Alec's first major retrospective exhibition, shown in Toronto in October and November 1953, in Ottawa in January 1954, and in Winnipeg from March 4 to April 4, 1954, is instructive about the way he painted. When it was displayed in Toronto and Ottawa this exhibit had eighty-five canvases painted in oil, dated from 1909 to 1953, four watercolours on paper from 1902, 1904, and 1905 (before Alec became a professional painter) and from 1925, plus thirty-six sketches (twenty-one of the smaller and fifteen of the larger size), for a total of 125 exhibits.[56] When the exhibition moved to Winnipeg, seventy-three items were dropped and nineteen new items were added, for a total of seventy-one exhibits. The earliest sketch of the larger size was dated 1937.[57]

Of the eighty-five canvases shown in Toronto, most paintings were either 20 by 26 inches or 26 by 32 inches, and a few were 32 by 40 inches. Only three paintings were very large, the largest 46 by 50⅛ inches. One large canvas was added to the Winnipeg showing. What these figures suggest is that less than 5 per cent of Alec's canvases were of major proportions, with his preference being to concentrate on intermediate sizes. He was always concerned about not overdoing the simplicity of his sketches when he moved to the larger surfaces presented by the canvas.

That first retrospective of Alec's was heralded as breaking completely new ground, for the works exhibited had been "selected from over five hundred paintings and two thousand sketches which the artist has completed and which depict scenes from places as separated as Algoma in Ontario and Great Slave Lake in the North West Territories to Picardy in France and somewhere in Quebec in early spring."[58] I asked Alec some questions about the 1953-1954 retrospective, which had included works painted as early as 1902. From what date would it be appropriate to consider him a professional painter? "Well, that depends on what you mean by professional," he replied. "I made the first worthwhile sale when I was twenty-nine years old, and that was in 1913."

I then asked him whether he could not be considered to have reached a stage of professionalism after he completed his six months

---

*The earliest sketches of the larger size in the collections of both the National Gallery of Canada and the Art Gallery of Ontario commence with 1937.

of studies at the Académie Julian in Paris. He answered that even though his efforts to sell his works in Europe and in Montreal, after his return in 1910, were not successful, he felt that he had acquired, during his stay in Paris, a measure of professionalism that constituted a basis for the development of his work in a new direction in Canada. Ever since this talk with Alec, I have accepted 1908 as the year from which his professionalism can be dated and have considered his earlier works as the products of his study period.

Alec mentioned that at an early stage he had concluded that water-colour was not his medium. Hence, he had concentrated on painting in oils, supplemented by the drawings that he considered notes.

The subject of figure work, in either painting or drawings, came up. Alec recalled that he had done three portraits of war heroes towards the end of the First World War when he was an artist in the Canadian War Records Office. He did sometimes place a small figure or two in a landscape, but this was an exception, apart from some of his Quebec paintings and drawings where he might include a figure on a sleigh or walking on a lonely road. (In over a hundred drawings reproduced in *A.Y.'s Canada*, only about a dozen show small figures placed casually in the landscape.) Sometimes there is a figure in a sketch that is omitted in a canvas. On occasion Alec had done drawings of friends or people he had met on a sketching trip. He had also worked from life models, mainly in the days before he became a professional painter, but the figure was not his favourite subject. The landscape or even a cityscape was preferable. As far as buildings were concerned, the more dilapidated they were the better he liked them. He complained that so many old farms were disappearing, he had to go farther and farther into the back country to find them.

I had seen hundreds of Alec's drawings during the fifties, but I never came across one of a female nude. I found this difficult to explain. Although Alec liked women and was not shy about it, there was something puritanical in his personality. He seemed to approach the female figure as an art object with reserve and circumspection.

It appears that I was not the only one who was puzzled about Alec's reluctance to draw nudes. Lawren P. Harris later told me about attending some weekly life model drawing sessions in Toronto in 1929 and 1930 in Charles Comfort's studio at 25 Severn Street. Other than Alec, Comfort, and Harris, George Pepper attended with his painter wife, Kathleen Daly. The sessions lasted two hours, and the model was paid $1.50 an hour toward which each of the five artists contributed sixty cents. While the other four artists regularly looked at each other's work, Alec kept his drawings to himself. If one of the artists wandered over to where Alec was drawing to look at what he was doing, Alec would close the sketch-book and sit on it. So his friends stopped asking him to show them his nude drawings. In fact, Harris said, he had not seen a single life model drawing of Alec's during that two-year period.

Another artist friend of Alec's saw some of his drawings of female nudes not long after these "classes" in the Comfort studio. She was attending a life model drawing session at the Grange at the Art Gallery of Toronto, and she was sitting next to Alec. "I was surprised," she told me, "that Alec was no good in drawing female nudes. He tried, but the drawings did not come off." And then she added: 'I suppose if he really had set his mind to it, he could have done it. But figure drawing was not important enough to him, so he let it be. He must have destroyed all these drawings."

I am quite willing to accept this explanation, for Alec himself told me that he was not good at figure drawing. But besides the artistic explanation, there may also be a psychological reason that has its roots in Alec's feeling about female nudes.

He was not a prude. Far from it. When I acquired a fine Holgate drawing of a nude, I showed it to Alec when he visited us. Our son Bruce, then aged eight, was present. He asked, "Isn't it rude to draw a woman in the nude?" Alec chuckled and replied, "It's only rude when you don't draw her well." He recognized that an artist could find great beauty in a woman's body and that some could capture the vibrancy of the human figure. He wrote that he was all in favour of figure painting from life, even though he did not practise what he preached:

> I hope, too, that figure painting from life may yet come into its own in Canada. It's a sad commentary on our sophistication and our culture that a model who is willing to pose nude is practically blacklisted by society. And those who do, a mere handful, find that they have to scuttle furtively to the studios, often working under assumed names. Most Canadian families would consider themselves disgraced if any daughter of theirs posed unclothed for an artist; yet those same people trek faithfully into the art galleries to be delighted by Rubens or any of the Old Masters who based their work on the eternal human figure. I suppose it's a hangover from puritanical beginnings.[59]

The question arises whether Alec hesitated to draw the female figure solely because he felt he could not do justice to it. Alec was in his forties when he last drew female nudes and apparently concluded that this was not his forte. Thereafter he concentrated almost exclusively on landscapes. Alec looked at women as individuals — as human beings with their own identity and purpose. He may have felt that if he drew a nude female, he was portraying an object and not a living person — and that he was not willing to accept.

Alec greatly admired Paul Cézanne not only because he, like Alec, had been influenced by Pissarro, but also because he, again like Alec, later broke away from French impressionism, with his work becoming more intense, more colourful, and more strongly accented. Cézanne showed great reluctance to draw nude models. Alec was quite familiar with Cézanne's lifestyle and this particular trait. I often wondered whether there was any link between the two painters as far as their attitude towards nude females was concerned.

I asked Alec whether in spite of his reluctance to draw figures or faces, he might like to draw the face of a professor. He said he would not be very good at it, but he would try. "Don't look so serious," Alec said to me, "I'm not going to bite you. I'm just trying to draw you with a faint smile." I burst into laughter. "That's better," he said, and in five minutes the drawing was done (see below). I protested a little, saying that I had more hair than Alec indicated. "That's the way I see you," he replied with a chuckle.

Alec was even more hesitant when I suggested he try a self-portrait. He didn't have a mirror with him. What about looking into the clear water? I suggested. We both laughed. Like a good sport, Alec did a quick self-portrait (see below), shaking his head and murmuring to himself, though loud enough for me to hear, "What a face. I like the hat better." When I asked him to sign the two drawings, he replied, "I'll just initial them to indicate that drawing faces is not my cup of tea." And he did just that. Incidentally, the self-portrait shows Alec wearing his famous painting hat.

O. J. Firestone   A. Y. Jackson

72

We had talked about drawings many times, but the Kingsmere Lake excursion gave me an opportunity to delve into the question more fully. Alec believed that a good painter must be able to do a good drawing. Some of the young contemporary painters appeared to be inclined to disregard this important principle of quality craftsmanship. As a result, some abstract works were mediocre or poor, even though the artists were talented. With a little more training and discipline, they could do much better.

Alec made a distinction between drawings and notes. Drawings were carefully executed, in pencil if done outdoors, sometimes in black ink when done in the studio. They took half an hour or longer to complete. Notes, on the other hand, were done in a few minutes, spontaneously, on the spur of the moment. Sometimes rain, snow, or wind interfered with completing a sketch outdoors. Alec would whip out his sketchbook, put a few "notes" on paper, and pack up. He would then use these quickie drawings as *aides-mémoire* to complete his sketch. Frequently they carried written notations about colours, textures, lights, shadows, and moods or other references that might be helpful to Alec when he looked at them in connection with painting his canvases. He preferred using sketches as a basis for painting canvases but when these were not available and he was attracted by a particular landscape, drawings had to suffice.

Painting directly from a drawing became particularly necessary when Alec did his canvases following his two trips to the eastern Arctic. It was difficult to paint outdoors because of the swarms of blackflies he encountered when he went north with Dr. Banting in 1927 and with Harris in 1930. The blackflies became mixed into the paint, which then did not look normal when it was applied to the panel.

Most of Alec's "drawings" were what he called notes. Some of them might have other written notations, such as a reference to the canvas painted from the drawing and the name of the person to whom the painting was sold. When he did draw figures he sometimes indicated who they were. A good example is his *September Mountains* (1958), which shows two people sitting in front of a tent and carries two notations: "A.Y.J. and John Rennie," and "September Mountains, Named by Geo. Douglas" (see page 74).

Another drawing, *Manotick Evening* (page 74) illustrates Alec's numbering system. The numbers from one to seven on the drawing had particular meaning to Alec. Two of them are explained — 2 means lights and 3 means snow. There is also the notation "move church" in the lower left corner. Alec would sometimes attempt to improve a landscape by altering its appearance. More often than not,

September Mountain

Manotick Evening

he would leave things out, for he said he believed in the principle "less can be more," but then he would add with a chuckle, "as long as you don't overdo it."

A few months later when we spoke again about drawings, I drew Alec's attention to the catalogue for the fourth exhibition of the Group of Seven, held at the Art Gallery of Toronto from January 9 to February 2, 1925. It indicated that Alec showed fifteen canvases and a number of drawings. Alec replied that he could not remember but that it was likely such drawings were of a finished nature, done in black ink, rather than hurriedly-put-down pencil notes.

Our talk turned to Algonquin Park. As we sat watching the calm waters of Kingsmere Lake, hardly moved by a ripple on this sunny, almost windless day, he contrasted the scene with the exciting wilderness of Algonquin Park. Ever since Tom Thomson had initiated him into the rugged beauty of the near-north in 1914 (Alec on his own had ventured into the Far North in the twenties), the park had held him fascinated. It was an unending source of beauty and inspiration. The most enduring and the most memorable of his visits to the park was the six weeks he spent with Tom Thomson in September and October 1914. The two men spent those weeks on long canoe trips, fishing, and painting while they lived in a tent. They were up at dawn, busy till dusk, and Alec was full of admiration for the energy and vitality displayed by Thomson, who was five years his senior.

In the years after the Second World War, Alec visited the park and frequently made his base at Canoe Lake, staying at the cottage of his old friends Charles (Chuck) and Dorothy Matthews. No matter that he travelled widely across the country, east, west, and north, he returned over and over again to the park. Understating his real feelings as usual, Alec once commented: "Algonquin's lakes and streams, log chutes, beaver dams, red maple and yellow birch appealed to me strongly."[60]

I told Alec about my camping trips in Algonquin with three friends, Murray Corlett, Harry Edmison, and Jim Milner, during and just after the war. Usually we started out at Canoe Lake, renting two canoes, and then proceeded with tent, packs, and supplies for two weeks of exploring the untamed wilderness, protected from human encroachment and man's urges to establish his mastery over nature. During these excursions, we felt close to the land, a feeling as strange as it was exhilarating to the four of us, all city dwellers.

On the first day of our outing, we usually stopped for an evening meal and an overnight stay at Ahmek, the boys' section of the Taylor Statten Camps. We would talk to the "Chief," Taylor Statten, and "Chubby," George W. Chubby who, as the manager, looked after the financial affairs of the operations.* His nickname referred both to his name and to his habit of continually smoking fat (chubby) cigars, Cuban when available.

These were beautiful camping trips, notwithstanding mosquitoes, blackflies, rain, windstorms, rough water, and treacherous portages. After returning to civilization unshaven for two weeks, we would compare results: who had caught more fish, and who had more mosquito and blackfly bites? Being fair-skinned, I usually won the bite contest, and I rarely did well in the fishing derby.

Alec was amused by these tales of the park he knew so well and he could match every one of mine with three of his own — except one. The year after I married, I took my wife to September Camp, the adult camp, after the young Statten campers had departed. We spent a happy week there, and we agreed that our children should spend their summers during their formative years at the Taylor Statten camps. When that time came, for seventeen years there were always one or two and for a few years three Firestone children at Ahmek or Wapomeo, the girls' camp.

I mentioned to Alec that the following year, 1964, our younger son, Peter, would be seven, old enough to join his twelve-year-old brother Bruce for a spell at Ahmek. Alec said that if he visited the park that year, as he expected to do, he would ask for my two sons. He added, "I don't think your boys have ever watched me paint. I'll ask them whether they would like to."

I forgot about that promise until a year later, when my wife and I picked up our two sons from the camp after their stay, and Peter reported the most exciting occurrence during his camp days. Alec had visited Ahmek and had been painting. He had asked for our boys. Bruce was away on a camping trip, but Peter was available. A counsellor-in-training fetched Peter and his counsellor, the young woman who looked after the bantam section — the only concession to female supervisory staff in an otherwise largely male-oriented camp.

Alec asked Peter how he liked the camp, and my son replied that he enjoyed swimming, sailing, and the "Council Ring" (a weekly ritual to familiarize the young campers with Indian customs and rituals). He wasn't so fond of the handicrafts that were taught at the camp or of walking, and that included the long walk from the sleeping cabin in the bantam section to the dining hall. This remark must have brought a smile to Alec's lips, for he was painting not very far from the dining hall.

---

*The story of Taylor Statten and his lifelong friend Chubby has been told movingly in *Taylor Statten*, by C.A.M. Edwards, foreword by J. Alex Edmison, published by Ryerson Press in 1960.

"Would you like to stay and watch me paint, if your counsellor says it's all right?" he asked. Permission was given, and Peter watched Alec paint for the next half-hour without a word being spoken. He still remembers as an adult the silence and the intensity with which Alec concentrated on his work.

My wife and I sometimes teased Alec about his forgetfulness, as did a few of his other friends. He admitted to some of it. Yet plainly when Alec wanted to remember something, even in his later years, he could and he did. He was also a man who would go out of his way to be kind to children and treat them as equals.

The afternoon had flown by. The conversation had been sparkling, sometimes happy, sometimes sad, with chuckles on Alec's part, hearty laughter on mine. I had had yet another view of Alec: his inner person, beautiful in its simplicity, searching, and in some ways unfulfilled. I wondered how a man with fame and fortune and with so many "friends" could feel so lonely as he obviously sometimes did.

I didn't ask Alec that question as we left the lake and got into the car to return to Ottawa, but I must have given him a compassionate glance, for he seemed to read my mind. Suddenly, he said, rather quietly, as if speaking to himself, "I have my painting."

We both knew what it meant. Man cannot be completely happy: he is fortunate if he has something that gives him a sense of fulfilment, and if he has a partner with whom he can share that fulfilment, the joy is even greater. Alec's life had not evolved this way, and he accepted his fate philosophically.

We were silent for a while driving home. There was one matter still on my mind. Knowing Alec's admiration for Cézanne, I mentioned his famous dictum, "Painting from nature is ... realizing one's sensations." I asked him whether he felt sometimes frustrated when he failed to achieve his goal in his paintings. Not frustration, Alec explained, but he felt a realization of man's inadequacy — his fallibility. Again this comment had a familiar ring. Later, I looked up a biography of Cézanne and found these words written to his son six weeks before his death in 1906: "As a painter I am becoming more clear-sighted before nature, but with me the realization of my sensations is always painful. I cannot attain the intensity that is unfolded before my senses. I do not have the magnificent richness of colouring that animates nature."

It seemed to me that two words summed up the sombre side of Alec's life, loneliness and fallibility.

CHAPTER 7

"Stupid Painter Forgets":
Visiting "Auntie Kay"

There were six children in Alec's family, two sisters and three brothers in addition to Alec. Alec's paternal grandfather, Henry Fletcher Joseph Jackson, came to Canada from England in the spring of 1846 and settled in Montreal. He married Isabella Murphy, and they had five children. The oldest son, Henry Allen, was Alec's father. Alec's maternal grandfather was a Scotsman who came to Canada in 1834 and settled in southwestern Ontario. His name was Alexander Young, and he married Anna Eliza Keachie. Their six children included a daughter named Eliza Georgina, Alec's mother. Alec was named Alexander Young after his grandfather.

The six children born to Henry and Georgina Jackson were Henry (usually called Harry), Ernest, Alexander, Isabel, William (Bill), and Catherine (Kay). Alec's two nieces whom we have met in these pages were the daughters of Harry and Coralie Adair Jackson: Naomi, who married James Walton Groves, and Constance (Ton), who married Robert Alexander Hamilton. They had another sister, Geneva (Didi), who married twice, to A.E.H. Petrie and then to Patrick D. Baird. Alec's other two brothers married and had families. Alec, Isabel, and Catherine never married. Alec continued to see a great deal of Harry and his three daughters and his sister Kay, who lived in Rawdon, Quebec, north of Montreal.

Edwin Holgate, one of the surviving members of the Group of Seven, lived in Morin Heights, Quebec, and Isobel and I usually visited him and his wife, Frances, once a year. In 1964 we arranged to make our annual visit on May 3, a Sunday. Thinking that Alec had not seen his old friend Edwin since the eightieth birthday party, I asked him whether he would like to join us on that day's excursion into the Laurentians. He thought about the suggestions and then said, "You know, Morin Heights is not too far away from Rawdon, where my sister Kay lives." We had often heard Alec talk with fondness about his sister, but we had met her on only a few occasions. It seemed to us that this would be a good opportunity to visit her if it were convenient. Knowing that Alec at his age was not anxious to write letters, I volunteered to write to her.

Kay's reply said: "I will be very pleased to see you and your wife and A. Y. on Sunday (May 3) at around three o'clock or whatever time you may arrive. I am sure Alex will be able to guide you to my place. The last time he was here, everything was covered with snow." That last sentence should have been a warning that things might go awry on our visit to Rawdon, but it did not ring a bell. Alec said he would draw a map showing us how to get from Morin Heights to Rawdon; once in the village he would have no trouble finding the place. Kay lived near the Heather Hospital.

We agreed to pick Alec up at nine o'clock. I knew the way to Morin Heights and relying on Alec's map to guide us from Morin Heights to Rawdon, I left my road maps at home — my first mistake that day! We were twenty miles out of Ottawa when I asked Alec about the map he had promised to draw for us. He looked through his pockets and couldn't find it. Then he exclaimed, "I remember now. I left it on the kitchen table."

We had no difficulty reaching Morin Heights, taking scenic Route 8 on the Quebec side of the Ottawa from Hull to Lachute and a secondary road north to Morin Heights. Our visit with the Holgates was pleasant, and time passed quickly over tea, raisin bread, and cakes. The two painter friends talked happily about common experiences, adventures and misadventures, and the fun we had all had at Alec's birthday party.

Edwin Holgate was leading a quiet life in the country, continuing to paint though his output had declined substantially in his sixth decade. For several years I had admired a large drawing entitled *Reclining Nude* he had done in 1929. The artist declined to part with it. His wife had been the model, for in those days he could not afford to pay a professional model. Besides, his wife had been a beautiful woman in her twenties when he made this drawing. When I raised the question again on this occasion and asked whether I could purchase the drawing, Holgate replied that he would leave the decision to his wife.

While Alec and Holgate were having an animated conversation, I approached Frances Holgate about the drawing. "I don't think Edwin would be happy to have a drawing of me in the nude in somebody's living room or bedroom," she said.

"But this isn't a portrait of you," I replied. "It's a figure drawing of a beautiful woman, one of the finest works of its kind ever done by Edwin. He did it with much love and with great artistic skill. It will live much longer than all of us. Wouldn't it be better for the drawing to be exhibited and seen by thousands of people who could admire Edwin's creative genius rather than continue being rolled up behind a filing cabinet in the studio, gathering dust?" Frances Holgate, who was a great lady, said with a gracious smile, "If Edwin agrees, I agree."*

Alec had estimated that it would take us about an hour to get from Morin Heights to Rawdon. We asked Holgate for advice, and he pulled out a map to show us the way. We were to get to the south-bound autoroute, go south to St-Jérôme, drive east on Route 41 to the intersection with Route 33, and then go north on this highway to Rawdon. A shortcut was possible if we were to take Route 18, but we would have to be careful not to miss a turnoff to the east after about ten miles on Route 18. The shortcut would save us ten miles out of a total of seventy.

Holgate estimated that it would take us about an hour and a half and offered us his road map, but Alec said he remembered the way. He had taken that shortcut the last time he had visited Kay; we wouldn't need the map.

We left the Holgates' at about two o'clock. An hour and a half later I was wondering whether we hadn't missed Rawdon. We stopped at a farmhouse and were told that we had passed the turnoff about fifteen miles back. We backtracked, finally arriving in Rawdon after four o'clock, more than an hour late.

It did not take us long to find the Heather Hospital, but Alec could not find his sister's house. We went to the end of the village; we drove through it again; we tried several side roads. No sign of Kay's house. Though we went through the village four times, back and forth, Alec still could not identify a house that looked like his sister's.

At first there was a good deal of laughter about it all. I speculated about the fun a newspaperman could have if he learned that Alec had got lost in the middle of the Laurentian Mountains, and made up headlines for such a story. Isobel suggested "A. Y. Jackson Lost in the Middle of a Village." I countered with "A. Y. Jackson Cannot Find His Sister." Alec's choice was "Stupid Painter Forgets." We laughed and laughed, but gradually that laughter became a sign of frustration, and Alec was getting really cross. He muttered things to himself that we couldn't hear. Then there was great stillness in the car. "Alec," Isobel said, "why don't you tell us how you really feel?"

He answered, "Because you're here." To which Isobel replied, "Never mind me."

"Damn, damn, damn, how stupid can I be!" he exclaimed. Again and again he said that the last time he had been in Rawdon it had

---

*This drawing, included in the Ontario Heritage Foundation gift, has been on exhibit continuously since 1964. The Holgates, being good friends of ours, helped us acquire fifty-seven items of Edwin's work, sixteen oils, nine watercolours, and thirty-two drawings.

been winter; deep snow had covered the ground, and farmhouses look quite different in winter than they do in springtime. Isobel asked whether he felt better now that he had said what he really wanted to say. He replied, "Yes, but I would feel even better if we would get to that damn place."

Finally we stopped at a garage, and I asked a young man whether he knew where Miss Catherine Jackson lived. "Yes," he replied, "she is just past the Heather Hospital."

To be on the safe side, I phoned her. She was relieved to hear that we were actually in Rawdon. "Go back to the Heather Hospital," she said. "You'll find a sign: 'Fresh Eggs for Sale'. Take the side road; don't stop at the first farmhouse but continue. I live in the second house beyond the farmhouse."

We retraced our steps and found the sign. "But that's not the house," Alec said, pointing at the farmhouse that we had passed about half a dozen times previously. "And my sister hasn't fresh eggs for sale," he added. But we continued on, and within a few minutes arrived at her home. Kay was standing at the front. She embraced her brother and welcomed us, although we were close to two hours late for our get-together.

After the greetings were finished, Kay offered us some rye, which she knew Alec liked. "Have a drink to revive your sagging spirits," she said. Alec's sense of humour was returning, and he remarked, "You want spirits to fight spirits." He poured the drinks. The first one was quickly downed, and Alec, acting as host, refilled the glasses. Kay had gone into the kitchen to check the dinner, and we settled comfortably in front of the fireplace. "Call me Auntie Kay," she said. "Everyone else does." We told her our day's experiences — to another round of hearty laughter, and Alec took the ribbing in good part. Isobel had brought Kay a bracelet set with Canadian stones, and she appreciated the thoughtfulness.

Kay told us she had been a secretary in a firm of architects in Montreal, but had always wanted to live in the country. This Rawdon, Quebec, farmhouse had become available when she had decided to retire, and she had bought it. It was old but sturdily built, and comfortable. The wood fire in the living room gave the place a warm glow — not just in a literal sense but in terms of genuine atmosphere. Kay was proud of the swimming pool she'd built after she'd acquired the property.

Living alone in the country was not a difficulty, since her nephew came to visit her quite often, she said, and her neighbours were all kindly folks. She had soon been made to feel at home. "I also have friends who drive to Montreal occasionally," she added. "I go with them sometimes, to enjoy the excitement of the big city. But as a way of life, I don't miss Montreal." She did not mind the loneliness of a single existence, she said, and as we looked from sister to brother, we could see that they were made of the same fibre: strong, sturdy, self-reliant — the kind of people who in years gone by pioneered in Canada, laying the foundation for future generations to achieve affluence and comfort.

Kay had prepared a thick soup, beef stew, vegetables, homemade bread, apple pie and cheese, and coffee. After dinner she showed us some of Alec's paintings that she owned. One was a large canvas. Several were very good sketches done in the twenties and thirties. In one corner she had three old sketches, painted in a very European style. Alec had done two of these in France and Belgium in 1908 and one in Montreal after his return from Europe in 1910. They were oils painted on panel, smaller in size than the panels he used when he moved to Toronto. Alec had given her these sketches before he enlisted in the Canadian Army in the First World War, and she had kept them in a drawer while she lived in Montreal. She had first put them on the wall when she had moved into the farmhouse at Rawdon.

The paintings had been neglected for more than fifty years, and their colours were hardly recognizable. I asked Alec whether it would not be advisable to have them restored, and he agreed. Then I asked Kay whether she would sell me the sketches, and I would look after the restoration. "I don't know whether I can sell them to you," she replied. "They were a gift of Alec's." When Alec said it was all right, we bought the three sketches. Alex explained briefly to us the occasions on which he had done these paintings, and later he added more information. They were entitled *Church at Etaples, Pas de Calais, Church of Jersualem, Bruges, Belgium* and *Lachine Canal, Montreal.*

We reached home after midnight. Our return journey was uneventful except that Alec was exceptionally quiet. Whether the reason was the good food, the ample drinks, or the exasperation he had undergone during the earlier part of the day, he never told us. A few days later, I showed him a letter Isobel had received from Kay: "I hope you all reached home safely after you passed Heather Hospital." She signed the letter "(Aunty) Kay." Alec had by this time regained his sense of humour and remarked, "Well, I haven't heard the last of it from Kay."

So ended our only journey with Alec in the "wilderness" of the Laurentian Mountains. The memory of good comradeship remains with us, and we saw a little more of Alec's character. When things were not going his way, he could lose his temper. But it was anger of a fleeting type. He held no grudges; he was willing to forget and to forgive, and that included his own shortcomings.

CHAPTER 8
Alec and His Women

Alec had many women friends and in several instances romance blossomed out of friendship. He appealed to women. He responded warmly to their overtures and, in some instances, was not even averse to taking the initiative. He courted the women he cared for in his own unique manner — ardently, but with a psychological holding-back that some of them sensed. He wrote beautiful letters. He gave them some of his paintings as presents. And most of all, he gave a great deal of himself in time, interest, devotion, and affection. The word "love" did not come easily to Alec, but when he used it, it came from his heart.

Alec's friends called him a realist, a down-to-earth person, yet there was also something of the romantic in him. He hid it well, but it was there, and it came to the fore on the few occasions when Alec was very much emotionally involved. In fact, there was a romantic aura around him that increased as he grew older. Women recognized it, and his charisma and appeal to the other sex grew with it.

Still, Alec never married and, like others, I wondered why. I already knew his invariable reply. When the question had come up in the company of others, Alec's answer was always that possibilities had existed in the past, but that he had been too poor to get married. Given the limited opportunities in Canada for a professional painter in the days before World War II, he was likely to stay poor. After fame and success as a painter did come, there was less time for women friends in his life.

Soon after the celebration of Alec's eightieth birthday I raised the question of marriage again, and he remarked with his customary chuckle, "Who would want to marry an old codger like me?" I did not know then that a warm friendship was developing into romance and that the question of marriage was not as hypothetical as Alec's answer implied.

The afternoon he and I spent lazily talking on the shores of Kingsmere Lake, Alec was in a mood to talk about his life, and he didn't seem to mind touching on personal matters. This was rare for him because he usually kept his emotional side very much to himself. I knew that Alec was fond of our four children, Brenda and Catherine, Bruce and Peter, so I started the conversation by asking him whether he didn't miss having a wife and family.

He would have liked to have had a daughter, he confided. (One way in which Alec expressed his particular liking for a young woman was to tell her that he would have been happy to have her as his daughter. He said this, for example, to Lovedy Burton, Ralph Burton's wife, and to Olympic ski champion Nancy Greene.) "What's the matter with sons?" I demanded. "Are we to consider them less important than daughters?"

"Well, no," Alec replied, laughing, "but it would be more fun to have a daughter." Then he went on predictably, "But if I had married I would have had to go back to commercial art. In my early days I didn't make enough as a painter to support a wife. I'm no woman hater, though — far from it."*

"The trouble with you, Alec," I said, "is that you were born fifty years too soon. If you had been born in 1932 instead of 1882, you could be married, your wife would be working and supporting you, and you could be painting to your heart's content." Alec replied that this was not done in his day and, furthermore, he was not so sure he'd like his wife to support him even if he were a young man today.

I told him a story related to this question that had come out in my seminar dealing with economic growth when we were discussing the will to work. A number of male students had taken Alec's view, but all the female students and one male student took the opposite stand. This one male student, who was working on his master's degree while his wife was working as a secretary and supporting him, had remarked, "You should try it, fellows. You'll like it."

Returning to his early life, Alec confessed that there had been several women whom he genuinely liked and considered marrying. The first time was before World War I, but he found himself faced with the same problems that his brother Harry had encountered. Harry, who was five years older than Alec, had also gone to work at the age of twelve at a lithographing company in Montreal. After their carefree trip to Europe in 1905, both of them had returned hoping to take up painting as a career. But when Harry decided to get married, he had no choice but to take a job in commercial art, and he worked in that field until he was about seventy years old.**

Alec's young lady of this period did not think much of his aspira-

---

*Alec said much the same thing in an interview with his reporter friend W. Q. Ketchum.[61]

**Alec seemed to feel a little sorry for his older brother. He wrote in *A Painter's Country*: "My brother Harry had the ambition to be a painter, but he got married and had to labour at commercial art until he retired ten years ago.[62] In his later years, Harry Jackson did some fine watercolours of mushrooms exhibited by the National Gallery of Canada in 1977 under the title *Mr. Jackson's Mushrooms*."

tion to be a full-time painter. Although Alec said he had a photograph of her around somewhere, I never saw it. Ralph Burton, who did see it, described her as tall, slender, and good-looking, dressed in a striped bathing suit that went down to her knees — the kind ladies wore early in this century. Alec had remarked to him, "That's the girl I wanted to marry. I proposed to her, and she said, 'You couldn't afford to keep me.' "

During this period, Alec made an oil sketch of a young woman standing on the shore of a lake against a background of low-lying hills and a livelier sky than he usually painted. She is tall and willowy and wears a skirt down to her ankles, a light jacket, and a bandanna on her head — a costume fashionable women wore in the days before the First World War. There is just a suggestion of facial features, reflecting the influence of French impressionism. As far as I know, this is the only oil painting of a woman by Alec that has been preserved. As he said to me repeatedly, he did not consider figure painting to be his forte. To have done this painting at all, he must have cared very much for the lady who was the subject, or she must have been very persuasive, as I had to be when I asked Alec to do drawings of himself and myself on our Kingsmere excursion. There is no evidence to link the painting with Alec's first great love — he was then twenty-five — but the possibility exists.

I told Alec of a remark Isobel had once made. Fond as she was of Alec, she observed that he would have been a difficult husband to live with, being as singleminded as he was, his kindness and graciousness notwithstanding. Alec agreed and observed, "Yes, a wife of mine would have had to come with me on sketching trips, rough country and rough weather, or she would have had to stay at home, waiting for me for weeks on end. Perhaps it's just as well I stayed a bachelor."

Even though he was a bachelor, Alec used to feel sorry for men who missed all female company. One of the occupants of the Studio Building was Thoreau MacDonald, the son of J. E. H. MacDonald, a good friend and fellow member of the Group of Seven. Thoreau was a shy person who led a lonely life. On one occasion when he seemed quite grouchy, Alec remarked to Harris in fun that Thoreau would be a happier person if he had a woman's company. "All he needed," Alec said, "was a good fuck."

As for himself, Alec remarked that he had had many women friends, and if he had married one, what would have happened to all the others? A number of the occupants of the Studio Building in Toronto were amused by the forms his popularity took with the ladies. Some would try to outdo each other in mothering him. They would arrange parties at his studio, providing the food and drink. They would invite people to their friends' houses for private showings of his sketches from recent trips. They came to visit so that he wouldn't feel lonely. All this he was happy to accept and enjoy, but there was one thing he *didn't* like — "cleaning time." Some of his women friends would wait until he went on a sketching trip. Then his top-floor studio would be thoroughly cleaned, old newspapers thrown out, garbage removed, and the furnishings put in their proper places. He complained he couldn't find anything. The message must have been pretty clear that Alec preferred living with his clutter to the probable house-cleaning instincts of a wife. On the other hand, he was both flattered and happy with all the attention. There was a saying among his Toronto associates : "He liked the stable of girls he could call on."

When I asked Alec who some of these women friends were in the twenties and thirties, he replied that they were all artists or connected with the art world. A few were married or got married later, "but there were enough single women around," he added with a smile when he noticed my inquiring glance, and I got the distinct impression that he was not referring only to platonic relationships.

He mentioned nine particular friends, five from Toronto and four from Montreal. I had met several of those who were artists, and knew a little about the remaining women from other sources. Of the nine, six were painters, all of them founder-members of the Canadian Group of Painters, two were sculptors, and one ran a book store that became the gathering place of Toronto painters and others interested in the arts. Knowing a little about these women helps the understanding of the artistic climate of the time.

In Toronto, one was Yvonne McKague Housser, who married F. B. Housser in 1935 after he divorced his wife Bess (later Mrs. Lawren S. Harris). Fred Housser was the financial editor of the *Toronto Star* and a good friend of Alec's. He became so interested in Canadian art he wrote a book about it in 1926.* Yvonne studied in Toronto, Paris, and Vienna and taught at the Ontario College of Art for about twenty years, resigning in 1949. She loved to paint northern landscapes, and this brought her in close contact with members of the Group of Seven. Later on she moved to figure and abstract painting. When I asked her about Alec, she remarked, "He was good company and a dear friend. He was not a charmer [and here she differed from what some of Alec's other lady friends told me]. I was charmed by Lismer, Harris, and Varley." Alec for his part greatly admired Yvonne Housser's continu-

---

*Alec described the book as "an absorbing story told so simply that people who had regarded us (The Group of Seven) as a public menace found themselves quite in accord with us."[63]

ous search for new ideas, her keen mind, and her willingness to experiment.

Isabel McLaughlin, daughter of Col. R. S. McLaughlin of Oshawa, one of Canada's pioneer automobile manufacturers, studied art in Toronto, Paris, and Mexico. She settled in Toronto in the twenties. In her paintings, she drew in part on creative imagination and in part on real life, so that Paul Duval described her as an artist who "possessed the most original vein of fantasy of all the Canadian Group founders."[64] Like Alec, she was a very private person, and she found him attractive. Alec was good company, generous in his criticism of younger artists, and helpful to her. We do not know how far this emotional involvement went, but we do know that the two were very fond of each other. A little of Alec's sentiment is apparent in his description of her: "reserved, shy of acclaim, paints a naturalist's world of flowers, weeds, sea shells, and marine denizens. She has been a moving spirit in keeping the (Canadian) Group [of Painters] alive, and we are much devoted to her."[65]

Frances Norma Loring, an American-born sculptor, studied art in New York, Boston, Paris, Munich, and Geneva. She moved to Toronto in 1913, and did most of her sculpting in bronze. Her work consisted mainly of figures and relief, including scenes reflecting Canada's part in the First World War. Through Alec she met Sir Frederick Banting, and he joined her circle of friends. She did a bust of Dr. Banting in the late twenties that was first exhibited in 1934.* Frances and her inseparable friend, Florence Wyle, used to invite Alec frequently to their studio-house and he attended many a late and lively party there. One particularly boisterous occasion was a farewell party given for Alec before his departure in July 1927 on his first Arctic painting trip. Alec sympathized with the difficult struggle of both women to survive as full-time artists at a time when few Canadians cared about art in their own country. So as friends, they understood each other and went their separate ways.

Florence Wyle, also an American-born sculptor, came to Canada in 1913 after having studied in Chicago. She settled in Toronto, made sculptures in bronze, marble, and wood, and did some work for the Canadian War Memorials. She included Alec among her close friends, though from all accounts romance never entered the picture. She made a bust of Alec in the twenties that was first exhibited in 1944.** It showed him in shirt, tie, and jacket. I thought the bust

---

*Acquired by the National Gallery of Canada in 1949, no. 5046.
**Acquired by the National Gallery of Canada in 1956, no. 6382.

looked rather sombre, and I asked Alec what he thought of it. "It's all right," he replied, "but I wish she had done me without a tie. She did Varley that way."*

That Alec felt very much at home with his two good friends Loring and Wyle — both strong individualists — is apparent from a passage in *A Painter's Country*:

> "In some ways the Loring-Wyle studio on Glenrose Avenue has been the art centre of Toronto. Originally a church, with additions tagged on to it from time to time, it was a most colourful place. The owners . . . made their living as sculptors, a form of art that fluctuates between an occasional big commission and long periods when medallions or busts or other odd jobs help to keep the fires burning. What wonderful parties they put on! Artists, musicians, architects, and writers were proud to be invited to a Loring-Wyle party."[66]

Norah Thomson De Pencier was the only non-artist among Alec's Toronto friends. Her friends described her as sweet but vague, with an inquisitive mind and a scholarly outlook. A physically attractive person, she was running the book department at Eaton's when Alec knew her. She would ask him question after question about art, and Alec, who was well read in art generally, was not only a helpful source of information but also a great raconteur full of yarns and stories. Being much younger than Alec, Norah soon developed a crush on him. Alec noticed this interest and treated her with kindness and true affection. Here was one lady who might not have turned Alec down if he had courted her with the warmth of which he was capable. Norah Thomson remained single for a long time until she met H. P. De Pencier, a widower, whom she married. It was a happy marriage, and it enabled Norah to translate her love of Canadian art into a significant art collection at her home in Owen Sound. Alec thought of Norah Thomson as a good friend, and he described her as a "book adviser" whose "interest in art resulted in Eaton's bringing in more good books on the subject."[67]

In Montreal there were four women painters whom Alec considered close friends. Interestingly enough, they were among the five women painters from Montreal who were founding members of the Canadian Group of Painters, the fifth being H. Mabel May, a figure and landscaping painter. She did not see as much of Alec as the other four painters did, and she spent a good deal of her time in later years in Ottawa and Vancouver. These five women were members of the

---

* Acquired by the National Gallery of Canada in 1959, no. 6383.

88

Montreal Beaver Hall Hill Group, founded in 1920, which also included Edwin Holgate, Randolph Hewton, and Albert H. Robinson. This group continued in existence for only four years. Afterward, it was Alec who gave inspiration to some of the women painters in Montreal; he did not seem to mind this arrangement, and his women friends were happy to go along. As another Montreal painter, Jacques de Tonnancour, put it, "One rooster in a hen yard, you know."

It is also noteworthy that all these ladies were English-speaking. There were few French-speaking women taking up painting as a profession, the one exception in the twenties and thirties being Louise Gadbois, who did some sensitive portraits.* Alec mentioned her name to me once as a former pupil of Edwin Holgate and remarked, "Too bad more French women aren't painters."

Lilias Torrance Newton, who had married in 1921, studied in Montreal, London, and Paris. She was a portrait painter of distinction and did both formal paintings (including portraits of Queen Elizabeth and Prince Philip) and informal studies. Lawren S. Harris and Alec were subjects for the latter.** The study of Alec shows him in a reflective pose against a background of a Quebec winter landscape, the kind he used to paint. Lilias Newton was a clear-headed and sophisticated woman, beautiful and self-confident. These qualities are quite apparent in her self-portrait, done when she was about thirty years old.*** She and Alec enjoyed each other's company and, as the First World War was coming to an end, they were close enough for Alec to refer to her as "my old friend Lilias."[68]

Moreover, Emily Carr, who became friends with several members of the Group of Seven after her first visit to Toronto in 1927 and who made two subsequent visits to that city, was amused that Alec seemed to have a soft spot for women painters, and she noted this in her journals: "Jackson patronized feminine paintings."[69]

Efa Prudence Heward ("Prue" to her friends) studied art in Montreal and Paris. She was a landscape, figure, and still-life painter. A gentle person, her poor health interfered with her painting. Still, she was determined to be creative, and she received a great deal of encouragement from Alec. He not only saw her regularly in Montreal but for a number of years, after the Group of Seven was dissolved in

*Together with Paul-Emile Borduas, Louise Gadbois was one of the few artists in Quebec who stood up for the French-Canadian cultural heritage before the Second World War.
**These were acquired by the National Gallery of Canada in 1943 (no. 4570) and 1948 (no. 4899) respectively.
***Acquired by the National Gallery of Canada in 1930, no. 3703.

1933, he also went every September to the Hewards' summer house in Brockville on the St. Lawrence. Prudence, sometimes with her close friend Sarah Robertson, would come up from Montreal and the three (and on occasion others as well) would go painting together. These were fulfilling and sometimes hilarious times for all concerned. Alec described Prudence's canvases as "rich, sombre, and powerfully organized."[70] Even though her works were sad and sometimes gloomy, a reflection of her struggle to survive and her determination to succeed, she was in Alec's judgment "one of the finest painters in Canada."[71] There was the quality of tenderness in Alec's relationship with Prudence Heward that comes from two gentle people cherishing what is in essence spiritual love.

Sarah Margaret Robertson studied in Montreal and was a landscape and genre painter. Paul Duval referred to her as one of the "most original colourists of her period"[72] in Canada, and Alec found her paintings "gay and colourful, full of sunshine and movement."[73] Sarah Robertson was a lively person, and she liked Alec. She and Prudence Heward were inseparable. This was an instance where two women with great affection for the same man were even more concerned for each other's feelings, so that neither would cultivate a relationship with him beyond a close friendship.

The fourth Montreal woman painter was Anne Douglas Savage. She was the woman Alec probably came closest to marrying. Alec was discreet, and on the occasion of the Kingsmere sketching trip he did not mention the name of this lady — nor did I ask. But it was no secret that of all the women painters Alec visited on his trips to Montreal, he saw one more often than the others. She was Anne Savage, whom I met after I started to collect paintings. Later on, Alec dropped some hints, and after talking to some of Anne Savage's women friends I was able to piece the story together. It was confirmed by the book written by her niece, Anne McDougall, *Anne Savage: The Story of A Canadian Painter*, which contains some of Alec's love letters to Anne Savage.

A native Montrealer, Anne was fourteen years younger than Alec. She studied at the school of the Art Association in Montreal under Maurice Cullen and William Brymner.* She was a member of the Beaver Hall Hill Group, artists who rented a studio in an old building on Beaver Hall Hill in the early twenties. These "young artists" whom

---

*Of the latter Alec once wrote: "Of all the artists I knew as a student, there was no one I admired more."[74]

Alec often saw when he visited Montreal or on sketching trips, had, he thought, "given prestige to the arts in Montreal."[75]

Anne referred to her landscape paintings, which were done mainly in the Laurentians, as "simple statements of things I have seen." Paul Duval described her as a lyrical painter who "added to the Group of Seven landscape tradition a sensitive line and quiet mood that were her very own."[76] In fact, her quietness was her strength. She taught art at Baron Byng High School in Montreal, later becoming supervisor of art for the Protestant School Board of that city and doing quite a bit of painting in her spare time, and also organized the Montreal Art Association's children's art classes, which Arthur Lismer took over in 1941. In 1933, Anne Savage was a founding member of the Canadian Group of Painters, the expanded group of landscape painters who continued for a period in the tradition of their predecessors, the Group of Seven.* Alec and Anne had a lot in common — their love for the land, their devotion to art, their fondness for children, and a high regard for each other's ability. They painted together and worked together.**

Anne and Alec met after he returned to Montreal in 1920; he was thirty-eight, she, twenty-three. With other women painters, she was part of the small art circle that formed around Alec. Of all those whom he met at that time in Toronto and Montreal, Anne Savage seems to have attracted him most.

After he moved to Toronto, he visited frequently in Montreal, and encouraged her return visits, also offering to let her use his studio when he was away. On June 7, 1925, she wrote: "Dear Alex, I was awfully glad to get your letter... I am looking forward to my visit very much. It will be the greatest delight and privilege to meet real people in the art world and see how they do things... It's most awfully good of you to give me the freedom of your studio. That should inspire some effort. Please don't shine it up and whatever you do don't clear anything out. I'll go down and have a feast every now and then. Sincerely, Anne."[77]

Her landscapes showed a continuous search for beauty, turning sometimes to nature, sometimes to fantasy. Alec's constructive criticism of her work was welcomed and appreciated, though his comments were occasionally quizzical, as when he suggested that in one of her paintings "the trees look like greyhounds on stilts."[78]

---

*She was invited to contribute one of her paintings to the seventh and last exhibition of the Group of Seven in Toronto in December 1931, at which Alec exhibited fifty paintings.
**For example, Anne Savage collaborated with Alec (and others) in illustrating *The Downfall of Temlaham* by Marius Barbeau, published by Macmillan in 1928.

In the second half of the twenties Alec's feelings appear to have reached a stage at which he thought he should use boldness in his amorous advances. But what he termed his "obstreperous" efforts did not get him very far. Anne wrote to him offering "good friendship" instead of love.

Matters continued on this basis for the next several years, but Alec's affection for Anne kept growing. After visiting her in Montreal in 1931, he wrote of the happiness he felt at just visiting and walking with her. The next year, there were two revealing letters. One seemed to put her outside the reach of ordinary mortals: "You are one of the few beings I know whose lives are so beautiful and serene that they rise above all the tumult and meanness of life."[79] The other letter, dated October 3, 1932, acknowledged her good wishes on his fiftieth birthday. It hints that he was thinking of marriage.

You have been a dear and constant friend . . . Perhaps you remember years ago when I was rather obstreperous. You wrote just a little severely to make me understand that our acquaintance was nothing more than good friendship and that friendship I have been very proud of ever since. But this birthday rather bewilders me. I'm a complex individual. I have many friends and contacts; for some reason I'm popular socially without wanting to be so very much and here I am getting on in years. Next door to me the horrible example of Williamson, soured, lonely and helpless . . . I don't know what little Annie Savage will make of all this and I wonder if she just wants to go on being good friends until the end of the chapter and I wonder if she realizes how pretty she looked in her green costume or if she knows how many girls come to tea in my studio and tell me I'm wonderful. But she has so much to do, her life is too full of good deeds to spend time in mere fancies.

With all good wishes, as ever,

Alex.[80]

Anne Savage's reply to this letter has not been found. Anne McDougall believes that this time she was more encouraging, asking Alec whether he could be more specific. This would be a fair request from a lady who had received a subtle hint that might be a marriage proposal and who wanted to know what her suitor actually had in mind. Alec merely replied on October 26, 1932, that someday he might be more articulate — hardly an ardent reponse.[81]

In the summer of 1933, Alec invited Anne to come with him on a sketching trip to Georgian Bay, and he suggested that she might bring

Lilias Newton along if she was free to come. Anne declined. Realizing his mistake, Alec issued a second invitation, this one to Anne alone. This time she accepted. Alec had been slow to realize that she didn't like playing second fiddle — or even first fiddle with the second fiddle tagging along.

Alec and Anne had an enjoyable time together camping, canoeing, and painting. In fact, Anne did some of her best paintings during that summer, inspired in part by the environment, in part by Alec's encouragement and stimulating company.

Nonetheless, romance advanced only slowly. It is hard to believe that two such sophisticated and sensitive people could have been so inept in letting what we assume were their true feelings be known. That ineptness was mutual, and they both knew it. Anne was sure she would be unable to talk if Alec were in her presence, and Alec wrote that when he wanted to tell Anne he loved her, "the words would not come."[82]

Although Alec continued to send letters full of romantic intention, they were in typical Jackson prose, written beautifully but apparently without an effective full commitment. Why he did not go down to Montreal and try to sweep Anne off her feet we will never know. One of his women painter friends has observed that perhaps Alec was not so sure in his own mind that he wanted to get married. Whatever his reasoning, Alec relied on his writing skills to express his emotions.

Here are excerpts from two of Alec's letters:

What do you want me to do, Anne? You are the dearest and sweetest soul I know and if you will be my wife I will try so much to make you happy. If you want me to help you as you say it seems the only way to do it. We can go on being friends for the rest of our lives as we would no doubt. Whether marriage would mean perfect happiness or not it is no use being afraid of life.[83]

It's true I have a lot of dear girls friends, Anne . . . Lil and Prue and Sarah and Frances, Florence and Isabel. I am very proud of their friendship and there is no reason for ever losing it. I expect you have a lot of responsibilities and it would be selfish to ask you to evade them, but perhaps I could share them with you. Then, Anne, you are an artist too, with all kinds of fine qualities that will blossom out if you had half the chance that others have.[84]

Anne's replies to these fairly straightforward marriage proposals have not been preserved, but when she refused him it must have been done gently. Alec's reply to the turn-down was philosophical and wist-

93

ful. He wrote to her late in 1933: "I am going to walk home with you from the Baron Byng every day while I am clambering over these miles of hills and so the best of good wishes dear and may the *bon dieu* keep on blessing you."[85]

We also know that Anne's decision was not reached lightly and that she had second thoughts later on, for late in the fall of 1933 Alec wrote: "Your letters up here have just made me so happy that any virtue to be found in the work I've done is due to you." Sometime later, Anne wrote: "My heart stands still when I imagine existence without you."[86] Was that not an indication to Alec that his love was being reciprocated?

In looking at some of Anne Savage's letters, one gets the impression that she looked at her relationship with Alec as something unreal with which she could not come to grips. But in 1944 she did write a letter that she termed "a whisper to your heart," which Alec could have taken as an indication that she had changed her mind about their relationship. (I know that this was the case because Anne confided her feelings to one of her women friends who told me the story after Anne's death.)

> ... You are the finest painter in the land, Alex, and still are. But it is you yourself that I'd like to talk to and somehow the last twice I've been perfectly helpless to express myself. But I am compelled to write this to you and you must forgive if I overstep the mark. But I can't just let it go on — and it seems very foolish to be tied by conventions on the last stages of the journey.

> Alex, you've always meant a very great deal to me. You've inspired me and helped me in every way, and I am very fond of you but I always was so afraid of imposing on you that my indifference has amounted to coldness and ingratitude.

> But I know what a hard life an artist is forced to live — that incessant pushing of the problem to be solved and the lack of interest on the public's part makes it one continual scramble — and then the need for emotional stimulus and the effort to be true to the art within you. All that is a struggle. But Alex, I also know that friendship which has stood the test of years if properly adjusted could become a bulwark against all ills and create a haven or a shelter which could face any tempest. I know that the spiritual life is the only real one — that the little things of wordly estate don't amount to a row of peas. But it is hard to find that perfect relationship. Perhaps it only exists in heaven.

To seek one's own personal happiness is hopeless but to be able to help someone else would be well worthwhile. I have my work — you have yours, and you would be as free as a bee and we could help one another and perhaps out of all this confusion and perplexity find our peace. Don't try to answer this. It is just a whisper to your heart, when you are away out at Banff and have a quiet moment. I shall be at Wonish a month from today — and remember, Alex, I'll understand. It is only what is best for you that will be best for me. And so may the *bon dieu* bless you and keep you safe — forever and ever.

Anne.[87]

I discussed this letter with Anne McDougall, asking her whether she read into it a hint of her aunt's hope that she and Alec could get together either in Montreal or in Toronto. Anne McDougall replied that she thought her aunt might have had such an arrangement in mind when she wrote of their individual work and ability to help each other. If they had been able to make this liaison, it probably would have been the best thing that could have happened to them.

I agree with this interpretation, but I am inclined to go further. Anne Savage finally realized how she felt about Alec, and she marshalled her courage to tell him. I look at this letter as a cry for companionship, for sharing life, whatever it might bring, with the man for whom she cared most. The conventions of her time still bound her so that she could not propose marriage, but she came as close to it as her conscience and pride would permit her.

Nothing came of this implied proposal. Had she waited too long? I. Norman Smith, who is a great student of human nature, concluded in his review of Anne McDougall's book that perhaps more than the timing was wrong: "Each of them, on separate occasions and years apart, suggested marriage. But both invitations were nervous, in a way pathetic. They seem to have been two strong, unselfish characters; neither wanting to hurt the other, but each uneasily aware of his or her own need, or assumed need, of independence."[88] If she had been willing to abandon that independence and if she had had the courage to say what was uppermost in her heart, undismayed by outdated conventions and inborn hesitancy, there might still have been time to make up for the lost opportunities and wasted years. Anne Savage could be a charmer, as the photograph on page 96 shows.

In the fifties Anne and Alec drifted apart, though they kept up their correspondence. While Alec was living in Manotick, Anne visited her sister, Mrs. Brooke Claxton, in Ottawa on several occasions. She never went to see Alec in Manotick, and he remarked that he was a little

Anne Savage, ca. 1952

hurt by her aloofness. It never seems to have occurred to him to meet her in Ottawa and invite her to come back with him to his studio. Still, Alec continued to have warm feelings toward her.

Anne Savage saw Alec for the last time at our house on May 5, 1962, when we celebrated Alec's eightieth birthday. There was a happy reunion. For a time the two sat together, Anne holding Alec's hands: two old friends looking back at what might have been. When she heard of his serious illness, his partial recovery, and his move to Kleinburg, she wrote to him on June 28, 1968, sending best wishes.[89]

Not too long afterward, Anne herself fell seriously ill. Alec heard about it in Kleinburg and wrote to her at the hospital. But the letter was illegible, and Anne Savage could only surmise that Alec wished her well. Shortly thereafter, she died. It was 1971 — too late for both of them.

In spite of their mutual devotion, the two remained apart. Anne McDougall offers other explanations for her aunt's behaviour. She writes that Anne was not strong physically because of thyroid trouble that developed in childhood. As a result, she tended to be bystander rather than participant, and her niece thinks that she may have avoided marriage as a result.[90] Moreover, in the fall of 1933, when they seemed closest to marriage, Anne Savage was also burdened by a sense of duty, real or imaginary. "Anne had a mother to look after. Perhaps, she [also] recognized in A. Y. a bachelor deeply committed to his painting, set in his ways that would mean a rough and tumble life for her, and perhaps unendurable confinement for him. Fourteen years her senior, he did not seem likely to change."[91]

I do not think that indifferent health, family responsibilities, and Alec's individualism were the main reasons why Alec and Anne Savage never married. Certainly they were contributing factors, but there was more to it. Both Alec and Anne were extraordinarily complicated people who sometimes were not sure of their own emotions — and when they believed that they did know them, each became too inarticulate to let the other know.

We have to ask, too, whether they were truly in love or merely thought they were in love. I suggest that there is a difference. True love puts the loved person ahead of everything else, and circumstances cannot change this feeling. Anne Savage may have felt that Alec only believed himself to be in love with her, and that was not good enough. There may be a moral in this: not to rely on words, whether uttered or written, as persuasive as they might be, but to search for the meaning that underlies these words — a matter of putting greater faith in the inner rather than the outer person.

Alec tended to put forward poverty as an excuse for not getting married. Moreover, according to the traditions prevailing in the inter-war period, a wife was expected to live wherever her husbnd wanted to live. In this case, Anne would have had to go to Toronto, to join Alec's bohemian existence in the studio at 25 Severn Street. Anne had a good job as an art teacher in Montreal, and after 1929, jobs in Canada, as elsewhere, were becoming increasingly scarce. She would have had to give up not only her independence but also her means of earning a livelihood. Thus it appears that both custom and practical considerations conspired to prevent two people who were very fond of each other but perhaps not truly in love from being married.

There were also some strong personal aspects to that relationship. Anne Savage was a gracious, kind, and considerate lady. She could not do enough for her students, friends, and family. But behind that endearing smile and warm personality was a strong will, an expectation that people should do what she thought was right. Although I saw Anne Savage only intermittently, I could not help but observe the schoolmistress traits in her as she gently steered conversation into channels of particular interest to herself. She was a subtle and persuasive person when she felt so inclined. With all her modesty, she had great confidence in herself as a person and in her judgement as a guide to living.

Anne Savage was a truly liberated woman. She could not see herself in any role subsidiary to a male, and she was much too wise to accept the assumption of the pre-Second World War generation that marriage was a partnership. Even though she was very fond of Alec, she preferred to remain single.

Sometimes, listening to Anne's friends talking about her romance with Alec, I wondered how she would have reacted to a marriage proposal from him if it had been pursued with all his vigour. She admired him as an artist and she saw in him a kindred soul regarding the role of the arts in modern life. Her questions to herself are not difficult to imagine: "Would I be able to paint when I felt like it, or would Alec expect me to cater to him? Would I be able to stand his disorganized way of living? His clutter? His tight way with money? How would we live? Alec does not earn enough to support himself. If he moved to Montreal, I probably could help support him, but would his pride and sense of independence let me do it? And he seems to prefer to stay in Toronto. If I moved there, wouldn't we starve? Which is more important, becoming Mrs. A. Y. Jackson or staying single and enjoying my freedom? Am I willing to play second fiddle to a man? Do I love him enough?"

She must have wondered whether affection and admiration were strong enough bonds for marriage when looking after Alec would have kept her from getting on with her own work. She probably valued her freedom as much as Alec did his. It seems probable that her views would have inclined her to say no to marriage in the early thirties and yes some years later when she had second thoughts on the matter. But by then it was too late.

I followed up the question of whether Alec's relations with Anne went beyond the type of courtship typical in Canada in the thirties among people of middle-class background. Basing her opinion on the correspondence between Alec and Anne and the talk in the family, Anne's niece said to me that she thought the relationship was platonic. I consulted some of Alec's Toronto women friends, and their answers revealed that Alec was such a private person when it came to his relations with female friends that they did not even know how close Alec and Anne had been until after their deaths. I also talked to some of

Alec's male painter friends, who suggested that he was a healthy and vigorous male who liked the ladies and could be expected to behave like any other normal male.

We do know that Alec and Anne went on a number of sketching trips alone that involved extended absences from the city. We know that Alec's upbringing was of the traditional kind but that his attitudes were bohemian; in his heart, he was a rebel against the established order. His conversation with Lawren P. Harris reveals how earthy Alec could be on the subject of sex. Whether Alec and Anne were lovers must remain undocumented, grounds exist to assume Alec made overtures in this direction.

I notice that in *A Painter's Country*, Alec referred to eight of these nine women rather warmly, calling them "good friends" or using affectionate terms. Yet there was no such endearment for Anne Savage. Was this Alec's way of showing a little resentment for having been turned down? We cannot know the answer, but we do know that Alec cherished Anne Savage's friendship for half century. Being the person he was, he would forgive, though he would not forget.

In her later years, Anne was a lonely person. She confided to a friend that if she had her life to live again, she would have been less career-oriented. The implication is that if she had, she might have become Mrs. A. Y. Jackson.

After he moved to Manotick and then to Ottawa, Alec had at least two romantic involvements. One of the two ladies seemed to cause him "some concern," as he laughingly put it; the other was "very nice" (again an Alec phrase).

The lady about whom Alec appeared to be "concerned" was Hazel Devereux, who lived in Combermere, near Barry's Bay, Ontario. Hazel was a big, obese, sloppy woman with a commanding personality and a heart of gold. She used to provide room and board for Alec when he came to Combermere on his sketching trips, two to three weeks at a time, during the sixties. Alec called this two-hundred-plus-pound lady Hurricane Hazel.

She was a good cook, and Alec enjoyed her meals. He usually gained weight when he stayed with her, only to lose it when he returned to his own cooking at his Ottawa apartment (I used to tease Alec about it). Hurricane Hazel had tremendous energy, and chauffeured Alec wherever he wanted to go to paint the neighbourhood of Combermere. She genuinely liked him and refused to take money for his room and board. Alec reciprocated her kindness with some of the sketches he did during each stay.

Hazel's husband, Bob, was an alcoholic who had had a heart attack. Alec felt sorry for the man, a kindly soul somewhat overwhelmed by his dominant partner. Alec liked to tell his friends with mock alarm that there was nothing he feared as much as a domineering woman, and if anything happened to Hazel's husband, he was afraid that he would have to leave the country, for she might then want to marry him. It was not easy to say no to a determined woman. Alec said he was "concerned," but none of his friends took him seriously, and when Hurricane Hazel heard about it she had a good laugh.

Alec was in earnest about the lady who was deemed "very nice," Elizabeth (Betty) Kirk, née Brine. A widow who lived in Buckingham, Quebec, she was born on Cape Breton Island and raised in Antigonish, Nova Scotia. She married W. B. Kirk, an investment counsellor, and they settled in Buckingham, forty minutes by car northeast of Ottawa, in 1946. Her husband had died in 1950, and she was raising her son (nine years old when she met Alec) alone. She worked as a secretary at the Thurso Pulp and Paper Company until 1963. When Alec met Betty Kirk in 1961, she was in her forties, youthful in looks and spirit. She was interested in art and had attended classes at the Ottawa Municipal Arts Centre in the late fifties.

Like Hurricane Hazel, Betty Kirk provided Alec with room and board when he was painting near Buckingham, and she accompanied him on sketching trips, doing a little painting herself. Alec encouraged her with his suggestions, and she appreciated the interest he was taking in her and her work.

Alec first mentioned her to me after he moved to Ottawa, saying that he had acquired a new sketching companion, this time a woman, who sometimes picked him up to go painting. Betty came to two parties Alec gave at his studio-apartment, and we met casually. It was not until June 1964, when I found Betty's name on his telephone list on the back of his Canada flag design, that I realized her importance to Alec. He would see her regularly when she came to Ottawa. Through the years, I learned not to make appointments to see Alec on Tuesdays — he kept that day free for particular visitors. He asked us to invite her to the party when we celebrated his eighty-fifth birthday at our house and he included her in the list he wrote out for us.

Betty Kirk enjoyed Alec's company and his stories. On her visits to Ottawa, she would take him for a drive, and they usually had lunch at the Green Valley Restaurant on the Prescott Highway or the Town & Country Restaurant on Richmond Road. Sometimes they went to see a film. Betty mentioned one in particular that had appealed to Alec —

The Incredible Journey, the adventures of a cat and two dogs in Northern Ontario, a part of the country Alec knew well. I asked Betty how she knew that Alec enjoyed that film, and she replied, "Because he watched it with rapt attention and because he didn't fall asleep."

As time passed, I began to notice a gleam in Alec's eye when Betty Kirk's name came up. He appeared to be very fond of her, and I gathered the distinct impression that he considered proposing to her and might have done so, though I never asked. I began to wonder whether he would be successful this time. Alec may have concluded that there was no harm in trying. After all, old age is no insurance that men may not make fools of themselves. And for Alec, a man of stout heart, strong mind, and a positive outlook on life, hope sprang eternal.

What drew Alec to Betty Kirk was not just the comfort and good food she provided when he stayed at her home in Buckingham. He also responded warmly to her good sense of humour, her kindness, and her unselfishness. What started out as a friendship seemed to change into a companionship that stirred emotions in Alec he had not felt for many years.

Again I asked myself, what might have been in Betty Kirk's mind? Being a sensitive person, she probably began to realize what Alec was thinking, though she may have been surprised when he actually popped the question. She knew she would face a dilemma. She liked Alec very much and did not wish to hurt his feelings, but there were other problems. What would her friends think about her marrying a man so much older? That she was marrying him for his money? Wouldn't Alec's friends make that assumption? Would Alec's family be unhappy that Alec's fortune would go to a stranger? And how might her young son feel when, instead of acquiring a new father, he would get a new grandfather? Would she be able to cope with that change in lifestyle, leaving the security of her Quebec village for life in the high society of the big cities, where crowds of people sought to honour one of Canada's leading painters? How would this new life affect her son?

And what about Alec, the man whose free-wheeling spirit caused him to roam all over Canada searching for new scenes to express his creativeness? Wouldn't marriage dampen that spirit? Alec might well think that marriage was the answer to the friendly feelings he had for her, but would it really be in his best interests? Would the marriage last?

After Alec's death I was hesitant to visit Mrs. Kirk and discuss with her what to my knowledge was Alec's last romance. Margaret Kennedy, whom I consulted when writing this book, counselled me repeatedly to see her, saying, "Show her what you have written about her and Alec, and hear what she has to say. It would be fairer to her to record what has actually happened than to speculate. Moreover, you could exchange reminisences about a man who was very dear to both of you."

I took this advice, and I had a useful and constructive four-hour interview with Betty Kirk in January 1978. Her dollhouse-like home, with its steep roof, was set back from the road and immaculately kept. There was a touch of grey in her dark hair, and she had a ready smile. A little shy at first, she became candid and friendly as we talked, and she added a number of things to the draft material that I had brought for her to read.

She began by saying that Alec had referred in an interview that he gave in 1971 to the possibility of marrying a widow without mentioning her name; "There was a widow, a delightful woman. She drove me all over the place. I should have married as soon as I had $20,000 a year. But it was too late, maybe. Hah! Ah!"[92] Although Betty Kirk's friends speculated about whether she was the lady in question, she never denied or confirmed it. But she told me, after reading my draft notes, that the question of marriage had come up. "Alec and I talked about it quite a bit. In fact, I was a little taken aback when Alec asked me to be his wife. He really cared for me, and I cared for him. He wrote me very friendly letters, and he gave me some of his paintings. On the back he would put 'To Betty with love, A.Y.'" She showed me a sketch called *Spring Freshet, Buckingham, Que*, dated April 1967, that bore this inscription.

"I didn't think marriage would work out," she continued. "You have mentioned some of the things, but there were other personal reasons." And she made two points in particular.

First, she said, she felt that she would not fit into Alec's bustling life. She was usually exhausted after Alec's visits with her in Buckingham. "He was set in his ways, and no woman could change him. Can you imagine me cleaning up MacLaren Street?" she asked, implying that Alec would have hated it. Second, both of her parents were ill, and she was accustomed to visit them in Antigonish three or four times a year. She would have faced divided loyalties.

My private reaction to her statements was that she could have surmounted the obstacles if she had so wanted. I was not an impartial observer, however, for I had hoped that Alec and Betty might get married. I genuinely believe it would have added to Alec's happiness, and it would have removed feelings of failure and frustration he may have felt. Also, Betty Kirk, loyal person that she was, could have helped Alec to live out his last six years in human dignity. Even though they did not marry, Alec was still lucky, for Betty Kirk remained his devoted friend to his last days.

I asked Betty how she met Alec and how their friendship developed. Here is her story.

"I visited my sister-in-law, Doris Brine, in Manotick early in February 1961. I wanted to meet Alec, and she introduced me to Ton Hamilton, who took me up to see her uncle who lived next door, up the hill. I said I admired his work and he was very nice to me.

"Two months later, I again visited my sister-in-law. I was returning by bus. As I was waiting at the bus stop, Alec joined me. I thought he wouldn't remember me, but he did, and we chatted. As I got on the bus, I asked myself, 'May I dare?' Then I turned to Alec and said, 'Will you sit with me?' He chuckled and joined me. I was lucky; I sat on his right, the side of his good ear. At that time I didn't know he was hard of hearing.

"Alec got off the bus ahead of me. He was going to a reception at the British High Commission, and somebody was meeting him to drive him there. As he walked away, he turned and waved to me, giving me a warm smile — what a thoughtful and sweet man! I made up my mind right then and there that I liked the man and I wanted to get to know him.

"Later that year, or it could have been early in 1962, I visited him again in his studio in Manotick. I inquired whether I could purchase one of his sketches, and he was kind enough to sell me one for sixty dollars. It is the only sketch I bought. All the other paintings were presents that Alec gave me.

"I asked him whether he would be willing to visit me in Buckingham, and he said he would be glad to. He moved to Ottawa in May 1962, and he wrote telling me about his new studio. I phoned him and arranged to pick him up on Sunday for lunch at my home. I asked some neighbours to join us, and we had a good time. Alec promised to return, saying this was good painting country and that I would be welcome to join him if I wanted to paint. This was the beginning of our friendship.

"He would come out three or four times a year, but after I stopped working in 1963 he would come more often. After that, I, in turn, would visit him more frequently in Ottawa, mostly on Tuesdays, occasionally on Thursdays."

It took a while for Betty to get used to the idea of being a close friend of a national celebrity. When she went out with Alec, she would notice people whispering and pointing at them. On one occasion, when they were having lunch at the Green Valley Restaurant in Ottawa and engaging in an animated conversation — necessarily a fairly loud one — admiring glances came their way from a neighbouring table. Finally, one of the observant young women walked over to

Alec and said, "Are you *the* A.Y. Jackson?"

"Yes," Alec replied, "I am Jackson," and he added a few kindly words to make his caller feel comfortable.

As Betty explained to me afterward, watching this little scene she had asked herself, "What am I doing here? Little me and that famous painter."

"Well, did you ever give yourself an answer to the question?" I asked.

"Yes," Betty replied. "I liked being with Alec because to me he wasn't a celebrity, just a good friend."

"I would do all the driving," she continued. "Alec would walk, talk, and paint. He was very active, and it was not easy to keep up with him. When I brought him home, he would have a nap while I prepared dinner. After the meal, I would wash the dishes and he would dry them. He liked my company, and he would follow me wherever I went. Then we would chat, and sometimes friends would drop by. Alec would be telling stories and stayed up till 1 a.m. Then he would get up at six. As fond as I was of Alec, that routine would have driven me up the wall, and after a three-or four-day visit of Alec's, I would be exhausted, needing time to recover."

I asked Betty whether she could tell me any stories about their visits together, and she told me several. First she referred to the famous laundry cardboard that had served as Alec's telephone list. "You discovered that Alec's design for a Canadian flag was on the other side and you arranged to have it sent to Mr. Pearson?" she asked. When I nodded, she went on, "Well, Alec told me about it and he remarked, 'Your phone number is on that list. If you get a phone call from the Prime Minister asking you for a date, don't accept it.'

"On one wintery March morning, we were painting at Notre Dame de la Salette, fifteen miles north of Buckingham. I was cold and got into the car to warm up. Alec, the hardy soul, kept on painting nearby. A truck passed by and then stopped. The driver, a farmer, came over and said: 'Do you have any paintings for sale? We have a big mirror over our mantelpiece. The wife and I want to replace it with a painting. They tell us it's the thing to do.'

"When I replied that I was not aware of any paintings for sale, he remarked, 'There's that painter Burton. He comes here sometimes to paint with an old fellow who is supposed to be famous, but I can't think of his name.'

"'Would his name be Jackson?' I asked. When he nodded, I pointed to Alec and said, 'There is that famous painter whose name you can't remember.' Whereupon the farmer looked embarrassed, went back to his truck, and departed in a hurry. Alec had not heard what had been

104

said, but when I told him the story later that day, he was amused, calling it a good joke."

On another occasion, Alec and Betty were painting near a highway. A school bus passed. A few minutes later it returned, and a number of children left the bus and came to them. The bus driver explained that some of the children had recognized Alec and had insisted that the driver turn around and give them a chance to meet him. When he refused, the children made such a fuss that the driver thought it would be better to arrive a few minutes late at their destination than to get there as nervous wrecks. The children were all French-speaking, and Alec was delighted to meet them and explain to them what he was painting. He also complimented them on their ingenuity in persuading the bus driver to deviate from his schedule just so they could say hello to an old man like himself. That little occasion made Alec's day, and he was very happy about it. It was gratifying to him to be sought after by young admirers.

On February 26, 1968, Betty and Alec were again painting at Notre Dame de la Salette, the last time they went out on a sketching trip together. It was a happy day for both of them, and the photograph on page 106 was taken on that occasion. Each did a sketch of the wintery landscape, and Alec gave Betty some pointers on changing the colour of the snow in the background to give the viewer a feeling of distance. She, in turn, admired Alec's sketch greatly, and he promised to do a canvas for her from it. When they came back to the house, one of Betty's neighbours asked whether she could buy the sketch. Alec said she could, with the understanding that she would receive it after he had done a painting from it.

But Alec did not get around to doing that canvas, for he was not well and became seriously ill late in April. After the move to Kleinburg, one of the first things he remembered was his promise to Betty to do a canvas for her of Notre Dame de la Salette. He insisted that a canvas be set up for him on an easel and the original sketch placed next to it. Then came days of agony. As much as he tried, Alec could not paint that canvas. He became very upset about it, and all those who watched him struggle to move the stiff fingers that would not respond to his creative mind were in tears.

Alec would not give in, and the struggle continued for almost a year. Finally, the McMichaels in desperation suggested that he might like to send the canvas to Betty as it was and visit her at some future date to add some "finishing" touches. Alec agreed, and the uncompleted canvas was sent to Betty.

The visit actually took place. Betty Kirk and her son Brine arrived in Kleinburg in early April 1971 to drive Alec and his nurse, Zita Wil-

son, to Buckingham, where he stayed for five days. He worked on the canvas for quite some time and it was improved, though it reflects the artist as the handicapped person he was in his later years and cannot be compared with the unconstrained compositions of earlier days. Still, this painting is historically important because it is Alec's only known canvas dating from the Kleinburg period, 1968 to 1974.

During this visit, Betty took Alec to see some places where they had painted together in happier days. Then, with the nurse, they visited the National Gallery of Canada. Alec was quite upset that so few paintings of the Group of Seven were on exhibit and that the War Collection concentrated almost exclusively on the Second World War. He made his annoyance clear, protesting in a loud voice that could be heard all over the gallery floor. "Fortunately," Betty said, "there were not too many people about." After the visit, Alec and Zita Wilson returned to Kleinburg by air.

Betty visited Alec two or three times a year during his stay in Kleinburg, with the last visit taking place at the nursing home near Kleinburg in February 1974, about two monthis before his death. It was sad to watch this once strong man shrivelling into insignificance, deprived of body and mind. Betty commented, "Some of his bright moments came when people asked for his autograph, for it meant to him that he had not been forgotten." At such times Alec also expected Betty to take him back to Ottawa, but then would accept his fate with resignation.

As a man and as her friend, Mrs. Kirk was entranced by him. "He was a charmer," she said. "He was a very kind and warm-hearted person. We felt very close. We didn't get married, but we became very dear friends. I am glad I brought happiness to him: he enlarged my life, he opened new windows for me. Those were fulfilling days for both of us. My friendship with Alec was one of the most wonderful things in my life. He and my husband are the two important men in my life."

CHAPTER 9

Alec and the Canadian Flag

Tuesday, June 9, 1964, we had arranged with Alec to join us for an early family dinner, and since I was free from professional duties that day, I went to pick up Alec about half an hour earlier than the agreed time. When I threw some pebbles against his studio window, our usual signal, he came to the window and beckoned me to come in. He was in his painting clothes, a brush in his hand. Did I mind waiting while he finished something? he asked.

I followed him to his easel. He had been working on a canvas, doing a small rock in the foreground. His brush went from paint to canvas, paint to canvas, and finally the rock took on the impression Alec wanted to give it. Suddenly he paused and stepped back a few feet to look at the part of the canvas he had just finished. He nodded. "It will do," he said.

As he cleaned his brushes and put things away, I phoned my wife Isobel to say we would be "a little late." A piece of greyish shirt cardboard lay next to the telephone — Alec's list of phone numbers. I studied it idly and found my home phone number entered three times and a fourth number I had used when I was working for the Canadian government also listed. Since I had left the public service on June 30, 1960, that telephone list dated back to 1959 or earlier. The names and numbers of some of Alec's family and friends, including his nieces, Dr. Starrs, Dr. Jeffries, Ralph Burton, Maurice Haycock, and Betty Kirk were on it. I asked Alec why he had put our name on the list four times, while everyone else's name was noted only once. Alec replied, "I'm forgetful. Every time I remember your number, I put it down."

"I thought your were putting us down four times as a reflection of how much you valued our friendship," I said, kidding.

"That, too," Alec retorted. "But the truth is, I'm just too plain forgetful."

I turned the cardboard over and I must have looked startled, because Alec chuckled. "You're looking at the Jackson flag of Canada," he said.

"When did you do this design?" I asked (the outline had been drawn in pencil, and the flag was painted in watercolour).

Alec reflected, "Well, I've been putting phone numbers on this sheet for the past five years . . . so I did the design while I was still in Manotick. That would make it 1959. Yes, it probably was that year. You know, I'd forgotten all about it. I haven't turned the telephone list over since I moved to this place."

The month prior, Prime Minister Lester B. Pearson had submitted the government's proposed design for a Canadian flag to the House of Commons — three maple leaves with a blue stripe at each side. I said that it was not nearly as good-looking a design as the one that Alec had produced.

"I agree," replied Alec. "The government or the people who work for it know nothing about art. My design is an artist's concept."

"We both like your design, Alec," I said. "Would you agree to send it to Mr. Pearson?"

"I'll do nothing of the sort."

"Why not?"

"Because I don't trust politicians. The government has probably already made up its mind, and it's going to get the design it proposed."

"Why don't you trust politicians?"

"Because they don't give a damn about little people. Anyway, this matter has become very political, as I see from the papers."

"But, Alec, shouldn't Canada have the best flag her people can produce? What would be wrong with considering an artist's design in addition to the ones prepared by 'experts'?"

"Well . . . but I don't see the point of getting involved. We'll just get a run-around. It's useless."

"What if we can make sure your design will be considered?"

"Bah, too much talk, no action."

So I proposed my idea. "As you know," I said to him, "I know Secretary of State Maurice Lamontagne well. If you were to sign this cardboard and date it, I could take it to him tomorrow and he could pass it on to Mr. Pearson. At least your design would be considered. It doesn't matter whether it's accepted by Parliament or not — but people should know that you felt keenly enough about the need for a Canadian flag five years ago — that you did a design of your own. Furthermore, you favoured the maple leaf as a symbol of Canada at a time when Diefenbaker was prime minister, and he and his colleagues couldn't visualize any other flag for Canada than one that prominently featured the Union Jack.* (Here was Alec, an English-speaking

*Although the maple leaf was a popular symbol for Canada, few people realized that it had been accepted as such both in colonial days and later when Canada became a dominion in 1867. The maple leaf was prominent in early coinage, became the emblem of the St-Jean Baptiste Society in French Canada in 1834, and was incorporated in the coats of arms of Ontario and Quebec in 1868, and in the Canadian official crest in 1921.

Canadian and a small *c* conservative, visualizing a flag in red, white, and blue, combining the colours of Canada with those of Quebec, with a symbol that was typically Canadian — the maple leaf — while Diefenbaker and those who supported him still clung uncompromisingly to the symbols of the British connection.)

And so went the conversation. In all the ten years I had known Alec, I had never pleaded with him as much as I did on this occasion, for the longer I looked at his design (see below), the more suitable it seemed to me in comparison with the one put forward by the Canadian government. Alec's proposal also showed three maple leaves, but his leaves looked like leaves. They were more natural in appearance and not as stylized as those in the other design. The leaves had easy, flowing lines — one could sense the gift of nature the artist was trying to portray — unlike the leaves in the government's proposal, with their stiff and sharply cut edges. There were about twenty points to each maple leaf in Alec's version, against thirteen in the government's (and the same number were in a later design that became known as the "revised" version). The stem was different. Alec's was thin, curving, and elegant, the other thicker, straighter, and heavy-looking. Whereas the government design had blue edges at the left and right ends of the flag, Alec's had a blue wavy line top and bottom. In both designs, the leaves were set against white backgrounds, but in Alec's design the leaves had a glow at the edges.

A. Y. Jackson's Flag for Canada

"Do the blue wavy lines represent 'from sea to sea'?" I asked.

"You might think so," Alec replied, "but what I had in mind were the rivers of Canada. We have them in every province and they helped us open up the country." Then he added, chuckling, "People in British Columbia won't like my flag. They may think that the upper wavy line represents the waves of the Pacific. They may not be happy with waves that are upside-down."

Alec finally agreed to let me take the drawing to Lamontagne, on the understanding that he himself would not be personally involved. (He later changed his mind and appeared as a witness before the House of Commons Special Committee on the Flag, and gave press interviews.) He signed the flag design, dated it "About 1959" and put a large red X in pencil over the names and telephone numbers. He added my name in pencil on the front side: "Return to O. J. Firestone."

I explained that it would be helpful to Lamontagne if he could take Pearson a letter addressed to the Prime Minister, signed by Alec, explaining what Alec had in mind when he painted the design. Alec agreed to prepare a handwritten draft which I would have typed. He would sign it, and I would deliver his original flag design to Lamontagne.

We both felt a bit guilty when we arrived at the house — we were very late, and Isobel remarked that our housekeeper had been making noises about the roast beef being overdone. We sat down to dinner right away, skipping Alec's usual rye and ginger ale in favour of wine. Alec traced the origin of his flag design, back to a little red maple tree he had painted in 1914 when he did his well-known sketch (and later canvas) *The Red Maple*. In the course of the evening I reached Lamontagne, and he agreed to the arrangements I had worked out with Alec.

The next morning, I phoned Alec about his letter to Pearson. He'd done part of it, and read me what he'd written. He had mentioned my name as the one who had discovered his flag design; I asked him to take my name out of the letter, since it was his flag and his letter. Alec first demurred, but then agreed. The letter was typed (see page 112), Alec keeping one copy and I the other. I submitted Alec's design and letter to Lamontagne on June 10, 1964. Lamontagne, in turn, passed both on to Lester Pearson the next day. Later, when a special House of Commons committee on the flag was established, Pearson himself sent Alec's design to the chairman.

That afternoon, I asked Alec whether he was sorry that I might be getting him involved in something that could shatter his tranquillity. "Never mind," he replied with a smile. "I'm used to excitement."

Then he added, "When you get the thing back, you can keep it as a present."

When I expressed concern that even with Lamontagne's and Pearson's promise, the design could get lost — there were said to be thousands of designs floating around — he volunteered to do another copy right then and there.[93] He said he would paint it at an angle, using a little more white around the edges of the maple leaves to distinguish the new watercolour from the old one. He searched for another cardboard and found one in a shirt recently back from the laundry. He then drew the flag in pencil, painted it with red, white, and blue watercolours, and the whole thing was done in less than ten minutes. He signed it in ink. I forgot to ask Alec to date the design, something about which on other occasions I had been quite careful.

192 Maclaren Street,
Ottawa.
June 10th, 1964.

The Right Honourable Lester B. Pearson, P.C.,M.D.,
Prime Minister of Canada,
Ottawa.

Dear Mr. Pearson,

Several years ago I made a design for a Canadian flag. It was not shown to anyone and I had forgotten all about it. I had scribbled some phone numbers on the back of it. A visitor to the studio the other day saw it and remarked he liked it more than the one being reproduced in the press, and asked if he could show it to Mr. Lamontagne. I imagine that back of my mind was the memory of camping with Tom Thomson in Algonquin Park just fifty years ago. I made a sketch which became a canvas entitled "The Red Maple" and was purchased by the National Gallery that same year 1914. It represented a tree with red leaves and the Ox Tongue River prancing by in the background.

The design under discussion at present is confounded by the idea of "Sea to sea". It should be horizontal, but it cannot be done. But when one thinks of how all this country was discovered and explored by men in canoes, running down or poling up rapids, and all the heroic adventures of brave men from LaSalle, Champlain, Mackenzie, Hearn Tyrill, Camsell and countless others, the wild river is far more associated with our history than any ocean and the rollicking line can be the expression of it on a flag.

Apart from that, I believe the leaf of the sugar maple in its natural state is much more beautiful than the simplifications made of it in most of the flag designs, also the blue lines at the top and bottom in my design separate the flag more effectively from whatever its background may be.

I trust you will forgive me for intruding my views into this rather confusing situation.

Yours very truly,

A. Y. Jackson

112

Lester Pearson was a man of his word: after Parliament approved Canada's new flag, I received a letter from the prime minister dated July 22, 1965, returning Alec's design. The original "Jackson Flag" is a valued piece of memorabilia in the Jackson Room. The second and newer version I have kept as a memento for my children. Alec later did several more versions of his original design in response to requests he received.

Furious debate raged for months in Parliament, and the media, and in heated public discussions across the country. Pearson, in his autobiography, described the flag debate as "one of the most bitter to arise in the House of Commons for a very long time (though not quite so violent as those debates in the 19th Century when they threw bottles at one another)."[94] The controversy even prompted threats of personal harm to the prime minister and his family — of the ten thousand letters Mr. Pearson received about the flag, ten containing threats were turned over to the RCMP for investigation.[95] To understand all the excitement that the flag controversy caused, it may be helpful to look at it in historical perspective.

In 1964, there were three years to go to Canada's centenary; ninety-seven years had passed since Confederation in Canada, but still there was no national flag. Canadian soldiers had fought in two World Wars under the Red Ensign, a red flag with the Union Jack in the upper left corner and the Canadian crest in the lower right. This flag was accepted by tradition but was not considered a national flag. On holidays the Red Ensign and the British Union Jack were usually flown together.

When World War II ended, the question of finding an acceptable flag for Canada was referred to a House of Commons committee, which sat in 1945 and 1946. Nothing came of its deliberations, even though Prime Minister Mackenzie King was keenly interested in having Canada adopt a national flag. The strongest stand on the flag question at that time was taken by John Diefenbaker, then a frontbench member of the Progressive Conservative Opposition, when he stated in the House of Commons in 1945 that any national flag for Canada would have to include a prominent Union Jack. This attitude remained the policy of the Progressive Conservatives during the next two decades and was the basis of their opposition to the government's flag proposals made in 1964.

The bitter dispute about which flag should fly lasted from spring 1964 to year's end*:

---

*This narrative is based in part on a Canadian Press report, "The Capsule History of the Flag Debate," and in part on the Debates of the House of Commons and the Senate as well as related government documents.

May 14	Prime Minister Pearson tells a few reporters at a confidential briefing that new flag legislation will be introduced in Parliament shortly.
May 17	Prime minister tells a hostile Canadian Legion Convention in Winnipeg that the time has come to adopt a distinctive maple leaf flag.
May 18	Mr. Pearson shows three maple leaf designs under consideration to a Winnipeg press conference.
May 27	The government introduces a House of Commons resolution for adoption of a design featuring three red maple leaves on a white background with narrow blue bars at the vertical edges.
June 15	The prime minister opens the formal flag debate. Opposition leader John Diefenbaker moves an amendment for a flag plebiscite at the next federal election.
June 17	Flag debate continues in the House of Commons.
August 13	The Progressive Conservative Opposition moves a sub-amendment to hold a flag plebiscite.
August 21	Mr. Pearson tells the House of Commons that three meetings of the party leaders have failed to produce agreement.
September 1	The Progressive Conservative sub-amendment is defeated, 118 to 69.
September 2	Another sub-amendment is moved by the Progressive Conservative Opposition asking that plebiscite results be announced on a national rather than provincial basis.
September 3	The NDP moves adjournment of the debate. The motion is defeated, 84 to 69.
September 8	Another motion by the Créditiste Party for adjournment is defeated, 85 to 64.
September 10	Party leaders meet again and agree to refer the flag issue to a fifteen-member special committee. The House of Commons sets up such a committee with a six-week deadline to submit its recommendations.
September 13	Mr. Pearson predicts in a TV-radio interview that Canada will have a new maple leaf flag by Christmas.

September 17	The flag committee holds the first of forty-five sessions and elects Mr. Batten (Liberal, Humber-St. George) as chairman.
October 7	The committee breaks its silence and announces that 4,200 designs have been received from the public and are being considered. Twelve expert witnesses are being called, among them A. Y. Jackson.
October 20	Word leaks out that the majority of the committee appears to be favouring the Jackson design as a compromise solution.
October 25	Another leak says that the majority of the committee has changed its mind and now favours a single red maple leaf on a white background with red panels on either side.
October 28	Mr. Diefenbaker says in a TV interview that a maple leaf flag is unacceptable because it denies the British and French heritage.
October 29	With four Progressive Conservative members dissenting, the special committee recommends a single red leaf design; ten Quebec Progressive Conservative members defy their leader and call for speedy approval of the committee's choice. The committee also urges adoption of the Union Jack as a symbol of Canada's Crown and Commonwealth ties.
November 30	The chairman of the Special House of Commons Committee opens debate on the first recommendation by the committee. The Progressive Conservative Opposition moves an amendment in favour of a flag plebiscite.
December 1	The Speaker rules the amendment in order, notwithstanding government objections.
December 3	A motion to adjourn debate, moved by the Progressive Conservative Opposition, is defeated, 129 to 55.
December 8	A second Progressive Conservative motion to adjourn debate is defeated, 139 to 68.
December 9	The NDP moves a modified form of adjournment, and their motion is defeated, 132 to 99. Léon Balcer, Quebec Progressive Conservative leader, and Créditiste leader Réal Caouette both ask the government to invoke closure to force a final vote.

December 10	Mr. Diefenbaker makes a final plea for a plebiscite to end disunity. The Progressive Conservative amendment for a plebiscite is defeated, 153 to 82.
December 11	A Progressive Conservative motion to adopt the red ensign as the national flag of Canada is put forward in the House of Commons. The government gives notice that closure will be applied at the sitting of the House on December 14.
December 12	The Progressive Conservative Leader of the Opposition in the Senate indicates that an extended flag debate is likely in the Upper House.
December 14	The House of Commons votes to approve closure, 152 to 85. The same night the motion to approve the new Canadian flag is carried 163 to 78, and the House adjourns at 2:15 a.m. (December 15).
December 17	The Senate approves the flag motion, 38 to 23, after a dignified and remarkably well-informed debate.
December 24	Her Majesty Queen Elizabeth II approves the specific flag design.

The final events in this struggle took place in 1965. On January 28, the new official flag of Canada was proclaimed, and it was first officially used on February 15.

Alec's contribution to the choices for a Canadian flag came close to becoming the flag committee's compromise solution. But "close" was not enough. The government did not endorse the Jackson flag. It stuck to its own proposal, saying that it was prepared to make changes in minor details.

On October 20, 1964, however, rumours had been flying that the Jackson design was a leading contender. Canadian Press wire service reported: "Famed artist A. Y. Jackson is on the road to becoming Canada's Betsy Ross. His flag design is reliably reported to be preferred by the majority of the members of the Commons flag committee. Informants say the committee will probably split nine to five to recommend to the Commons that the 82-year-old Canadian painter's maple leaf flag design become Canada's flag and that the Canadian red ensign be used to mark Canada's Commonwealth connection."[96]

Nevertheless, the course of history had taken a different turning. Five days later word had leaked out that the majority of the committee's members had changed their minds in favour of a single maple leaf, the design later recommended to the House of Commons and ultimately approved by Parliament.

Meantime, Alec gave several interviews to the press, commenting on his design and on flag designs generally. He said that he was in favour of a distinctive Canadian flag with the maple leaf as the key symbol, rather than the beaver or an abstract design such as a tricolour. His own design, he said, had come from the painting *The Red Maple* (by then owned by the National Gallery of Canada) which showed a small maple tree with bright autumn foliage against the background of a river. He did not like the government's design in either the original or the revised version. The leaves "look like they were cut out of leather, and a paralyzed maple leaf is not a maple leaf at all. And I don't like the stems either; they are like tree branches." Furthermore, he did not like the single maple leaf design (the flag that was finally adopted). "You have to think how a flag will look through a telescope from three to four miles away. One maple leaf from that distance might look like a circle or something, and the flag would not be distinctive. The three leaves would make it distinctive." His own choice, he said, would have been green leaves rather than red on the grounds that the combination of green and blue would be more distinctive than red and blue, and, "when leaves turn red they are ready to fall . . . but I don't think that there is any chance of that being accepted."[97] (Interestingly enough, there were three green maple leaves in Canada's official Coat of Arms from 1921 to 1957, when the colour was changed to red.) But he did not wish to push his own design. "The government has apparently decided on a flag, although it is not a very good one."

Although urged by the press to divulge the name of the person who had discovered the flag design after he had forgotten all about it, Alec kept his promise to me and did not do so. All he was prepared to say was that the design was "recently submitted to the government by a friend."[98] But my name did surface. An enterprising newspaperman, J. R. Walker of the Southam News Service, got the story, reportedly from somebody in the prime minister's office, and included it in an article that appeared in the *Winnipeg Tribune*.[99]

I have two footnotes to add in bringing this narrative of Alec's contribution to the choice of the Canadian flag to a close. In January 1965, I met the High Commissioner of Pakistan at a reception. He remarked that Canada was a lucky country indeed — that when Pakistan achieved independence in 1942, with a constituent assembly serving as legislature, it had taken only half an hour to approve a national flag. "You Canadians could afford to luxury of nine months of Parliamentary debate to decide on a national flag — at a time when the world faces poverty, hunger, illiteracy, epidemics, high unemployment, and subsistence living for hundreds of millions of people. You lucky, lucky people," he repeated.

Some time later when I saw Alec, I told him of the High Commissioner's comments. "Canadians are slow," Alec said. "We like to talk. Sometimes it takes too damn long to make up our minds. We had to wait ninety-seven years for a flag. We're lucky! We could have waited one-hundred-ninety-seven years." Nearing his eighty-third birthday, he was as pragmatic and positive as ever, in his dry humorous way.

CHAPTER 10

Of Sketch Boxes, Snowshoes, and Painting Hats

When Alec decided in 1962 to move from his Manotick studio-house to Ottawa, he said (as most people do when they move) that it was a good time to get rid of a lot of old junk he had been accumulating over the years. Yet I noticed when I first visisted Alec at 192 MacLaren Street that the place was even more cluttered than his Manotick home had been. The new place was smaller, and not all his things had places.

For the next two years Alec kept mumbling about getting rid of things. On one such occasion early in 1964, I asked, "What, for example?"

In reply he pointed to a sketch box he had used for fifteen years. "I have a new sketch box now. I haven't used the old one since 1950." He continued, "Look at this old pair of snowshoes. They've seen better days. I have no use for them now."

I said that if he didn't want them I would be happy to take the sketch box and the snowshoes and put them in our Jackson Room. Alec was willing to give me these, though he drew the line at his painting hat. He wrote on the inside panel of the box in ink: "Sketch box used by A. Y. Jackson for fifteen years, 1936-1950." He added five different-sized brushes and a palette-knife. Then he took a roll of masking tape, cut off two pieces, signed them, and attached them to the snowshoes. He handed me these items with a sad smile, saying, "Something to remember me by." It was one of those rare occasions when the hidden character came through and his true feelings showed. He could be close to a person without saying much.

Before I left him that day, we talked more about sketch boxes and snowshoes. Alec told me he had designed the sketch box himself. In his early years of outdoor painting, he had used 8½-by10½-inch birch panels, a small size handy for travelling by canoe.[100] Later on, when he relied more on car transport, he changed the size of his panels to 10½ by 13½ inches, and it was at this stage that his specially designed sketch box had come in handy. His niece Naomi, a keen observer of her uncle's habits, described to me in 1967 his method of organizing his paints on the base panel. On his sketching trips early in the year, before the snow was gone but with the first thaws of spring in the air, Alec would go out with

> his bear-paw snowshoes strapped on top of his rucksack for use when the snow became softer that day. In the rucksack he carried his drawingbook for 'notes' and his handy lightweight little 'Jackson sketch box' in which two birch sketch panels formed the cover, while the bottom served as a palette. To save weight, the paint was already squeezed around the edges, starting in the lower left corner with cerulean blue, then French ultramarine, viridian green, and yellow ochre; in the upper left corner an immense glob of flake white; along the top, chrome or cadmium yellow, cadmium orange and red; rose madder or thalo red rose, and finally burnt sienna.[101]

As Naomi observed, this was a simple range indeed to achieve the subtleties which became the hallmark of Alec's paintings.

Except for the day at Kingsmere Lake, I did not accompany Alec on sketching trips and so was not familiar from first-hand observation with the way Alec operated on his outdoor excursions. My knowledge came from what he told me and from observations made by others.

When Alec came back from a sketching trip and the paint was not quite dry on his panels, I noticed tiny pieces of wood stuck into the paint of the panels. Alec picked away the bits and touched up the spots. That was his method of keeping wet panels apart: "How else could I bring all these newly painted sketches back?" He said he was using the Banting method of transporting wet sketches. The little pieces of wood I'd seen were parts of a broken matchstick, Dr. Frederick Banting's invention.[102] Banting broke a wooden match into five pieces, and before the paint was too dry he put the pieces right into the paint, one in each corner and one in the centre. When they were finished, the sketches were tied into a bundle, and there was no difficulty with the paint being disturbed. The broken match pieces were later removed in the studio and some touching up done if necessary.

Alec was proud of his sketch box design. He told me that he had once asked the owner of an art supply store whether there would be a market for a sketch box such as he'd designed. It could be produced inexpensively, he'd said, and might become popular with art students and people who were taking up painting as a hobby. According to Alec, the store owner replied, "You better stick to your painting, Mr. Jackson. You would starve running a store selling art supplies." Alec added he could have replied, "There were years when I didn't do much better as a painter, either." But he had refrained from saying so.

Alec had painted a great deal in Quebec in the late twenties and early thirties, taking Dr. Banting under his wing. On those trips, snowshoes were part of his equipment. He used two types, one pair four and a half feet long, the other just over three feet long (he gave us the shorter pair for the Jackson Room). Alec became well known to the *habitant* farmers in some of the Quebec villages, who called him Père Raquette (Father Snowshoe).*[103] What Alec liked about those simple folks was that they did not look at him as an eccentric *anglais* but as a person who was doing what he wanted. Nobody questioned him, asked what he was doing and why (unlike some city people). Alec had little patience with what he considered stupid questions. He once told me about a lady who had seen a picture of him on his snowshoes. "How quaint," she remarked, adding, "don't you prefer skiing?" Alec looked at her straight-faced and replied, "Well, it may be quaint — but have you ever tried painting with skis on?"**

To Marius Barbeau, a close friend of Alec's, the term Père Raquette was more than an affectionate greeting by *habitant* farmers. It was a symbol of Alec's understanding of the people of rural Quebec and ability to adapt himself to their way of life, a man who preferred the peacefulness of the land to the bustle of the big city. Barbeau explained that the name Père Raquette "characterizes the man of the country who moves slowly but surely over the snow, and for whom the snowshoe is not an article of sport, but a necessity. A man of this type is well planted, is sure of eye and foot, like a hunter tracking the deer, or a woodsman who, in the spring, runs the maple and makes sugar. In descending a hill, if he cannot follow the skier from the city, at least he climbs the slope more easily, jumps the fences and finds himself unhampered in the underbrush. And the painter using snowshoes can station himself comfortably while he sketches a landscape .. Père Raquette... takes pleasure in searching the soul of the people of ancient Quebec. He enjoys the simple life which, though rough at times, does not lack charm. In it he finds peace and an awakening of the imagination which are essential to an artist whose inspiration thrives on the unknown."[104]

I asked Alec how long he had been snowshoeing. He had started at age eight, he replied, and had stopped at seventy-five because of "too

---

*Alec seemed to remember that the first person to call him Père Raquette was Edwin Holgate, when the two of them with Clarence Gagnon went on a winter sketching trip around Baie-St-Paul in the mid-twenties.[105]

**In fact, Alec at one time did consider taking up skiing and giving up snowshoeing: "There is plenty of snow for the old snowshoes, but I fear it is their last season; the gut is beginning to break, so I am thinking of taking to skis and keeping up with the younger generation."[106]

damn many barbed wires." Alec did a sketch of himself on snowshoes to immortalize Père Raquette.* It shows him from the back, warmly dressed for the winter in snowboots, trousers, lumber jacket, and battered ski cap, on snowshoes with a palette in his left hand and a brush in his right, as if he were painting a winter landscape. There is a barn with a snow-covered roof in the distance. This sketch was reproduced in *La Presse* in 1935 and the London *Evening Free Press* in 1960.

The name Père Raquette stuck. Forty or so years later, in 1970, the last time Alec attended a National Gallery opening in Ottawa, Mrs. Eric Brown, widow of the former director of the gallery, in her opening address affectionately welcomed him by this name.

The other item of sketching gear Alec gave us was the painting hat he had been wearing when he drew the portrait of himself at Kingsmere Lake. It came to the Jackson Room in a roundabout way.

On Monday, May 10, 1965, we had a birthday dinner (a week early) for A.J. (Cass) Casson, who was in town with his wife, Margaret. There were fifteen of us, including Alec. Alec mentioned to me that he had received an invitation from P. B. Baird to join some members of the Alpine Club of Canada on a climbing expedition at Pangnirtung Pass on Baffin Island. This was to be Alec's third trip that far north; he had visited the eastern Arctic in 1927 with Dr. Banting, and Baffin Island in 1930 with Lawren Harris. Thirty-five years had passed, and Alec was now eighty-two. I asked whether he wouldn't find the trip too strenuous. "Well, I'm young," Alec replied, "young in spirit, and I'm willing. Anyway, I'll leave the mountain climbing to others and concentrate on painting."

"How will you be able to paint if you get too tired?" I asked.

"Only two things keep me from painting. One is if people talk to me while I'm painting. The other is fog."

In his letter to P. B. Baird[107], Alec mentioned the hazard of fog; he left out the reference to people talking. He told us he was planning to be away more than a month; he promised to write to us and, if possible, would keep a sketch and/or some drawings for us.

Alec kept his promises. First, he sent us a card from Frobisher Bay dated July 6, 1965, commenting on fog, cold weather, snow in the mountains, and the compensating feature of being together with "a nice group of people." Second, he brought us a sketch and three drawings from his trip to the Arctic. He had done more than one hundred sketches on the trip — a number of them with the names of members of the Alpine Club marked on the back, and others for his Montreal dealers. The promised sketches were to be sold at one hundred dollars

---

*This painting is in the McMichael Canadian Collection.

each. Meanwhile, Alec would paint a fairly large number of canvases from them. During these months, dozens of visitors saw the sketches and wanted to buy them, offering much larger sums, but Alec turned all offers down. These sketches were not for sale, and the canvases too had all been promised.

Since it took Alec several months to finish all the canvases he wanted to do, some members of the Alpine Club grew nervous and inquired by letter or phone when they could expect their sketches. While Alec rarely answered letters at this time, he would answer the phone. His reply was always, "Never fear. I have your sketch and you will get it soon." He was true to his word. In due course, all the rightful owners received their sketches, much to their delight.

The Jackson works that entered our collection as a result of this trip were the oil sketch *Frobisher, Baffin Island*, and one ink and two pencil drawings. He also brought us an unexpected gift.

For nearly two decades, sunshine or rain, hot or cold weather, Alec had worn a brown suede felt hat (except in wintertime when he wore a ski cap) on his sketching trips. As the years went by, that hat became battered, soiled, and worn, but Alec was attached to the hat and did not wish to exchange it for new headgear. I teased him about it — "The only way you'll get rid of it is if you lose it."

To which he replied, "I'll try not to — I'm too fond of that old contraption."

But the hat did get lost on the trip to Frobisher. It was only found again as the result of a determined effort on the part of the whole party. Naomi Groves reported on the "lost" hat:

A. Y.'s spontaneous humour is of a concrete visual type. He never fails to come up with a funny answer at the drop of a hat. And speaking of hats, A. Y. has had some of the best. There was his ripe old brown suede hat that had been to the Yukon several times and on the 1965 flight to Frobisher Bay got lost somewhere during the night. A great search by all the mountain climbers finally located it under A. Y.'s own feet, slightly more battered than before. "Not hurt a bit," says A. Y. clamping it on his head. "Nothing can hurt that hat; it's my best."[108]

After Alec returned, he told me about the episode and added that the time had come to get a new hat. I laughed and reminded him that we had a common interest in that hat. "I wonder how many people realize how small your head is," I mused. Alec chuckled and retorted, "A good thing that my art is not judged on the basis of the size of my head."

Alec bought a new hat, and he gave me the old one for the Jackson

Room, for all to see. The inscription in his handwriting on tape on the inside band of the hat is fading, though it still is legible. On several occasions, high school students visiting the Jackson Room have asked, "Did the hat fit Mr. Jackson? His head looks much bigger in the photographs."

Alec is now long gone, but a little thing like an old hat brings his memory back to life. The young look at his paintings as part of the heritage left by a great Canadian artist. They look at his old painting hat as a memento of A. Y. Jackson, the man.

CHAPTER 11

The Eighty-third
Birthday Party

Alec was eighty-three years old on October 3, 1965. The next day, his Toronto friends gave him a birthday party to be followed by another get-together with Robert and Signe McMichael in Kleinburg, described as a "happening." Before Alec left for Toronto, we asked whether he would like to have another birthday party in Ottawa. He replied, "Ever since I turned eighty, I seem to be celebrating my birthday two or three times with different friends and in different places. I don't mind being reminded of my age if it's in good company — so let's get together."

We agreed to hold the party at our home on Saturday, October 23. This time, Alec left the choice of the guests to us. There were to be forty of us at a buffet dinner.

On the evening of the party, after drinks and dinner, we were ready to cut Alec's birthday cake. Isobel led the singing of "Happy Birthday, Dear Alec." Alec blew out three candles and received three kisses from the ladies. The cake was served, and we raised our champagne glasses in a toast to Alec's continued health and well-being. It was then after 10 o'clock.

We had asked Charles Comfort and Henri Masson to offer some comments about Alec as a colleague and a friend, and they were willing. Alec's reply to the speeches and the rest of the proceedings, including some amusing banter, were taped. We kept the original tape, and we gave a copy to the Main Library of the University of Ottawa.

This was the second occasion on which Charles Comfort paid tribute to Alec celebrating his birthday at our home. This time, however, he was speaking as a private citizen whereas on the previous occasion he had been director of the National Gallery of Canada. The other speaker was Henri Masson, a successful landscape, figure, and genre painter who like many of his colleagues had had to struggle for years to make a living as a full-time professional artist. Like Alec, he lived long enough to see the demand for his works exceed the supply; unlike Alec, however, Masson allowed market forces to play in bringing about a balance between the supply of and demand for his oil paintings, watercolours, and pastels. He also did fine drawings, but the Canadian public had not yet reached the stage of appreciating black charcoal drawing as much as their more colourful sisters in other media.

Masson, who was born in Belgium in 1907, came to Canada at the age of fourteen with his widowed mother. Largely self-taught, Masson started to work as an engraver in 1923, and continued in that occupation until 1945, when he left the "security" of a regular job to become a full-time painter. He had a dedicated wife, Germaine (whom he married in 1929), and three children. To supplement his earnings from professional painting, he also taught art on a part-time basis.

Masson never regretted the move. He became a very much sought-after artist whose works were exhibited widely and found their way into many public galleries in Canada and abroad as well as a number of private collections. He had a particular affection for Alec, who had bought one of his drawings at an exhibition in Toronto in 1937 to encourage the young artist. The previous year, Henri Masson had done two chalk drawings of Alec. He kept one* and the other joined our collection (see page 127). Both drawings were done spontaneously at a luncheon at our house on December 20, 1964, at which Henri, Germaine, and Alec were present. Masson drew them while Alec was asleep after lunch, sitting in his chair. When Alec woke up, Masson added the finishing touches around the eyes. Alec chuckled, nodding approvingly at the drawings, and said something like, "You never can tell what will happen when you close your eyes."

Masson was known for being outspoken and straightforward in tackling issues and people, and was an exceedingly well-read person who liked music. His *Les Patineurs à Hull* (Skaters in Hull) was to be seen by more people in Canada than any other Canadian painting up to that time when the Canadian government printed it on an issue of 105 million eight-cent Christmas stamps in 1974.

I used my introductory remarks at the party to put on record Alec's painting achievements in the course of his professional life as he had passed them on to me. Then I called on Henri Masson. He talked with ease, humour, and great warmth about Alec.

Everyone knows that we love Alec. I have known him for some years. We know he is the revered and the beloved old master of this country. I wish just to say a few words. I belong to the generation which followed the Group of Seven. I sometimes call it the neglected generation, the generation of the Depression. Since we came

---

*Reproduced on page 109 of Hugues de Jouvancourt's *Henri Masson*, published in Montreal in 1976.

after the Group of Seven we were completely overwhelmed by several events. First, we were neglected by the "museum boys." Then we were overwhelmed by a new trend — non-objective art. We were said to have been left behind in the advances in style of painting that were taking place, the "Continental," and the so-called International style.

As far as the Group of Seven is concerned, Jackson, Varley, and MacDonald have always been my favourites. I was browsing

Henri Masson, *Drawing of A. Y. Jackson*
Ink and crayon on paper, 16¾″ x 14″

around the studio a couple of weeks ago, and I found an old catalogue published by the National Gallery of Canada in 1936. This was the year the Group of Seven had an important retrospective at the National Gallery. I am sure Alec remembers. There were nine members of the Group of Seven, which sounds rather strange and funny. There were six members of the old guard, minus Johnston, plus Casson, Holgate, and Fitzgerald. The last three have also made a significant contribution to Canadian art. *Entre nous*, I will add that Holgate suffered from having too much money, and he did not paint enough. It is too bad that such a beautiful painter is a bit neglected; but his problem was he did not produce enough, and he was not as well known as the other members of the Group. But today, collectors are trying to get his canvases, and of course, like most of us, he is getting older too.

What I wish to say is that in 1936 in Ottawa, we didn't know your work very well, Alec. As you are well aware, Ottawa is a provincial town. It was particularly so three decades ago. I was young then, twenty-nine. I was trying to paint and to make a living. I was already married with two children. Life was difficult. I must admit, I was then not an admirer of the Group of Seven. I found them rather rude and crude, a bit commercial, some of them, though not all of them. I was particularly fond of two painters: my old teacher, Franklin Brownell (1957-1946), who was a conservative man but still a lovely painter (he is almost forgotten today); the other was J. W. Morrice (1865-1924), who painted mainly abroad and was a friend of Matisse.

When I saw the Exhibition of the Group of Seven at the National Gallery of Canada in 1936, it came as an immense shock to me. It was a great revelation to see the range of variety, the colours, the compositions. I still remember this experience vividly, and it changed my mind about the Group's contribution to the Canadian art scene.

I was always a sort of a rebel. I didn't want to paint the so-called "wild" Canadian landscape. I stuck to painting Hull scenes, and figures — monks, priests, skaters, and other types. After I saw the Group of Seven show, I could not shake the shock I experienced. So I undertook to do a number of woodcuts that year. As you know, I was an engraver. I could not make a living with painting. I painted in my spare time and I made my living with engraving. I made some woodcuts that were strongly influenced by A. Y. Jackson. I found some of them last week in a drawer in my studio. They date 1936 and 1937. I kept painting. After 1936, I was, like many other painters, strongly influenced by the Group of Seven. What was exciting was the fact that here was a generation that discovered Canada. It saw the country with a new vision, away from the Continental and from the French vision. The latter I still admire. In fact, I believe that Alec was the most French of the Group of Seven. He had that touch, that way of seeing things which were not stiff, the sort of stiffness that came from too many years spent in commercial studios in Toronto.

Alec to me was always my favourite landscape painter. When it came to draftmanship, my favourite was Varley. Alec remains, in my estimation, the most Continental and International Canadian painter of that generation — in the true sense of the phrase, his technique of seeing things. For his was not only a Canadian vision, it was also a true painter's vision.

I had my first show in 1938 at the inevitable Picture Loan Society in Toronto, run by that formidable character Douglas Duncan. He had peculiar habits. He would cash a cheque every five years — don't take me literally — and he would send out a cheque every ten years. From that show, I sold three small things. The oils were bought by the owner of the Gallery. One drawing was bought by A. Y. Jackson. This of course remains in my memory as a very dear and a very touching gesture from the old master. I didn't know Jackson, although I was elected to the Canadian Group of Painters. As you know, the Group of Seven was disbanded in 1933 when I was twenty-six years old. I was about thirty when I first met A. Y. Jackson. I had my first show in Ottawa in 1939. It represented ten years of work. I sold one sketch for fifteen dollars. This was our life then. Those were the years which Alec, the old master, knows much better than I do. But he, of course, was already established and became ... the elder statesman of the Canadian art scene.

We still admire him. We still love him. I ask all the girls here to give him a big kiss on the cheek and to wish him many more years from all of us.

To emphasize the bilingual character of Canada and Alec's fluency in French, Masson added in that language, "Although most of the Toronto painters are little known in Quebec, Jackson is well known there." He concluded in ringing tones, "Vive, Jackson!"
Speaking from notes, Charles Comfort brought us up to date with events since Alec's eightieth birthday and referred to some different aspects of our friend's qualities.

129

A. Y. Jackson's birthday, and quite properly so, has become a popular Canadian calendar event. It is now celebrated at all seasons of the year as the exigencies and the opportunities of the occasion demand. I have celebrated his birthday with him and others on a remote island in Georgian Bay in mid-summer. Three years ago we observed his eightieth birthday in this house in May. The number of celebrations far exceeds the number of years being celebrated, and they may occur in any part of Canada... Our popular friend is well on the way to rivalling St. John the Baptist... in the wide acclaim which surrounds the observance of his natal day...

To begin with, about the man himself. We all know he is a friendly person.... He meets people easily, no matter what their rank or age. Further, as a painter he is a dramatic and passionate poet-patriot who has devoted his life to interpreting this country in a visual big-book vocabulary which is uniquely his own but which can be shared by everyone. His accomplishments are so much a part of our development as a nation that the separate stages of that development have become synonymous, revealing to us our own emergence as a nation. For instance... in the season 1909-10, he painted *The Red Barn** and *The Edge of the Maple Wood*. These canvases were among the first painted statements which announced in a visual way a new national consciousness. Progressions out of these were *Terre Sauvage* of 1913 and *The Red Maple* of 1914.** His purpose in these and other paintings of the period and the countless canvases that followed up to this very day has been to capture the beauty and majesty and character of this country.

As is well-known, A. Y. was one of the original members of the Group of Seven. It was he and his rebellious colleagues who created the most vital and significant movement in the art of painting in Canada beginning approximately half a century ago. The advent of the Group was a landmark in our cultural history representing what we describe today as a breakthrough which for once and all had dispensed with hide-bound traditionalism and moribund practices. It was they, the Group of Seven, who helped release the spirit of national consciousness in this country, long before the Treaty of Westminster, long before the Commonwealth, long before the paramount problems of today were even thought of.

---

*This painting was purchased by the Montreal art dealer, William Watson, who turned down the Canadian Government when it wanted to buy it to present to Princess, later Queen, Elizabeth, on the occasion of her visit to Canada.[109]

**These paintings were purchased by the National Gallery of Canada in 1939 and 1914 respectively.

It has been my good fortune to have known personally each member of the Group of Seven and those who subsequently became identified with them. It was also my privilege to view the first exhibition of the Group, at the Art Gallery of Toronto in May 1920.

Here in the Firestone home tonight we have the unique experience of finding as part of the Firestone collection excellent examples of all members of the group and those identified with them, with some exceptions, of course. Particularly well represented is the guest of honour, A. Y. Jackson...

A. Y. is a man who knows and loves this country, from southern Alberta to Baffin Island, where he spent some time earlier this summer. In speaking this evening with his niece, I gathered it was a most successful expedition. A man who knows the Indian secrets of the Skeena River, and of northern British Columbia, he is familiar with the people of the lower St. Lawrence and the townsmen and the villagers of St-Fabien and Rivière-du-Loup, the fishermen of the Restigouche and citizens of that unique crossroads of Canadian international capabilities, Ottawa...

Alec, I offer you the *felicitations* and the congratulations of everyone present on this occasion marking your eighty-third anniversary. May you be spared to enjoy many more.

After the speeches, I called on Alec. He was slow in getting up; he looked hot and a little flushed. I turned over the microphone to him, since we were taping the proceedings. Seeing the uncertain stance of his friend, Comfort got up to stand next to Alec.

Alec began by saying that after listening to all the revelations of his colleagues, he felt "like a dumbbell." He made several wry remarks, usually with a serious face. This was a habit he had acquired when he wanted to note his listeners' reactions. If they laughed, he joined in. Comfort, who knew Alec well, looked on amused, and one of our friends took a picture of them at just such a moment (see page 132).

Alec referred to a number of his experiences: life in Montreal after his return from France and Italy in 1910; his move to Toronto and joining the group of painters later to be the Group of Seven; his friendship with Tom Thomson; his war service; the Group of Seven Exhibition in 1920; his friendship with Dr. Banting; painting in Alberta and in the Barren Lands; the painting he did for Premier Joey Smallwood of Newfoundland, showing a mountain consisting of 300 million tons of iron ore (he quoted Smallwood's famous remark: "I

Jackson and Charles Comfort

didn't know I could move mountains"). But to these familiar stories he added some revealing personal remarks.

Alec was most effective when implying that he didn't know much and didn't paint as well as he might. This notion was in line with his principle that "Less is more." On this occasion he used this self-deprecating approach as he tried to place the quality of his art in perspective, replying to the complimentary remarks made by the speakers. He said, "We used to be told that artists do their best work when they are just about starving, like Van Gogh. That accounts for any shortcomings of my work. I did not starve enough."

Alec didn't explain how he could have eaten much less than he did in the hungry thirties, when often his only good meal in a week was the Sunday luncheon to which he was asked by one friendly family or other. But the reference to Van Gogh is indicative of his admiration for that artist; Alec described him and Piet Mondrian as "probably the most important Dutch painters of the past hundred years." Although he was quite right about Van Gogh's poverty, he also understood that he differed from him in temperament. His own happy-go-lucky nature made it possible for him to roll with the punches while keeping his long-term objectives in mind and refusing to take no for an answer when the public showed nothing but the profoundest apathy toward his work. How different was he from Van Gogh, whose despondent mind could not cope with his failures!

Looking back over his eighty-three years, Alec felt that he had been very lucky: "A lot of people have been nice to me . . . A lot of people have looked after me... I have just been lucky." Here was a reflection of his attitudes toward others. When people responded to his jovial and down-to-earth personality with equal warmth, he always seemed to be surprised — pleasantly so, but surprised, nonetheless. He did not take people for granted. Though he might not care to talk much to some people, he would neither talk down to them nor cater to them to obtain favours. He did not ask to be given anything; he preferred to give, whether giving meant a word of encouragement, support for worthy causes, or bringing joy to others through his art.

It was hard for Alec to feel ill-used by the harsh side of life. He took poverty, grief, illness, and death in his stride, stoic in his belief that he was alive to fulfil a creative purpose. Having achieved what he was determined to do, it was in his temperament to look back over the eighty-three years filled to the brim with exciting experiences and rewarding accomplishments and to recall the whole sequence of events as a happy dream. Alec knew he was living reality, but his spirt transcended that reality and forged a link with his dream-world, so that reality and dream became an integrated whole, bringing excitement to Alec the man and peace to Alec the dreamer.

What Alec was saying to us with those few words was, "I have lived a full and rewarding life. I have been happy to share my creativeness with other people, and to bring joy to their lives. People have been very kind to me, perhaps more than I deserve. Even after I am gone, my works will live on and give pleasure to future generations."

But was life to be taken seriously, even most of the time? Not if one could help it, Alec's answer seemed to be. "One crazy thing after another is happening to me, you know... Life is just a kind of a great big joke... I don't seem to be able to be miserable," he told us.

A philosophy of life put simply and clearly — why go through life with a big frown on your face when you can be smiling? Why not use your sense of humour and be sensitive to the needs of others? If I can be happy, you can be happy too; you don't have to be miserable unless you persist in remaining miserable.

Alec tried to put this homespun wisdom across to as many people as would listen. Initially, few people paid attention to what he had to say, in his own words or in his paintings. Later on, interest grew as Alec became recognized as a fine artist and a great teller of tales. But what most people saw was the outer Alec: a jovial personality, a friendly chuckle, warmth and compassion for others. There was also an inner Alec, smiling at the world's concentration on material things and in the process missing real living — the beauty and fulfilment that come from being creative, letting the spirit roam, whether it seeks adventure, learning, culture, or any other form of human development. To Alec, there was more to life than making a living or raising a family. The real test seemed to be how to solve the mystery of making the outer and the inner man into an integrated whole. For as long as there were conflicts between the two sides of humanity, man was likely to be miserable most of the time.

Alec concluded his remarks, "I certainly appreciate this party. I think it is wonderful of all you people to come here to celebrate my birthday. I hope to see you here next year, and the year after," and everyone joined in his laughter. "Thank you all from the bottom of my heart."

At this point, Isobel got up and gave him a warm kiss on behalf of all the ladies present and said, "God bless you." We were all very moved.

CHAPTER 12

Canadian Art
in the Jackson Era

The story of the first exhibition of the Group of Seven, at the Art Museum of Toronto in 1920 (later the Art Gallery of Toronto and still later the Art Gallery of Ontario), has been told many times. I shall not repeat it. I would like to draw on Alec's comments, though, to discuss certain aspects of it and some of his views on Canadian art in general. The catalogue of that first exhibition is not easy to come by, as I discovered, necessary though it is for a thorough study of the exhibition. Quite early on in our meetings I asked Alec whether he had a copy, and he said he would look for it. He couldn't find it. The library of the National Gallery of Canada did not have a copy: it was a young art library with rather meagre holdings of documents, I was told; given time and money, it would do better.

Alec suggested trying Miss Sybil Pantazzi at the Toronto Art Gallery. On my next visit to Toronto I went to the gallery's library and approached Miss Pantazzi with another of Alec's observations, namely that the Art Gallery of Toronto had the best documentation in Canada on Canadian art. Miss Pantazzi's rather sombre face broke into a shy smile, and she soon produced an original copy of the catalogue. It was a folder, six pages in all with a self-cover noting that the catalogue was for sale for ten cents, a two-page foreword, and three pages listing the artists, the paintings, and the prices of the works that were for sale.*

I told Miss Pantazzi that the National Gallery of Canada was without a copy of the catalogue and that if she wanted to be kind to her Ottawa colleague, she should send her a photocopy. Soon thereafter the National Gallery Library had a copy of the catalogue available for public perusal; some time later I was told by Dr. R. H. Hubbard that there had been a copy of the catalogue all along at the National Gallery — it had apparently not been in the library when I asked for it. Meanwhile, Alec found his own. The catalogue, signed by Alec, is now in the McMichael Collection, where it was taken when Alec moved to Kleinburg in April 1968.

---

*In subsequent catalogues of the Group of Seven, prices of the works for sale were not mentioned.

The paintings exhibited by the group, according to the catalogue, totalled 121 works, consisting of seventy-seven canvases and forty-four sketches, and they were on display from May 7 to May 27. Of this total of 121 exhibited works, eighty-eight were for sale and thirty-three were not. In the latter category were several portraits by Harris and Varley and a few paintings for which previous commitments had been made. Alec, Harris, and Varley would not put their sketches up for sale because they all thought of them as spontaneous impressions to be used later as materials for larger canvases. Two other members of the group, Lismer and Carmichael, felt sketches were completed works that should stand on their own merits, a view apparently shared by Johnston. MacDonald took a middle position: some of his sketches were for sale and some were for showing only. Later on, Alec, Harris, and Varley changed their minds and were prepared to sell their sketches.

Three Montreal painters, described as "invited exhibitors," had been asked to show with the group. They were R. S. Hewton, Robert Pilot, and Albert Robinson, and they exhibited a total of seven works. There were thus 128 paintings in all shown at the 1920 exhibition, of which ninety-five were for sale. Viewers were advised that among the works for sale, "some of the pictures . . . may be hired, preferably by clubs and educational institutions."[110] Anyone interested was asked to get in touch with MacDonald at the Studio Building, 25 Severn Street, Toronto.

All of Alec's eleven canvases were offered at two hundred to three hundred dollars each, except one, *Northland*, which had a ticket of eight hundred dollars. Alec's prices were generally lower than those of Harris, Lismer, and Carmichael and within the range of prices charged by MacDonald and Varley. Johnston's prices appear to have been a little lower than those asked by Alec. Of the three invited painters, Alec's good friend Hewton followed his pricing policies while Pilot seems to have priced his works below and Robinson above the levels that the Group of Seven considered appropriate for works of new and not-well-known artists coming on the market.

Alec mentioned that some of his canvases were smaller than those painted by several other members of the Group. He would have been quite satisfied if he had been able to sell his works at those lower prices, but his hopes came to nothing.

The exhibition catalogue does not use the name "Group of Seven" in the title, but the forward, written by Harris, begins: "The group of seven artists whose pictures are here exhibited, have for several years held a like vision concerning Art in Canada."[111] I asked Alec whether the artists had been considering the name "Group of Seven" as they were getting ready for their first exhibition. He said no, not as such; theirs was simply a group of friends getting together for a joint showing of paintings.* The name was used by the press after the first exhibition, and it stuck, even after the group lost one member and later added three others.

I turned to the three invited artists. I wondered why they never joined the Group of Seven, particularly because another of Alec's friends, Edwin Holgate, also from Montreal, joined the group later on. Alec pointed out that Holgate became a member in 1930; the question of the other three had arisen much earlier, and at that time there was no general agreement among the members of the Group regarding admitting non-Toronto painters. In the catalogue he prepared for the Group of Seven exhibition in 1970, Dennis Reid refers to Alec as having "foreseen a 'Canadian Group' including painters from Montreal, as early as 1921."[112] He quotes as evidence a letter that Alec wrote to Eric Brown, the director of the National Gallery, on April 24, 1921, which is in the possession of the National Gallery.**

The foreword of the catalogue spoke of the possibility that the Group might face criticism and indifference, for the artists were presenting to the public new works, described as "vital and distinctive," that might not appeal to viewers and collectors whose sentiments were traditional. I asked Alec which of the two he had feared more, criticism or indifference. "Indifference," he replied. "We had a lot of criticism and we were able to cope with it. We could reply, and we did. But indifference meant that the public would not be interested in our paintings. They would not be seen by enough people, and galleries and collectors would not buy them. Artists cannot exist without a market."

While criticism of the Group of Seven remained severe in Canada, the beginning of a change for the better could be seen in the reaction to Canadian art at the British Empire Exhibition at Wembley, near London, in 1924. The National Gallery assembled and sent to the exhibition for the Canadian Section of Fine Arts 270 works by Canadian artists, including twenty-four, less than ten per cent of the total, by the Group of Seven.*** It was mainly members of the Group who got the rave notices in the British press.[113]

---

*The name "Group of Seven" was used for the first time in the second exhibition of the group at the Art Gallery of Toronto, May 7 to 29, 1922.

**In this letter, Alec added: "I would like to see it [the Group] increased to ten or twelve members."[114]

***Three oil paintings by Alec were shown, including *Entrance to Halifax Harbour*, subsequently acquired by the Tate Gallery.

"Bold landscapes . . . a real triumph . . . memorable vision . . . vivid colour . . . unusual appeal . . . new emotions that flood the mind . . ." were some of the phrases used in the reviews.[115] "There is something almost formidable about this type of art," one read. The reception for the Canadian works was enthusiastic generally, with the new "national school of painting" being given special mention. The reviewer for *The Times* wrote: "Emphatic design and bold brush work are the characteristics of the Canadian section." After mentioning Tom Thomson, he went on: "Similar qualities — of bold simplification and emphatic statement with full brush in strong colour — are to be seen in the works" of some of the members of the Group of Seven.[116] In the *Daily Chronicle* a reporter wrote: "These Canadian landscapes, I think, are the most vital group of paintings produced since the war — indeed this century."[117] The *Morning Post* stated that the works of some of the painters of the Group of Seven and several others "are the foundation of what may become one of the greatest schools of landscape painting." In New York, a writer for the *International Interpreter*[118] reported:

I shall not be surprised if these Canadian pictures — the landscapes, I mean — make something of a sensation in British art circles. They are so fresh, so elemental, so delightful and daring in colour, so simple in design, so decorative, so synthetical. They seem to be the work of natural painters, uninfluenced by tradition, inspired solely by the wild splendour in form and colour, of the scenes among which the painters live. Looking at these landscapes, those who have never visited Canada are offered at a glance a survey of the great undeveloped land.

Such a picture as Lawren Harris' *A Gray Day in Town*, beautifully painted, fresh and clear, although there is something of humour in the title, shows plainly how primitive life can look even in places where men dwell. Such a picture as J. E. H. MacDonald's *The Solemn Land*, simply and broadly painted, could only have been done through a strong emotion before the thing seen — this Solemn Land. And the same may be said of A. Y. Jackson's *Entrance to Halifax Harbour* — nature compelled this breezy, rough, outstretched scene. The theme dictated the technique; the entrance of Halifax harbour lives on this canvas.[119]

In Canada, the selection of the paintings for the exhibition stirred up a bit of controversy. It reflected the differences in opinion as to what constituted good Canadian art between the traditionalists represented by members of the Royal Canadian Academy and the young rebels, the Group of Seven. Alec described this controversy thus:

Briefly, the authorities of the British Empire Exhibition, to be held at Wembley in 1924, invited the National Gallery of Canada to send an exhibition of Canadian paintings to England. The invitation was accepted. Instead of co-operating with the Gallery, the Royal Canadian Academy insisted on controlling the exhibition. On this demand being refused, the executives of the Academy advised its members to boycott the exhibition. If the executive had consulted the members before taking this action, there would have been no Wembley controversy at all, for in spite of the efforts made to secure a boycott of the exhibition, more than half the Academy painter members exhibited, including five members of the Council ... The President of the Academy, Horne Russell, wrote to the London *Times* explaining why the Canadian exhibition was going to be a failure. When the press notices arrived from London they were so enthusiastic about Canadian pictures that the detractors of Canadian art at home could only splutter. They had been so sure that the exhibition, constituted as it was, would receive the most adverse criticism. As many of our newspapers failed to publish the favourable reports on Canadian art at Wembley, the National Gallery reprinted them in a booklet.[120]

The enthusiastic comments received by the Group of Seven painters in London led to a somewhat more favourable attitude in at least some Canadian minds. When a critical editorial appeared in the Toronto *Star*, the *Canadian Forum* rose to the defence of the Group:

The editorial is clearly inspired by the hostility to the newer Canadian painters which still lingers in certain quarters. The fact of the matter is that this hostility is rapidly becoming out-of-date and ridiculous. The English notices of our pictures at Wembley have established the newer painters in a secure place.[121]

After the Wembley showing, the pictures went on tour to galleries in Leicester, Glasgow, and Birmingham, with a selection also displayed in the following year at the British section of the International Exhibition in Ghent, Belgium. When I asked Alec how he'd felt about the Wembley Exhibition, he replied that he and the other members of the Group had been very pleased by the favourable reaction from British reviewers and the British public, and he added: "The sad thing was that our work could not be recognized first at home. But then, that's nothing new. Many Canadian artists, writers, actors had similar experiences. Wembley helped us, though. More people began to look at our works and some favourable reviews appeared. Still, sales were hard to come by."

Interestingly enough, a second Wembley exhibition was held in 1925, and an almost entirely new collection of Canadian paintings was sent to this exhibition. There were 187 works, including thirty (or about fifteen per cent of the total) by members of the Group of Seven.* In the foreword to the catalogue, the National Gallery observed:

> This second exhibition at Wembley of the work of Canadian artists opens with a justifiable feeling of confidence based upon the success of its predecessor in 1924 ... That it came well out of the comparison and earned praise from all critical judgement for its qualities of originality, frankness, and an indigenous Canadianism were matters for extreme satisfaction throughout Canada.[122]

All the works except a few on loan were for sale, and interested viewers were advised that "prices may be obtained on application."

British reviews were as favourable as they had been the year before. For example, the reviewer for the *Nottingham Guardian*, wrote: "Outstanding ... in the ensemble is the striking collection of modern Canadian art, testifying to the native strength of Canadian landscape art."[123] The weekly *Observer* noted: "The 'Group of Seven' ... now at Wembley ... have it all their own way. They practically fill the two rooms with their daring, decorative and intensely stimulating landscapes."[124]

In the *Yorkshire Herald*, the reporter was overwhelmed:

> Here is youth, vitality, a freshness of outlook, a courage that is like a tonic ... These young 'giants at play' have a fresh way with them, and a manipulative skill that is remarkable. Startling and unreal some of their subjects look to our eyes. But it is a great matter that these young eyes that have looked at primeval forests, vast tracts of snow, and dramatic scenes should have the courage to state what they saw in their own terms — terms of pure colour as befit clearer skies than our own.[125]

Alec had not mentioned the second Wembley Exhibition in *A Painter's Country*, and I asked him why. He replied, "We were honoured by the confidence Eric Brown had in our work, and we knew he was going out on a limb in supporting us. When we again received those favourable reviews in England, we wondered about their effect on Canadian attitudes. They helped, but criticism, a good deal of it quite ignorant, continued. The British reviews became old hat and people went on with their old ways."

---

*Three oils and four drawings by Alec, all new works, were included in this exhibition.

It was again a mixture of criticism and indifference that Alec felt he had to attack in the late twenties. The climate of acceptance for the Group of Seven in Toronto had improved — without any significant increase in sales — but the attitude in Montreal continued to be unfavourable and at times harshly critical. This prompted Alec to say, in an interview in Montreal on September 10, 1927, "There is no more bigoted place than Montreal." He continued: "I mean what I say . . . It's certainly true of Montreal in art. About the only freedom they have in Montreal is for booze. Certainly the Group of Seven could not exist in Montreal." When the reporter asked, "You mean there would be no sale for their pictures?" Alec replied, "That's only a secondary consideration. I mean that the Group of Seven couldn't get an opportunity to exhibit their work here. They wouldn't be allowed the use of an art gallery. Apart from some of the French papers, there is nobody in Montreal who could write an intelligent article pertaining to our work. Montreal has simply never given us a single sign of an opening."[126]

The *Montreal Standard* thereupon rose to the defence of Montreal with an editorial:

> We decline to make an argument of the fact that some of the most famous art collections in America, including world-celebrated pictures, have had their home in Montreal, whose rich men have been generous buyers as well as discriminating connoisseurs. It is true that from these collections Mr. Jackson's masterpieces have been conspicuously absent, but we do not put this down so much to bigotry, or lack of culture, as to failure to understand the message of Mr. Jackson and the Other Six. The 'Group of Seven' has painted some of the greatest riddles in the world. It is a rash man who will not ask for more than one guess before he decides what the 'Group of Seven' has been doing to the canvas. Is it a Headcheese or Sunset Behind the Old Mill?[127]

I often heard Alec telling stories about the first Group of Seven exhibition, but I never heard him talk about the tenth anniversary exhibition held in April, 1930, at the Art Gallery of Toronto. I had thought that this exhibition was quite important. It looked backward, observing what the Group had accomplished, and it looked forward, pointing the way in which the members felt they could further advance the course of painting in Canada, broadening its scope and extending its influence nationwide. So, I asked Alec, why this neglect on his part?

Alec answered that he'd found people were more interested in the Group's struggles than in its accomplishments, and that he got more enjoyment out of telling stories that poked fun at the academicians, art critics, and the not particularly far-sighted collectors (a bit of a dig at the Montreal well-to-do who preferred Dutch art to the French impressionists and Canadian art).

I asked what some of the main differences were between the exhibitions of 1920 and 1930. What prompted the Group, for instance, to invite thirteen new contributors from various parts of the country to the 1930 exhibition and drop the three from Montreal who had exhibited with them in 1920?*

There were some subtle differences and at least one plain one, he replied. In 1920, the members were newcomers who had to fight criticism, ignorance, and indifference. In 1930, they were much better known; they had received a good amount of acclaim. Nevertheless, they were still struggling to be recognized for artistic qualities — and struggling to make a living. Painting continued to be a part-time occupation for most of the artists, a full-time painter such as Jackson being a rarity.

Another difference was that the Group had become more venturesome, in a variety of ways. Alec had travelled across Canada from east to west and into the North, all the way up to the eastern Arctic, and his travels showed up in his work. Harris had started to experiment with abstraction, which was exciting artistically but subject to severely adverse public reaction. Lismer had done some major canvases at Georgian Bay. Two younger members had been added to the group — A. J. Casson, who did some fine work, particularly watercolours, and Edwin Holgate, who, like Varley, showed great sensitivity in painting the human figure. Alec mentioned, and the catalogue confirmed,[128] that Holgate was exhibiting as a member of the Group of Seven in 1930 (he had taken part in previous exhibitions as an invited contributor).**

As to selecting the invited contributors to the 1930 exhibition, the emphasis was on youth.*** In 1920, the three artists who had been asked to show with the group were contemporaries.**** These younger artists in 1930 were ones whose work was felt to be in harmony with that of the Group. They included Emily Carr from Victo-

---

*I am reporting here the substance of what Alec told me along with subsequent reference to the 1930 catalogue and other published material.

**Holgate's status seems to have been a somewhat confusing matter. In 1960, the National Gallery of Canada noted that he was a member of the Group of Seven between 1931 and 1933. Sixteen years later a publication of the National Gallery[129] gave 1930 as the year of Holgate's becoming an official member of the group.[130]

***This was also true for some of the earlier Group of Seven exhibitions.

****This was true of Robinson and Hewton. Pilot was sixteen years younger than Alec.

ria, Lemoine Fitzgerald from Winnipeg (who was to become a member of the Group in 1932), and George Pepper from Ottawa, all three fine artists whose work had been a struggle carried on in great loneliness, away from the two main centres of art activity, Toronto and Montreal. The Group wanted to encourage them.

The main difference, perhaps, was that the 1930 exhibition was a much bigger show. The Group of Seven was exhibiting this time with some other groups, which indicated a broader approach. Also, it was a practical solution to the financial problem, for money for exhibitions was scarce. The other groups were the Canadian Society of Painters in Watercolour, the Society of Canadian Painter-Etchers, and the Toronto Camera Club.

The thirteen invited contributors, with the number of works each showed, were as follows: from Toronto, Bertram Brooker (two), Bess Housser (two), Thoreau MacDonald (one), Yvonne McKague (two), Doris Mills (two), and Kathleen Munn (eight); from Montreal, Prudence Heward (two), H. Mabel May (three), Lilias Torrance Newton (two), and Sarah M. Robertson (one); from Victoria, Emily Carr (five); from Winnipeg, Lemoine Fitzgerald (two); and from Ottawa, George Pepper (two).[131]

Besides these thirty-four works by guest contributors, ninety-one works were shown by the members of the Group of Seven (then numbering eight) as part of their own show. The Canadian Society of Painters in Watercolour exhibited seven watercolours each of Carmichael and Casson.* The Group of Seven show, therefore, contained 125 works including those of invitees.

In 1920, the members of the Group had exhibited a total of 121 works, whereas the works of invited contributors amounted to seven, or a little more than five per cent. In 1930, the members of the Group showed ninety-one items,** and other artists contributed more than a third of the whole Group exhibition. Thus, not only had the Group acknowledged that there were promising younger painters coming along in various parts of the country who were as interested as they themselves were in interpreting Canada to the Canadian people, but its members also appeared to feel that the quality of work of the younger artists was up to their own high standards.

In the catalogue, members of the Group noted the great change. Since 1920, they wrote, "a great forward movement in art in Canada has made itself felt, and exhibitions of all Canadian Art Associations

---

*The catalogue listed prices for these watercolours: Carmichael's at between $35 and $75, with one at $275; Casson's between $35 and $75, with one at $150.

**This excludes the fourteen watercolours exhibited by Carmichael and Casson as members of another group.

are impregnated with the sincere spirit of adventure. Youthful painters are asserting more than a mere preoccupation with topographical
and natural features of the Canadian scene. They are cutting trails ...
The most significant trail has been cut into the spiritual and national
life of the country, challenging apathy, and giving a new rhythm to
the forward stride of a people."[132]

At the 1930 exhibition it appears that all the paintings for sale were
canvases, except for six drawings which had not been shown in the
1920 exhibition. Of the eight Group of Seven artists, Carmichael exhibited seventeen; Casson, seventeen; Harris, fifteen; Holgate, nine (including one drawing); Jackson, fifteen; Lismer, eleven (including five
drawings); MacDonald, two (he was in failing health); and Varley,
five. Seven of these ninety-one works were not for sale, being on loan
from their owners (three Jacksons, three Harrises, and one Carmichael). I asked Alec about prices. He said that they had changed hardly
at all during the decade because all the members had many paintings
for sale and there were few buyers. Moreover, the continuing adverse
criticism from "experts" still hampered sales somewhat.

Alec was particularly annoyed about the criticism that had come
from the city of his birth, Montreal. After more than thirty years, it
continued to rankle. I could understand why when I looked up the
reviews of the show after it had moved to the premises of the Gallery
Association of Montreal, opening May 3. S. Morgan Powell, art critic
of the *Montreal Star*, was devastating: "The outstanding feature of the
exhibition is the monotony of the pictures shown. Most of them
appear to be done in the same style, and a casual observer might be
excused for thinking that most of them came from the same brush ...
slovenly drawing in many of the pictures ... painfullly crude, the average canvas . . . is one of gloom, creating a most unwelcome and
unpleasant atmosphere of depression."[133]

While not as acerbic as Powell, some other Montreal criticism also
had adverse connotations: "Press and platform propaganda has
invested the painting of this Group with an importance out of all proportion to its performance, as indicated by the present show ... It cannot be regarded as an inspiring exhibition."[134]

A Vancouver art critic was particularly hard on Harris: "In his
present contribution, [Harris] comes to a pathetic stillness, his works
appear to be cut out of marble, as if life had turned him, in his quest
for spiritual values, away from the realm of physical beauty."[135] The
same critic was more approving of Alec's recent work, in which "fresh
subjects, fresh interest and decided techniques [have] brought new
interest ... He may [have] abandoned the wilderness but he has created a whole symphony from the theme of life."[136]

It is clear from these reviews that after ten years of struggle and some acceptance by the art community and the public, opinion in the country was still widely divided over whether the work of the Group constituted a genuine creative effort of lasting value. This lack of consensus, coupled with the onset of the Great Depression, was to have a devastating effect on the earning capacities of the members of the Group of Seven.

My conversations with Alec about the fortunes of artists led me to talk with him about the connection between his field, art, and mine, economics — if there were any. Alec felt that creative artists should have an opportunity to pursue their chosen calling if truly gifted and willing to make the necessary sacrifices to achieve what they set out to do. Yet because artists too have to live, the question arises, how can making a livelihood be reconciled with dedication to the pursuit of art as a career?

The first step was the period of learning, and here Alec felt that the art school system in Canada had developed sufficiently to offer adequate opportunities to seriously interested young people. Bursaries for study at home and scholarships for travelling and studying abroad could ideally be more plentiful, but a basically satisfactory system already existed in Canada, subject to continuing improvement.

The difficulties arose when it came to making a living after the initial learning process was completed (Alec ackowledged that a true artist kept on learning until he stopped painting). Only a limited number of painters and sculptors working full-time could survive in Canada. The majority were part-time artists who had other jobs in teaching, commercial art, or administration. Some relied on government handouts (Alec called the Canada Council the rich uncle of Canadian artists), but these were limited and unpredictable.

Considering this situation, Alec asked whether the answer to the dilemma was for young people who wanted to become full-time artists to accept abject poverty and continuing efforts to survive as a way of life — as had been his own experience until recent years.

I replied that times had changed greatly. When Alec had faced his hardest struggle in the twenties and thirties, the Canadian population was largely comprised of the first generation following a pioneering society engaged in nation-building in a harsh northern country, a task that required not only blood, sweat, and tears but also hardiness and the will to survive, the hostility of nature and American pressure from the south notwithstanding. In such a situation, the first priority of Canadians was to make a living and to achieve a lasting national identity. Culture and interest in the arts were luxuries that only the privileged few could afford.

It took another generation, the one that came after the Second World War, for Canada to be ready to take a greater interest in the art of her native sons and daughters. Governments, institutions, and people were more likely to support arts and letters. Grants and purchases of works meant that larger amounts of the nation's income were being spent on encouraging the arts and helping artists. It was true that the proportion in relation to Canada's growing GNP was infinitesimally small, but the fact of the matter was that interest and support expanded as awareness of a finer side of life grew and people became more aware of their heritage.

The point I was making was that there was a link between art and economics. Society not only had to be *ready* for art, it had to be able to afford it. In the first half of the twentieth century, Canada was not ready to support the visual arts to any significant extent because people attached a lesser priority to this cause and felt — if they thought about it at all — that encouragement of the arts would have to wait for increasing wealth and higher incomes. This stage of affluence was reached in the second half of the twentieth century; artists working in this period would not have to struggle as hard as their colleagues of the previous generation or two.

With this Alec agreed, though he seemed to be of two minds. He remarked wistfully, "Life could have been easier. But I have no regrets. I'm glad for the new generation of painters. They have better opportunities to make a living as professional artists." Then he added with a wry smile, "Still, a little struggle has never hurt anyone."

One day we talked about how long it might take an artist to achieve recognition after he or she had arrived at artistic competence. It all started when Alec remarked that it had taken the Group of Seven fifteen years to be recognized with regard to their artistic achievements and perhaps thirty years in terms of the market. Many European artists had received recognition only after death; in Canada, this proved to be the case with Tom Thomson and Emily Carr. After Thomson died in 1917, his masterpiece, *The West Wind*, was offered to the Art Gallery of Toronto for six hundred and fifty dollars, but the gallery turned it down.[137] (The painting is now worth over five hundred times that amount.) Emily Carr, the greatest painter on the West Coast in the first half of the twentieth century, died in abject poverty. Her works started to sell well only after her death in 1945.

To explain these phenomena, I described to Alec the concept of the time lag as we use it in economics. To move from an idea (an invention) to the implementation of that idea (an innovation), to the production of a new commodity, and to its successful marketing may take one year or ten years, or the whole process may never materialize. It is not only the artist, even if he is a genius, who may have to wait to be recognized. The concept of the time lag applies also to the inventor, the investor, and the businessman. Alec appeared interested in this drawing of a parallel between business and the arts.

Some time later, Alec presented me with an autographed copy of his book, *A Painter's Country*. When I brought the book home and read the introduction, I noted two sentences in particular: "It would be interesting to know how much of Canadian art is going to survive the passing of the years," and "while scientific truths can be demonstrated immediately, it may take thirty years or more before an artist's contribution can be estimated."[138] Although these passages did not fully reflect our conversation and were in the Jackson style, they did have a familiar ring.

The time lag was ended for the Group of Seven painters in the fifties and sixties, since their works were in demand all over the country. In 1963, when I was a member of the Royal Commission on Health Services, I met Dr. Malcolm Taylor, principal of the Calgary Campus of the University of Alberta and a senior adviser to the committee. After one of the committee sessions, Dr. Taylor told me that a new library was to be built at the Calgary campus, to be opened the following November. He had been approached to mark this occasion with an exhibition of paintings of the Group of Seven and some Western painters. The Glenbow Foundation would make the works of the Western artists available; would my wife and I be willing to lend some works of the Group of Seven? We were pleased to do so, and Charles Comfort, director of the National Gallery, agreed to use the gallery's facilities to crate and transport the works, to "enhance the opening of the new university library."

I consulted Alec and Casson about the selection of the paintings. We chose thirty-seven oil paintings representing all ten painters who were at one time or another members of the Group of Seven, six large canvases, nine medium-sized paintings, and twenty-two sketches. Twelve of the works were by Alec.

The University of Alberta was planning to have a catalogue for this exhibition, and I was asked to prepare the part of the foreword dealing with the Group of Seven. Before I sent it off to the editor, I showed a draft to Alec and asked his opinion. At first he did not say much because, as I discovered later, he did not want to hurt my feelings. Nevertheless, he did not seem to like what I had written, and he eventually came out with his comments: the text was too long; I was a romantic, and my story of the Group of Seven did not reflect the harsh realities; my description of the group's spirit, their love for the land and search for freedom, was not quite adequate. If I would consult Harris's introduction to the catalogue of the first Toronto exhibition, Arthur Lismer's notes on the group, and his own *A Painter's Country*, I might learn better what he and the others had been trying to say in their painting.

I agreed with Alec about the first point, but felt that I couldn't respond to the second without further lengthening the introduction. I did, however, decide to take him up on the third point. I went back to *A Painter's Country* and found, "We have attempted to interpret Canada and to express, in paint, the *spirit* of the country" (my italics here and below).[139] Lawren Harris said in the 1920 catalogue: "The Group of Seven artists whose pictures are exhibited here have for several years held a like vision concerning art in Canada. They are all imbued with the idea that an art must grow and flower in the land before the country will be a real home for its people."[140] In the catalogue of the second Group of Seven exhibition there appeared the statement: "These are still pioneer days for artists and after the fashion of pioneers we believe wholeheartedly in the *land*. Some day we think that the land will return the compliment and believe in the artist not as a nuisance nor as a luxury, but as a real, civilizing factor in national life."[141] Alec had said in the *Mayfair* article, reflecting his deep personal attachment to nature: "I'm perfectly happy to be put down with my pack up among these lovely rivers and lakes, perhaps two or three hundred miles from the nearest human being." And Arthur Lismer, referring to Alec's part in the group, said, "Jackson has done more than any other writer or artist to bind us to our own environment, to make us vitally aware of the significance, beauty and character of the *land*."

In spite of Alec's reservations, the editor of the Calgary catalogue kept all of what Alec had called "that romantic stuff" and had left out all the factual material about the Group of Seven! When I showed Alec a copy of it, a little smile appeared and he said, "I see there are some more romantics around besides yourself."

That exhibition, which was the first including all members of the Group of Seven in Calgary's history, showed also the work of eight western artists: Emily Carr and Sam Black from British Columbia, Henry George Glyde, Illingworth H. Kerr, and Stanford Perrot from Alberta, Wyona C. Mulcaster from Saskatchewan, and George Swinton and Franz Johnston from Manitoba. Johnston was an adopted Westerner whose home was Toronto, but he had been principal of the Winnipeg School of Art between 1920 and 1924. I myself would have chosen instead of him Lemoine Fitzgerald, a native Winnipegger and principal of the Winnipeg Art School between 1929 and 1949. Fitzgerald as well as Johnston had been a member of the Group of Seven for a brief period, Johnston between 1920 and 1922 and Fitzgerald in 1932 and 1933. Fitzgerald was also a founding member of the Canadian Group of Painters.

In the fall of 1966, I visited the Museum of Modern Art in New York. I met one of the curators of the museum and asked him what criteria were used to select the many abstracts by American artists housed in their collection. He replied that they used the best judgement they could in deciding what was quality and what was not. It had to be remembered, also, that as a representative museum they had a social as well as an artistic function. "The best test," he added, "is the test of time. If in a hundred years three out of a hundred of our American abstracts survive, we will have done well."

I discussed my impressions of the museum and this conversation with Alec. He observed, "Good art is timeless."

"What do you mean by timeless?" I asked.

"People change," he replied. "and so do their attitudes and tastes. Good art survives change." Some years later, I read a passage of Julian Huxley's in *Essays of a Humanist* that spelled out what Alec had said: "A particular work of art may be timeless in the sense that men can continue to enjoy it in spite of lapse of time and change of circumstance."[142]

Alec was not a religious person in a formal sense. His moral principles were of a high standard, and they guided his life, but there was also his insight as an artist that gave him a vision of his destiny. He believed in the evolution of art as a process that could contribute, as long as it were good art, to the enrichment of human life. It could also broaden man's perception of beauty and deepen his emotional reactions to it. He saw men's mortality in the broader context of the immortality of man's creativeness.

Would his own art survive in the Canadian context? Alec rarely talked about this question, for he kept his inner thoughts largely to himself. But on one occasion he let me see a glimpse of that vision.

I had come early to pick him up, and he was putting some finishing touches to a part of an uncompleted canvas. Suddenly he put his brush down, looked at the work, and said, "That won't do. I shall have to do better tomorrow." As he cleaned his brushes and put things away, I remarked on the high standards that he set himself. I said it was quality in art that would survive.

Alec mused for a time about whether the Group's work would have the staying power of a century and beyond, then threw back his head, his eyes alight as with prescience. "I think they will."

CHAPTER 13

An Artist's View
of Canadian Artists

Alec was always willing to talk about groups of painters — painters in Quebec or British Columbia, or Painters Eleven in Ontario, or abstract artists, or younger painters in general. He was more reluctant to comment on the work of a specific artist or express a critical view of some of the one-man exhibitions we attended together. Whenever possible, he would make a positive comment; in other cases, he would just make some non-committal noises.

Looking back, I now realize what a predicament I created for him when I passed on to him a request I had received from J. E. (Jack) Nutter, manager of the main branch of the Royal Bank of Canada in Ottawa. Jack was trying to induce the bank's head office to take more interest in encouraging the visual arts in Canada and, specifically, to buy a few paintings by Canadian artists for the bank's premises. In mid-1965 he asked me to ask Alec to write out his list of the twelve leading Canadian painters. Such a list, Nutter reasoned, could help bring bankers and artists closer together.

I considered this to be a worthwhile objective, and passed on the Nutter proposal to Alec. Alec demurred, asking, for instance, what Nutter meant by "leading" painters. I said I supposed this meant Canadian painters, currently active, whom Alec held in high regard and whose works might be acceptable to a conservative institution such as a bank. Alec protested that he was being asked not only to name painters he considered well-qualified but also to decide who might or might not be acceptable to a bank. This could exclude some rather good abstract painters, and he was not sure whether he wanted to be involved in such an exercise. "Let me think about it," he concluded.

I did not hear from him about it for several months. Past experience told me that when Alec said he wanted to think about it, the answer was more likely to be no than yes. But on my first visit to his studio after he returned to Ottawa that fall from his sketching trips, he pulled out a piece of paper and announced with a grin, "Here's your list."

"What made you decide to do it?" I asked.

"It may help a few artists to sell some paintings," he replied. "And people who don't know much about Canadian art might become

acquainted with the many fine painters in this country." The list he
handed me read:

A.J. Casson
W A Ogilvie
J. de Tonnancour
Alan Collyer
Robert Pilot
Molly Bobak
Wm Kurelek
Jean Paul Lemieux
Alex Colville
Paraskeva Clark
William Winter
Ed Hughes

"It was a difficult choice to make, and I had to leave out a lot of
good people," Alec added.

I asked him to explain his choices — but there I ran into difficulties.
Although he made complimentary remarks about a few of the artists,

he refused to be drawn into specific discussions of their merits, so my notes from that talk are particularly fragmentary — a few phrases such as "organized his work well" (Casson), "compassion for Quebec" (Pilot), "sensitive" (Ogilvie), "appealing rhythm" (Molly Bobak), and "subtle" (Paraskeva Clark). He was looking rather tired and our discussion broke off inconclusively.

Early in November '65, Jack Nutter arranged a luncheon in the bank's dining room, to which Graham Towers, the former governor of the Bank of Canada, Alec and myself were invited. At lunch, I handed Alec's list to Jack, and after a bit of good-natured banter, the basic question emerged: would bankers put greater value on money than on good art? Graham Tower's advice was "Never underestimate a banker." Jack Nutter thanked Alec for the list and later he forwarded it to head office. In due course, the bank did express greater interest in Canadian art. It probably would have done so without Alec's guidance, but he felt happy to have made his own contribution to a worthwhile cause.

Two months later, at his studio, I asked Alec whether he had seen much of the painters on his list. Very little, he said, except for Casson. These painters were younger artists — anyone under sixty was a "younger" artist to Alec. None of them travelled in the way he did, and their paths did not cross very often. He kept up to date with their work, however, and had followed their artistic careers.

He launched into a story about having arranged a party for Paul-Emile Borduas with some friends of his during the fifties when he was still in Toronto. It was his first meeting with Borduas, and they spoke in French. In the course of the evening, Borduas turned to Alec and inquired, "By the way, do you paint, Mr. Jackson?" Alec replied that he did, a little. The purpose of the story, I gathered, was to show how lonely an existence most artists lead — Alec being an exception — and they did not necessarily know what some of their colleagues in other parts of the country were doing.*

What I have done in the following pages is to incorporate the isolated phrases from our conversations in the fall of 1965 into comments on five artists we talked about that day, drawing on Alec's comments at other times, my personal knowledge of the artists' works, and some published material. I offer my apologies to the five artists concerned if my reconstruction does not do full justice to their work; all I can say is that Alec spoke highly of them, as he did of the others on his list.

Alec also said that art was a possible means of linking different cul-

---

*In 1960 Alec repeated this story to Brian Magner, who reported it in a magazine article.[143]

tures — specifically, he spoke of how desirable it would be if there were greater cross-fertilization among French-Canadian and English-Canadian painters. Then he sighed and remarked, "I tried for half a century, but I didn't get very far." Subsequently, I found out that Alec, when opening the first show of the Beaver Hall Hill Group in Montreal in January 1921, had urged French-Canadian artists to work with their English-speaking colleagues, and that he'd "told them about the group in Toronto, urging them to do for Quebec what the Group of Seven was doing for Northern Ontario."[144]

Alfred Joseph Casson was sixteen years younger than Alec. As early as 1920, Alec's influence on Casson became apparent when, as Paul Duval observed, "a strikingly similar treatment could be found in the way Casson painted snow scenes."[145] Casson was the first to admit that the one artist who'd left the "deepest impression with him"[146] in the twenties was A. Y. Jackson. According to Casson, Alec encouraged him to paint green compositions, saying that he was "one of the few artists he knew who could handle that colour successfully."[147]

Alec had a high regard for artists who could master "green," which he found the most difficult colour to tackle in a landscape. He included Casson, Emily Carr, and Goodridge Roberts in this group. His own preferred seasons were winter (the snow-covered landscape), spring (as the snow was leaving, when the soil had a fresh look and river waters were cascading down), and fall (with its glory of rich colours).

Alec thought highly of Casson, and on several occasions spoke about what were, in his opinion, Casson's leading qualities: that he was an able and technically competent painter who organized his work well, devoting considerable time and effort to advancing the cause of struggling artists by helping build stronger and more cohesive art associations in Canada. Alec also referred to Casson's great ability to use watercolours, a medium that did not appeal to him, and he called Casson "one of our foremost painters" — high praise indeed.[148]

Casson was on friendly terms with all the members of the Group of Seven, and he exhibited with them before he joined the Group, at the Wembley exhibitions of 1924 and 1925, for instance. He became a member of the Group in 1926.

In 1966, Alec introduced Casson to one of his favourite painting places, Grenville, Quebec, and to his friends the Putnams. The two drove from Ottawa, staying with the Putnams at their remodelled farmhouse. Casson, who had painted all his life almost exclusively in Ontario, was so much taken with the picturesqueness of the landscape in the Grenville area that he painted there six consecutive summers, visiting the region without Alec after his illness. Casson did "150 oil sketches while based on Grenville, more than he had ever done of any one specific place."[149]

W. A. Ogilvie, or "Will" to his friends, came to Canada from South Africa as a young man of twenty-four after having studied art in his home country and in the United States. He met Alec early on, and they painted together at Georgian Bay.

Alec praised Ogilvie's sensitivity and choice of colours and the quality and the variety of his compositions.[150] He described Ogilvie's work as a war artist during the Italian campaign as having the same quality as that of Charles Comfort, and he used the term "outstanding." In the post-war years Ogilvie's landscapes painted in watercolours had a lyrical quality, a poetic sensitivity. Others seemed to share Alec's views about Ogilvie's creativeness — J. Russell Harper described some of his studies as "brilliant."[151]

Alec had known Robert Pilot from his Montreal days, when Pilot had come from his native Newfoundland to study art under his stepfather, Maurice Cullen. Alec thought so highly of Pilot's work that he persuaded his friends to include Pilot among the invited artists in the first exhibition of the Group of Seven. In fact, I gathered the impression from talking to Alec that if it had been up to him, Robert Pilot might have been included in the Group of Seven at a later date when the Group considered an increase in membership. Robert Pilot submitted two paintings for that exhibition in 1920, and they were offered for sale for the modest price of forty dollars each.

Alec described Pilot's paintings as imaginative and sincere, important qualities if an artist's work was to stand out among that of his fellow painters. In the thirties Pilot had achieved an international reputation while still a young man (he was born in 1897), and exhibited in Europe, the United States, Australia, and South Africa. Pilot, according to Alec, had genuine compassion for the Quebec landscape and the *habitant* farmer, and he painted both the city and the country with true love.

Alec had a particularly soft spot in his heart for Molly Bobak (née Lamb), who had come from British Columbia and was living at that time in Fredericton, New Brunswick, with her painter husband, Bruno Bobak. Both Molly and her husband had been war artists, and Alec was always amused about the fact that working for the army had brought a pair of artists together.[152] Molly Bobak used to call him Uncle Alex, and when she and her husband were house-hunting after they left the service, Alec let them to stay at his place in Toronto for several months while he was away out West.[153]

On November 15, 1965, Molly and Bruno Bobak were in Ottawa to meet their public at exhibitions at two galleries, Molly showing paintings at the Wells Gallery and Bruno showing drawings at the Robertson Galleries. They had arrived in Ottawa the day before, and they came to our house for drinks. Alec wasn't feeling well and could not come, so we took Bruno and Molly to see him. An animated conversation ensued, with a good deal of reminiscing and some funny remarks from Alec.

Molly was quite concerned about how frail Alec looked: she was accustomed to seeing him in robust health, with a tanned and weatherbeaten face. She asked me to let them know when Uncle Alex's health improved and he was able to paint. (Alec had told us that the most annoying thing about being sick was that it kept him from painting.)

Keeping my promise, on December 11, 1965, I wrote to Molly: "Alec Jackson's health has been improving. He is now back in his own place [he had been in the hospital]. He has started to paint again but is taking it much easier. We had him for luncheon at our house last weekend. We talked about you and Bruno. Alec remarked: 'I hear that Molly and Bruno Bobak did very well in their Ottawa exhibitions. I am glad. They are both fine young painters.' " On January 29, 1966, I wrote to Bruno: "We saw A. Y. Jackson last week. His health has improved but he tires more readily than he used to. On the doctor's orders he is taking it easy."

Alec described Molly Bobak as one of Canada's best women painters of the younger generation. She had become a romantic painter in the true sense of the word. She had a great feeling for people and how they fitted into space. Her paintings had an appealing rhythm.

Alec admired Paraskeva Clark's courage and her competence as an artist. She had received a very good professional training in Leningrad before she came to Canada in 1931, and although she had been influenced by the French impressionists, she soon struck out on her own. She became a bold and uncompromising painter, willing to innovate and to explore new forms of expression. Alec described her as a subtle and intuitive painter with a fine colour sense. The fact that she set high standards for herself made her critical of a great deal of the Canadian art she saw, which she considered mediocre — or worse. She was one artist Alec said he'd prefer not to cross swords with[154] because not only was she outspoken but because she also knew what she was talking about.

It was inevitable that Alec's opinion of the other members of the Group of Seven should come up from time to time in our discussions. I don't remember the exact words, but I recall the gist.

Lawren Stewart Harris and Alec got along well; their secret was mutual respect. Still, there were many things on which they didn't agree. Alec could never fully understand Harris's mysticism and dreamy thoughts. To Alec, who was a different type, life was hard reality, not just something to philosophize and write about: it was to be lived. But whatever Harris's thoughts and feelings, Alec felt, he was one of our finest painters, forthright, original, and thought-provoking. He wrote well, and the members were happy to have him act frequently as spokesman for the Group. He was also a very generous person. If it hadn't been for him and Dr. MacCallum, there wouldn't have been a Group of Seven. He was a lonely man, at times quite unhappy, and he seemed to feel frustration more keenly than most of the Group. But his personal disposition didn't hold him back as a painter.

Although Alec and Harris were temperamentally quite different, they could work well together. For example, in 1924 they went to Jasper Park and then into the back country, to Maligne Lake and Tonquin. This was a beautiful part of the Rockies — miles and miles of mountains, lakes, forests, and pastures, the kind of panorama that might interest the travelling public. So they did a number of drawings of this scenery, each one doing half. They suggested to the CNR that they might do some decorations based on the drawings, either for the railway or for one of their hotels. The railway officials were interested, but — no sale. Harris didn't mind, but Alec said he could have used the money.[155]

Alec described James E. H. MacDonald as "our poet-painter, a romantic who loved his country dearly." To him the Canadian landscape had a special meaning — something to be revered, something to be explored, something to be captured in colour and set in the perspective of changing times. (Alec was particularly taken with one of MacDonald's drawings in our collection, *Lake McArthur, B.C.*, done in 1928. It had these notations in his handwriting: "I and seventy noughts to show the number of items in the universe.")

"Dr. MacCallum helped MacDonald," Alec once remarked, "as he helped me. MacDonald's training as a commercial artist stood him in good stead, but he really blossomed out when he could devote more time and effort to painting landscape and mountain scenes. Those Rocky Mountains were a hell of a difficult thing to paint, but MacDonald did it effectively, combining boldness and delicateness with a touch of understatement that made his paintings so appealing.

"It was a pity he couldn't earn enough money to live on from his paintings. He did book covers, posters, and what other work came his way. I think he got great pleasure out of decorating St. Anne's Church in Toronto, and he did several fine murals. He was not very strong and as his health gave way, he painted less and less. He was the first to go. He died the year before the group was dissolved in 1933."

Alec thought very highly of Arthur Lismer's work, which beginning in the twenties, had become particularly challenging, gay and sombre, full of movement and colour. He felt very close to Lismer, whom he admired for his devotion to the young. He was a good teacher. As a painter he was well trained, and he had an extraordinary colour sense. Alec said of him, "I would have liked to see him paint more, but I guess teaching was his first love. We had a lot of fun together. Under his prickly exterior was a heart of gold and great dedication to causes and to people he liked." Alec once wrote: "If MacDonald first visualized a Canadian Art movement, and Harris supplied the vigour and enthusiasm which brought it into being, then it can be said of Lismer that he carried the Gospel of Art for Canadians to every corner of the country."[156]

Lismer was the only member of the Group who was always accompanied by his wife on his travels. He felt that she needed looking after, but Alec thought she was stronger than Lismer was. For years he painted on the west coast of Vancouver Island, where the Lismers had a summer place. But his favourite painting place was Nova Scotia, particularly Cape Breton Island. In his later years, Lismer grew impatient, so that some of his paintings appear to have been done in a great hurry and give the impression of being unfinished. Alec said his *September Gale* in the National Gallery, which he painted in 1921, was Lismer's best work.

Alec referred to Frederick Varley as a romantic and a bit of a rascal. He added, "Some of my women painter friends in Toronto used to say they wouldn't trust Varley around the corner. His heavy drinking did not help his painting either."

I had visited Varley in Unionville, near Toronto, early in 1960. I saw Alec after my return and reported that I had found Varley greatly changed, his health failing and his mind slipping. "Too bad," observed Alec. "It must be hard on him. He was such an intense and restless person." Alec thought that some of his best works were his paintings as a war artist during the First World War and his portraits, which reflected his passions and emotional feelings.

When he talked about Francis Johnston, Alec appeared to be a little less enthusiastic than he was about the other members of the Group. He had been rather put off when he heard that he changed his name from Frank to Franz. He observed, " 'Frank' is a respectable name. I guess he wanted to sound bohemian, also to make more money. Can't blame him, because I know what it means to be poor. I guess he did make more money than I did selling those pretty little pictures of his during the twenties. You know, he resigned from the Group in 1924. After that his paintings were of the commercial kind. Too bad!"

Alec described Franklin Carmichael (he called him Frank), the youngest member of the original Group, as a lyrical painter of great ability and a fine craftsman.[157] He was really a part-time painter, relying on work as a designer and later as an art teacher to earn his livelihood. Alec remarked, "His watercolours were well designed and his oils showed imagination, especially when he started to paint landscapes with intricate patterns of tree forms and foliage. But then he changed his style, and his later work was less appreciated."

When we talked about Edwin Holgate, Alec's affection for him always surfaced. He called Holgate a good friend, and said he liked going on sketching trips with him. "He was always so gentlemanly and courteous and willing to put up with a rough guy like myself. He was a little slow when it came to painting and quite often said, 'Alex, I can't keep up with you.' I always felt that Holgate was a good painter. If it had been up to me, he would have become a member of our group in the twenties [he was an invited contributor in 1924] rather than in 1930 when he joined us. He was as much at home in painting the landscape as he was in doing portraits."

I asked Alec what he thought of Holgate's nude drawing of his wife that I had acquired the day we all visited the Holgates in 1964. He replied, "That's a fine drawing, sensitive and strong. Edwin loved Frances very much, and he wanted to do justice to her. She was a beautiful woman. I was very fond of both of them."

Lemoine Fitzgerald, who was the last to join the Group of Seven, was liked by all the members, Alec told me. He was a shy man; but at the same time he had a keen interest in advanced ideas, and his style changed quite a bit. He moved from figurative work to geometric patterns, and later to abstract painting. But in this he had less staying-power than Harris did. He was a quiet man, an intellectual who could both paint and draw well. His problem was in part that he liked living in Winnipeg, and there he was somewhat off the beaten track. His contacts were limited and his visits East infrequent. Alec said, "We asked him to exhibit with our group and become a member because we wanted to encourage him, to feel less left out of things."

On a number of occasions Alec and I talked about abstract art and non-figurative Canadian painters. He did not make the distinction between abstract and non-figurative as it has appeared in the literature (abstract — a derivation of nature to such an extent that the original object or scene becomes unrecognizable; non-figurative — creation entirely from imagination, the product of inner feelings, emotions, and visions). To Alec, all abstract painters were non-figurative.[158]

Our discussions started when I asked Alec early on whether he had ever been tempted to change to abstract painting; his reply was that he was happy with what he was doing — he only wanted to do it better. But he did comment over the years about non-figurative painting and its adherents in Canada.*

Alec's views on abstract art and non-figurative painters seemed to fall into several groups.

Abstract art was fine if it was good art, and he was all in favour of it. But if it was not good, it was "rubbish."[159] Alec used this description in private conversation. He was careful in using it in statements that might be published because he did not wish either to appear to be a stuffed shirt or to hurt, unnecessarily, the feelings of the many abstract painters in Canada.

Abstract art excited mainly younger painters. It gave them a new freedom to express themselves, it opened up new vistas, and it provided them with new opportunities to experiment. Alec was all in favour of change and of competent artists to bring it about. He was not, however, in favour of change for the sake of change but rather of change to achieve new meaning in life and a different cultural expression for the artist. With his own experience in mind, Alec observed, "There's no use in older painters trying to do it — they only make fools of themselves. If an older painter swings, it means he's not sure of his convictions."[160] There were, of course, exceptions to this principle, and Alec mentioned one himself. He referred to Lawren Harris in 1928 becoming "interested in the idea of abstract art," which Alec defined as "the beginning of an era in which there was complete freedom for the creative spirit." Later, Harris "abandoned completely painting from nature, and devoted himself to non-objective art."[161] (Note that "abstract" and "non-objective" are interchangeable in Alec's terminology.)

---

*Two limitations should be noted. The first is that these reports are not original with me. What Alec told me he mentioned to others as well. Some of the observations have already appeared in various publications. Where I have found such references, I have noted the sources. What I have done is compile Alec's views on this subject. Second, some of the things Alec explained to me may appear to be banal to an art professional — an art historian, for instance, would probably have offered a more integrated presentation of these recollections.

Some of the abstract painters in Canada were "very talented" though perhaps misguided, in Alec's view. He wrote in 1954: "When I see so many of our younger artists — many of them very talented boys — struggling to out-Rouault Rouault, well, I just don't understand it. We've got half a continent as our backyard here, much of it terribly exciting stuff. I can't believe that its inspiration has ended and that nature had no place in Canadian art."[162] Georges Rouault, of course, was the French painter who, in the mid-thirties of this century, began to paint small canvases on which the paint was thickly applied, with the lustre of enamel, giving a three-dimensional impression such as one gains in looking at a relief. When Alec made this statement, he may have had in mind the work of Alfred Pellan, Paul-Emile Borduas, Jean-Paul Riopelle, and Marcelle Ferron. On other occasions, Alec could be complimentary in a typical Jackson manner. For example, when visiting an exhibition at the Robertson Galleries in Ottawa, he observed, pointing to an abstract painting: "This is not the way I would do it, but I like it."

Abstract painting was certainly worthwhile and should be encouraged if it constituted good art, but Alec did not think it was in the best interest of the artistic development of this country to concentrate almost exclusively on non-objective works and to neglect the Canadian landscape with its many unique and inspiring features. He said in an interview: "It's too bad seeing this country going to waste. There is no use having a big country and the artist never seeing it. No one is doing it. They're too busy doing abstracts."[163]

Alec was sympathetic to the difficulties some of the modern painters faced in finding public acceptance of their abstract work, for he remembered well the criticism that he and the other members of the Group of Seven faced when they broke with tradition and came forward with new ideas in the twenties. He genuinely believed that the artist must provide leadership, and his counsel to the public was to take its time in formulating judgements and to look, and look again and again. Nevertheless, on occasions, Alec wondered whether modern art was not "too far advanced for the average Canadian,"[164] and whether patience would really resolve the problem of recognition and acceptance.

One abstract painter of whom Alec thought a great deal was Harold Town of Toronto. Alec was asked to address the Cornwall Art Association when they were celebrating the completion of a new mural by Town. He referred to some of the Canadian abstract painters as "very brilliant people." Non-figurative art, developed by modern painters, was "a sign of life, pure and exciting." Alec is reported to have added, with a twinkle, "Probably each time you see it [abstract art], I won't say you'll like it more... but you'll dislike it less."[165]

Alec once remarked that Harold Town was one of the few abstract painters who did not look down on the Group of Seven and who, in fact, had shown a great deal of perception in writing about Tom Thomson in relation to the Group.* Many years later, Town, with David Silcox, was responsible for what turned out to be one of the best books on Canadian art so far published.[166] When asked what made him work on the book, Town replied, "It was A. Y. Jackson who got me started. He had read my short 1965 essay on Thomson and he remarked that 'This is the best piece about Tom Thomson I've read.' "

Alec favoured international exchange among artists and cultural cross-fertilization but, as a great believer in Canada, he had one regret: Canadian artists doing abstract painting had lost their identity. This non-figurative work had "ceased to be Canadian art. It's international art, being done elsewhere."[167] He regretted that Canadians found it necessary to bring in American adjudicators to decide what was good art and what was not. "What is wrong with our judgement? Why can't we believe more in ourselves?" he asked, apparently feeling that abstract art contributed to this dependence on outsiders. In 1959 he complained: "There are now so many non-objective artists that not half of them can get their work in exhibitions, and it has become necessary to bring in Americans to decide between the wheat and the chaff. And of course they have not the slightest interest in anything that is Canadian in feeling."[168]

Speaking more generally, Alec raised the question of whether Canadian artists could not develop an abstract art that would draw inspiration from the vigorous spirit and exciting beauty of their country. He mentioned as an example Jack Shadbolt of Vancouver, who had exhibited with the Canadian Group of Painters in 1950. Shadbolt had shown in some of his abstract works great understanding and deep feeling for the wilds of British Columbia and their native people. Alec remarked that the idea he was expressing went back roughly four decades. He had discussed the matter with Lawren Harris when the latter was beginning to move in the direction of abstract paintings, and they had both agreed. After some searching, I found this comment from Lawren Harris: "Our way is not that of Europe and when we evolve

---

*"Unquestionably, he [Tom Thomson] was mainly responsible for taking that hardy band of painters called the Group of Seven into the wilderness; and though he hadn't a quarter of the instinctive skill of Jackson or Varley, there is in his work an irrevocable quality — a joy, a solemn gaiety, a sense of youth — that makes him the natural symbol of his time."[169]

abstractions the approach, direction, and spirit will be somewhat different."[170]

As far as the modern realists were concerned, the basic honesty of the artists, their strength of conviction, and the power and vitality that flowed from the integrity of presentation — if well done — appealed to Alec. Among that group, Alex Colville ranked high, and for this reason Alec included him on his list of twelve leading Canadian painters.

Even though Alec stuck consistently all his life to the painting scheme he had set himself, he remained a modern man who accepted change if change was for what he deemed better, and he encouraged others to follow the new trends, which in the period after the Second World War increasingly led toward non-figurative art. But there was enough nostalgia left in him, as well as a prophetic gaze into the future, to plead as well for a middle-of-the-road course — the best of yesterday, today, and tomorrow. Alec had a quiet way of helping newer generations of painters, and that was to go to the exhibitions and galleries and buy works of various promising young artists. Sooner or later these artists heard about it, and they always remembered Alec's kindness. Some of these, to my knowledge, were Léon Bellefleur, Molly Bobak, Glitta Caiserman-Roth, Henri Masson, Emily Coonan, and Ralph Burton. When Alec died, Henri Masson recalled how much Alec had encouraged him by paying fifteen dollars for one of his drawings at his first show in Toronto in 1937. "He didn't have very much money during those Depression years, yet he bought the drawing," Masson said. "It was the only one I sold outside of two works to the gallery owner."[171] Alec never felt so poor that he would not help another artist.

I mentioned earlier that in his later years Alec did not like to be outspokenly critical of the work of some fellow painters. But in his own way he could make his views quite clear. Here is example of what we may call "gentle criticism." Alec and Henri Masson were viewing a number of the paintings of a fellow artist. Alec looked at several of them, all of the same size, hung in a straight row like chocolate soldiers. He pointed at one of the paintings and said, "Hm, he [the artist] had a good day when he did this one." It was his way of saying that that particular artist's work was uneven but that he occasionally turned out a good painting. Alec could paint his praise with a faint brush.

CHAPTER 14

Alec and the National Gallery

After Alec moved to Ottawa, Isobel and I frequently took him to openings at the National Gallery of Canada. We did not always leave together because he would meet friends he had not seen for some time and stay behind to talk to them. They would usually see that Alec got home. Our arrangements were quite informal, and that suited Alec as well as us.

The National Gallery was an important force in Alec's life. First of all, it was a buyer of his work, and the income from these sales was sometimes crucial. The gallery also made his work available to the public, and this was of considerable significance throughout his career. Acquisitions of his paintings by the National Gallery can be grouped in two periods — 1913 to 1938, when Alec was struggling to survive as a professional painter, and 1939 to 1958, when his fortunes were improving.* During the first period, the gallery acquired ten paintings, nine through purchase and one as a gift. During the second period, it acquired fifty-one works, thirty-six through purchase and fifteen as gifts (including one given by Alec and eleven by Dr. Mac-Callum). All ten paintings of the first period were major canvases, while in the second period sketches made up the larger group. All told, during the forty-five years covered in the catalogue by R. H. Hubbard, the National Gallery acquired sixty-one oil paintings by Alec. Few painters are as well represented in the permanent collection of the National Gallery as A. Y. Jackson.

I was surprised to discover in 1962, on a visit to the drawings section of the National Gallery, that there were no pencil or pen-and-ink sketches by Alec. I reported this to him, and he said that he didn't think his "notes" were important enough. I did not share his view and said so, but Alec felt that he could not take any initiative in the matter. Isobel and I therefore agreed to donate three drawings out of a group we had acquired from Alec to the National Gallery. Alec

---

*The figures given here exclude, with one exception, war paintings and drawings, and they end with 1958. There were substantial acquisitions later than 1958, particularly of drawings.[172]

helped us choose *Pangnirtung*, done in September, 1930, *Great Bear Lake*, from September, 1938, and *Ashcroft, B.C.*, done in September, 1945, all pencil drawings on paper, and they were presented to the drawings section. We received a letter from the Chairman of the Board of Trustees dated May 28, 1963, thanking us for the gift and advising us that the three Jackson drawings had been placed in the permanent collection of the gallery.[173] Alec was pleased and so were we.

Alec was a wholehearted supporter of the gallery's objective of encouraging the visual arts to bring citizens and this art form together. In his later years his comments on the gallery were not as outspoken as they had been earlier because so many of the gallery's administrators were his friends, but he continued to try to prod it in the right direction. When at the age of eighty-four he was asked in an interview what he thought of the National Gallery, he said that it "was not one of the great galleries of the world," but added that "the National Gallery here is doing a good job, but could do more with more adequate funds."[174]

These were mild comments indeed, for in private conversations with me, Alec was critical of the gallery on a number of scores, all the way from insufficient emphasis on quality in new acquisitions to some one-sidedness in exhibition policies, both in Canada and abroad. His reference to the inability of the National Gallery to do the job for which it was responsible because of inadequate funds was really a veiled criticism of the place that government had given to the encouragement of the arts in Canada.

The whole question of government support was fully explored by the Royal Commission on National Development in the Arts, Letters, and Sciences (Vincent Massey, chairman), which reported in 1951. When Alec and I looked at its findings, we found some of the figures startling.[175] For example, the National Gallery in 1951 had four professional employees — the director and three assistants. Some American art museums that had only local or regional rather than national responsibilities employed ten times as many professionals. It had appropriations of $75,000 for acquisitions in 1950-51 and $260,000 for operating expenses in the same period. Some American galleries had two to four times as much to spend in these categories, as the figures in the table on page 165 show.[176]

The National Gallery was asking at that time to be allowed to increase its professional staff to eight and to receive additional funds with which to fulfil its national responsibilities more effectively. It was proposing a program that included, besides acquisitions and exhibitions, greater efforts in the way of "active education and demonstra-

164

	Number of Professional Employees	Purchase Fund ($ 000)	Operating Expenditures ($ 000)
National Gallery of Canada	4	75	260
Philadelphia Museum of Art	46	—	798
Cleveland Museum of Art	45	157	494
Museum of Fine Arts, Boston	43	317	955[177]

tion." The Massey Commission fully endorsed these proposals and made comprehensive suggestions to the government to expand substantially the funds, staff, and facilities available to the gallery.

Although the government gradually implemented some of the recommendations of the Massey Commission, adequate financing and an effective organization for the gallery continued to have recurring problems. In 1959, Alec rallied to its aid. In an interview he said, "If we are going to have a National Gallery that is worthwhile, we will have to have an appropriation of $10,000,000 a year."[178] This was fifteen times as much as the gallery was getting at that time. In the fiscal year ending March 31, 1959, total operating expenditures were $571,884 and purchase funds for works of art amounted to $93,172. Interestingly enough, some of the political support the National Gallery did receive came from the least expected source, the Social Credit Party, which even though it was strongly oriented to private enterprise, criticized the government for its failure to provide the gallery and its director with an adequate budget.[179]

The Liberal Party when in office claimed that it had a continuing interest in supporting the National Gallery. In a heated exchange in the House of Commons, Judy LaMarsh, then Secretary of State in the Pearson government, reminded Michael Starr, Progressive Conservative member for the riding of Ontario, that when he was Minister of Labour in the previous government, he had stated that "his government did not have any interest in the National Gallery."[180] But this was not the view of the Progressive Conservative Party when in opposition. Speaking in the House of Commons, welcoming the appointment of Jean Sutherland Boggs as the new director of the National Gallery of Canada, Gordon L. Fairweather, Progressive Conservative member for Royal, urged that the House "ensure that the Gallery has an adequate budget." Furthermore, Fairweather suggested that members of Parliament "should not interfere with the selection of its acquisitions."[181]

In 1958, Alec had summed up his opinion of the politicians' neglect of Canadian art in these words:

One cannot say that our country has done much for art; of all our Members of Parliament in the past fifty years there have been no voices raised to appeal for greater assistance to the fine arts. Neither Mackenzie King nor R. B. Bennett took the slightest interest in art; indeed, in the Bennett regime, Eric Brown was afraid the National Gallery would be closed down for reasons of economy. What saved it was the smallness of the grant the Gallery received.[182]

Over the next decade, he felt he had little reason to change his mind, and the six-million-dollar da Vinci painting affair in 1966 only reinforced his views.

Alec's high regard for the people who ran the National Gallery had its beginnings in the days before the First World War after both he and Harris wrote letters to the newspapers criticizing the Gallery for neglecting promising Canadian artists. Sir Edmund Walker, president of the Canadian Bank of Commerce, had become chairman of the board of trustees of the Gallery in 1912, in effect the governor of the Gallery reporting to Parliament. He asked Alec and Harris what they were complaining about. He learned, as Alec put it, that "our intention [was] to paint our own country and to put life into Canadian art. Sir Edmund said that was just what the National Gallery wanted to see happen; if it did, the Gallery would back us up. The Gallery was as good as its word."[183]

Under Sir Edmund, Eric Brown was the first full-time director of the Gallery, appointed in 1910 and continuing till 1939. His task included choosing Canadian works for the permanent collection "generally from all exhibitions of Canadian art," a guideline designed to avoid favouritism for any particular group. But Brown gave substantial support to the Group of Seven and Emily Carr, for which he was subjected to a great deal of criticism. Alec, as his friend, rose to his defence, saying in a letter to the Toronto *Mail and Empire* that those who had asked Prime Minister R. B. Bennett to oust Brown because he was favouring certain artists (the Group of Seven) were defenders of the status quo and included many artists whose works were "dull and monotonous."[184]

Brown's successor was H. O. (Harry) McCurry, another good friend of Alec's, who continued in the tradition of his predecessor as director between 1939 and 1955. According to Alec, one of the most farsighted projects that McCurry undertook, with his help and that of Casson, was to encourage the production of silkscreen prints of paintings by leading Canadian artists for free distribution to the armed forces abroad and later for sale to the Canadian public.*[185]

---

*One of these was Alec's *The Red Maple*. Ten thousand copies were made of it. I purchased one of them, and that was how I took my first step in collecting Canadian art.

McCurry was followed by Alan Jarvis from 1956 to 1959, the most dynamic Gallery director up to that time. Jarvis, a sculptor by profession who had written a great deal about Canadian art, was articulate and very literate and had wide cultural interests. Although Alec did on occasion frown at what he considered far-out policies initiated by Jarvis, he admired the leadership he gave to the Gallery and his willingness to stand up to shortsighted politicians.

Charles Comfort was director from 1960 to 1965. He was an old friend of Alec's who had moved from Winnipeg to Toronto and had taught at the University of Toronto since before the Second World War. Comfort was a scholarly person who had acquired a wide reputation, both nationally and internationally.

When Charles Comfort reached retirement in July 1965, the trustees of the National Gallery had difficulty in agreeing on a successor. As a result, the position remained vacant for almost a year with Doctor W. S. A. Dale carrying on as acting director. Early in the spring of 1966, the choice was narrowing down. One of the leading candidates was Jean Sutherland Boggs. When I was visiting Alec in his studio, I asked him whether he had heard about Jean Boggs being considered for the senior position. He said he had, and we discussed this possibility. Admitting the high professional qualifications of Miss Boggs, I raised a flurry of questions.

First, how would she do in a job that was politically sensitive? Had her earlier work really equipped her to deal with the many problems she would be facing as director of the Gallery? Would she be able to cope not only with a government that attached a low priority to Canadian culture but was also tight when it came to money, both for the acquisition of new works and for operating the Gallery? How would she get along with another woman, secretary of State Judy LaMarsh, under whose jurisdiction the National Gallery was placed? Miss LaMarsh had a good sense of humour, was a formidable debater, was inclined to be stubborn, and liked to win when involved in an argument. She knew little about art — she herself made the point repeatedly when speaking in public — and she did not possess particularly heavy influence in the Cabinet or with the Treasury Board, the cabinet committee that had the final say about monies to be spent before the estimates were approved by Government and submitted to Parliament.

Further, how would Jean Boggs deal with the considerable strife among the curators and administrators that had become more pronounced as the Gallery marked time for about a year, with little government encouragement and without enough money or the leadership that a permanent director could give? Would she be able to assert her authority as the first woman director in the eighty-six-year history of

167

the National Gallery? Would she bring inspiration to a dispirited group of people, dedicated to the advancement of the visual arts in Canada but with little practical knowledge of how to go about it? Would she be able to bring order to a loose organization that had acquired the reputation, rightly or wrongly, of financial mismanagement and inadequate professional control? Would she run the Gallery as a one-person show, as some of her predecessors had tried to do, or would she be able to put together a strong team and work in harmony with the senior people?

And would Jean Boggs get along with Canadian artists? Since she had done her graduate studies in art history in the United States and had taught at American universities for a decade and a half (Skidmore College, in New York, Mount Holyoke College in Massachusetts, and the University of California), would she not have a natural bias towards American art? How much did she know about Canadian art? Would she be able to support the young artists who were searching for new forms of expression, at the same time bearing in mind the contributions that others had made to Canadian art in the past?

How would Jean Boggs get along with the Canadian public? Would she be able to communicate effectively enough so that people in Canada would understand better what the National Gallery was trying to do? Would she strive to make it easier for people to see works of art in Ottawa, elsewhere in Canada, and abroad? Would she be able to arouse sufficient public interest in the arts so that people would write to their Members of Parliament or to the newspapers in support of some of the programs that the National Gallery was putting forward?

We had quite a talk; it took over an hour. I have summarized what Alec said. In essence, he was strongly in favour of the Jean Boggs appointment.

In dealing with my first questions Alec emphasized that the government was stingy with money when it came to art. It had its priorities mixed up. What artistic value did the public buildings built in increasing numbers by the Canadian government across the country have? Were they not drab in their outside appearance, commercial-looking with their steel, concrete, large-windowpane, high-rise structures? And how about the insides, utilitarian in layout, unimaginative in colour schemes, lacking works of art — sculptures, murals, paintings?

If government officials did not know any better ways of bringing culture to people who were visiting their offices, at least they could strengthen the National Gallery by giving it more money and providing the director with greater authority. With more money and authority, Jean Boggs could be a dynamic director. It would not be easy to work out an effective relationship with an argument-loving woman such as Judy LaMarsh. Smiling, Alec added, "Judy LaMarsh may surprise us all. Being good at arguing, she may get more money for the National Gallery than her predecessor, Maurice Lamontagne, got." Lamontagne, Alec continued, "knows more about Canadian art than LaMarsh will ever know, but he is not a fighter. He is a gentleman. Few gentlemen ever win arguments. He is just too nice a person to be a successful politician."

"What is a successful politician, in your opinion?" I asked.

"One that gets things done and gets re-elected. Not that I particularly like politicians, but I guess we have to live with them."

When we returned from this digression to the main theme of our discussion and Alec saw the look of doubt on my face, he asserted, "Well, I think LaMarsh and Boggs will make a good team. It's about time we had a woman director of the National Gallery. Don't you think so?" I admitted I did. Alec noted Bogg's leadership qualities in her three years as curator at the Art Gallery of Toronto. She brought a fresh spirit to a gallery whose structure had become fossilized and whose relations with artists were increasingly strained. Jean Boggs was a determined woman who could put together a strong team, and could work with the people she'd gathered. She was not an administrator, but she would probably get a good person and let him or her look after that part of the work under her direction. She could be relied upon to stand up for the Gallery to politicians and bureaucrats alike.

Alec also observed that Jean Boggs was a first-class scholar, which few Canadian artists would deny, and had also had close contact with Canadian and American museums and galleries. Her main interests were European and American art, but this did not mean that she would neglect Canadian art. She would probably be inclined to favour modern works, he thought, but she was also a fine art historian who understood the significance of the evolution of art. Alec reminded me that Jean Boggs had achieved international acclaim when she participated in bringing exhibitions of the works of Delacroix, Canaletto, and Picasso to Canada. Her catalogue, *Picasso and Man*, was outstanding scholarship.

On the matter of relations with the community, Alec observed that Jean Boggs was very conscious of the importance of bringing art to the public. She would probably encourage extensive travelling exhibitions, and she knew how to communicate with people. She had acquired valuable experience with her CBC radio series, "Listening to Pictures."

I was frankly amazed by the scope of Alec's replies, and sat silent for a moment. I wasn't accustomed to so much eloquence from him — he must have felt strongly about this matter and must have been considering the subject with care long before I asked the questions.

169

I was particularly struck by his statement that it was time for a woman to be appointed director of the National Gallery. For a bachelor who was at heart a traditionalist, it was refreshing to hear him advocate the entry of women into areas of responsibility that in the past had been the prerogative of males. His fervour for the cause of women would have both delighted and amused women liberationists if they had invited him to speak on that subject.

I asked how he knew so much about Jean Boggs. "I've known about her achievements in the United States and observed the good work she's been doing in Toronto these last few years," he said, then added with a grin, "I hear things. If she's appointed, Jean Boggs will make a great director — and she'll last."

"Would you be willing to say publicly what you said to me?" I asked.

"Don't worry. Nobody will ask an old man like me for my views. There are quite a few people who say I'm out of date and in a rut. But if I'm asked, I certainly will speak up for Jean."

At home after that discussion, I said to my wife, "It looks as if Jean Boggs is going to be the new director of the National Gallery."

"How do you know?" Isobel asked, to which I replied that I had just listened to Alec and that he had made a most convincing case.

On May 4, 1966, the trustees of the National Gallery of Canada announced the appointment of Jean Boggs as director of the Gallery. Speaking in the House of Commons the same day, Judy LaMarsh referred to Jean Boggs as a person who could be expected to give leadership to the National Gallery, and added: "I think all Canadians interested in the development of the National Gallery and the furtherance of our cultural life in general will be pleased at the appointment of a Canadian of such national and international stature. For my own part, I need hardly add that I am particularly happy to see a woman filling such a senior position among our cultural agencies. She is, in fact, the first woman to head an agency with the status of Deputy Minister."[186]

Alec proved to be right in more than one way. Not only was Jean Boggs appointed as the director, but she also held the position for ten years. And further, she proved to be a match for politicians and bureaucrats who made life difficult for her, and she stood up to criticism from artists and art critics, both the well-meaning and the belittling kinds. Much was achieved under her directorship at the National Gallery, some inadequacies and shortcomings notwithstanding.

Alec was asked in interviews several times how he felt about the job she was doing at the Gallery. His comment to W. Q. Ketchum is typical of his replies. After asserting that he was an admirer of Jean Boggs, he added, "She has had a lot of museum experience, allied to competence, very good taste, and arouses goodwill owing to her personality."[187] For me, the affair was further confirmation that Alec had good judgement, and it proved to be right in many of the things we discussed over the years.

In speaking to a meeting of the Kitchener-Waterloo Business and Professional Women's Club on May 15, 1966, Judy LaMarsh floated a trial balloon: how would Canadians feel about acquiring a six-million-dollar painting that equalled in quality the famous *Mona Lisa*? She did not name the painting in this talk,[188] but reporters soon found it out; it was the *Portrait of Ginevra de' Benci* by Leonardo da Vinci. The minister's proposition caused public discussion and heated argument about the virtues of spending public money for good art to an extent unparalleled in this country's history and, in a minor way, Alec and I became involved in this debate.

The portrait in question was small, 14 by 15 inches, and had been painted on a poplar-wood panel approximately five hundred years before. It was of exquisite quality, and was owned in 1966 by Prince Franz Josef of Liechtenstein. It was possible that it might become available for sale, and there was no Leonardo da Vinci painting anywhere in North America.

The public reaction to the minister's attempts to ascertain the people's feelings about art in Canada came as a great surprise to her. There were considerable numbers of letters to editors and to members of Parliament; there were open-line radio shows; there was widespread comment in the press and over the broadcast media; there were continuing questions in the House of Commons and some debate.

The minister's own mail was, as she termed it, "suprisingly heavy," with response running half in favour and half against spending six million dollars on a painting.[189] The critics said that there were more urgent needs in Canada than art, that the money could more usefully be spent on raising old-age pensions or unemployment insurance benefits or on housing. The proponents of the purchase claimed that it was time Canada did more for the arts, and they supported the principle of excellence that would be associated with acquiring one of the world's leading works of art.

Even the opposition parties were amazed by the strong and widespread reaction to the minister's questions. They had not thought that Canadians would be that interested in art — as a comment by Reid Scott, New Democratic Party member for Danforth, indicated: "This announcement by Judy LaMarsh, in particular, for some strange reason seems to have evoked a fantastic response, certainly in my experience, both pro and con. We have seen much the same reactions as the minister has outlined."[190]

When the minister first raised the matter, she stressed that she was expressing her own views, for she had not discussed the matter with the prime minister or any of her other colleagues. When she was pressed in the House of Commons to explain her reasons for having raised this question, the minister responded in part:

> It was my opinion that the National Gallery, which really is not very old and which I think has never spent more than $100,000 on any one acquisition, might benefit in very many ways from being the setting for a very fine jewel in the world of painting. I do not know that the owner of the painting in question would be prepared to sell it to Canada, or whether the price I have suggested it might be worth would be acceptable to him. I do not believe that most Canadians feel this kind of investment is a bad one . . . I cannot think of any better way to teach people that Canada has an appreciation for the very finest objects of art than by providing a home for a work of art such as this. It seems to me that, as the Bible says, man does not live by bread alone, and we need a goal in our cultural life which perhaps does not exist at the moment. Canadians often think they do not deserve the best, that they are second-rate and the best that is in the world cannot be ours. I know that voting money in this amount for such a purpose is not very common for this or any other country. But if this amount of money was spent on something which could be put on display next year at Expo, it would be a terrific drawing card and would be the diamond in the sceptre of the National Gallery's existence.[191]

Miss LaMarsh was also criticized for having brought up this matter before the new director of the National Gallery, Jean Boggs, had assumed her duties and without consulting her. When Miss Boggs started to do her job, however, she spoke out in favour of the minister's idea. There the matter remained, with no indication of government support.

I brought a clipping of the public controversy about the da Vinci painting to Alec and asked him what he thought about the arguments. Alec was all in favour of the purchase, calling the painting one of the greatest art treasures to come on the market in decades. He pointed out, looking back, that Canadians had sometimes bought paintings of lesser quality because they were penny wise and pound foolish. He illustrated his thought with the mistakes some collectors, particularly in Montreal, had made in buying Dutch art instead of works by French impressionists or post-impressionists.

Although Alec agreed that six million dollars was a lot of money, it was worth it for a masterpiece like the da Vinci, which in his opinion would be the greatest painting in North America. Canada should give herself this birthday gift for her centenary in 1967. I agreed with Alec, and I pointed out that in economic terms six million dollars was about one-hundredth of 1 per cent of Canada's GNP, estimated at fifty billion dollars for that year (over the years, Alec had become accustomed to my use of the concepts of national income and GNP). He felt that it was time something was done about this matter and suggested that he might write a letter to the *Ottawa Journal*. It would help the cause and it would assist the newly appointed Jean Boggs, who was advocating the purchase.

The letter appeared as the first communication in the *Ottawa Journal* letters page on June 22, 1966, under the heading "A. Y. Jackson Favours Purchase." The last communication on the same page was entitled "That Painting." In this letter, an irate taxpayer, speaking for what he claimed was the majority of breadwinners living in Ottawa, stressed that he was "bitterly opposed to such a purchase" and that the money would be better spent on badly needed things such as housing.

What happened to the da Vinci painting? It was purchased in February 1967 by the National Gallery of Art in Washington, reportedly for $5.8 million. The *Ottawa Citizen* published a cartoon on February 21, 1967 showing two ladies (Jean Boggs and Judy LaMarsh) watching an empty picture frame with the notation "Reserved for Leonardo's Ginevra de' Benci" being removed. It has the caption: "She's run off with an American." The American was John Walker, the director of the National Gallery of Art in Washington.

I showed the cartoon to Alec and asked him what he thought of the whole affair. He replied, "We're just not ready for great art, just as the public wasn't ready for the Group of Seven in the twenties and the abstract painters in the fifties."

As part of the centenary celebrations in 1967, the National Gallery organized an exhibition under the title "A Pageant of Canada." Conceived by R. H. Hubbard and organized by Roy Strong, the gallery had spent three years assembling nearly three hundred items for this special event. They came from many private and public sources including museums in England, France, the United States, and Canada. The emphasis was on art and objects concerned with the history of Canada from the early sixteenth century to 1867.

The opening took place on October 26, 1967, with Governor-General and Mrs. Roland Michener in attendance. The main speaker was the Marquis de Montcalm, of France, one of the Exhibition's main contributors and a descendant of the French general who died on the Plains of Abraham in 1759. Alec was invited to the opening and the festivities, a black-tie affair. Isobel and I also attended.

To the Editor of the Ottawa Journal

Sir - When Miss Judy LaMarsh first suggested that Canada should purchase a Leonardo da Vinci painting for six million dollars I thought she was merely joking. Preposterous. - but not quite.

Consider in what other way spending that amount of money would add to our National prestige or make our National Gallery the envy of every art gallery in America.

Being cautious has long been a watch word for Canadians and particularly in the Arts. when in earlier days when great paintings were much more available. the miserable little doles were spent on art. resulting in our acquiring next to nothing. while Americans bought paintings that are worth today a hundred times what they paid for them.

There will not likely ever by another Leonardo on the market -.

Yes six millions seems preposterous. but when one considers that our Gross National Product this year will amount to over fifty billion dollars what better investment could we make to celebrate our Centennial year.

The Americans admire us for creating the Shakespeare Theatre at Stratford. and the Simon Fraser University in Vancouver is going to make them sit up.. and now to own probably the greatest painting in America. What an opportunity!

Yours - A Y Jackson

After the opening, there was a champagne and caviar party on the eighth floor of the National Gallery building. Alec was surrounded by well-wishers. After a while, as the crowd around him was thinning out, I asked him whether I could bring him a glass of champagne and some caviar. He replied, fairly loudly, that if he had a choice he would prefer rye. Several bystanders around us who heard the remark started to laugh, and one gentleman said to Alec, "Right on, Mr. Jackson. Who needs all that foreign stuff, French or Russian? Give us good old Canadian whisky."

Alec just smiled and as we walked on he mumbled rather quietly but loudly enough for me to hear, "Too presumptuous. Not enough Canadianism." These five words reflected Alec's attitude. His tastes were modest, and he felt a little out of place in all the to-do the Gallery had stirred up. He also seemed to think that Canada's centenary could have been celebrated in a more Canadian way, which to him was simpler and thus more dignified, by having Canadian food and drinks served. This was his rather quiet way of protesting against offering champagne and caviar and making this a black-tie occasion.

When I asked Alec later what he thought about the exhibition, he remarked, "Historically important and meaningful — but they should have let Bob Hubbard do the show." (This was a reference to the fact that Roy Strong, the director of the National Portrait Gallery, was an Englishman and it illustrated Alec's belief that a Canadian could have done as good a job, if not better, to meet Canadian cultural needs.*)

On January 23, 1969, Isobel and I were invited to the opening of an exhibition entitled "A New Look at the Group of Seven," consisting of the MacCallum-Jackman donations to the National Gallery. The Governor-General, Roland Michener, was officiating at the opening to which Alec, who was by now residing in Kleinburg, and Robert and Signe McMichael were also invited.

Dr. James M. MacCallum, who had been such a help to Alec and other members of the Group of Seven, had donated to the National Gallery 134 paintings, mainly by Tom Thomson and the Group of Seven and including eleven works by Alec. Mr. and Mrs. H. R. Jackman of Toronto donated to the National Gallery the murals that Thomson and members of the Group had painted on panels installed in the original MacCallum cottage on Georgian Bay. The Jackmans had bought the cottage after Dr. MacCallum's death in 1943, and more recently, the panels had been dismantled, restored, and transfer-

---

*As an aside, it should be noted that Dr. Hubbard was also involved in organizing "300 Years of Canadian Art, An Exhibition in Celebration of Confederation," which opened at the National Gallery of Canada on May 11, 1967,[192] and that it would have been difficult for him to be responsible for the organization of two major exhibitions in the same year.

red to Ottawa. Twenty-one of them were on exhibit. To show the panels in something like their natural habitat, the gallery carpenters had built a cottage living room on the fourth floor of the National Gallery. Dennis Reid acted as the co-ordinator, and he had prepared a fine catalogue. Five hundred people attended the opening.

We found Alec changed a great deal. He still recognized his friends, but much of his vitality was gone. His sense of humour was still alive, however, as revealed by an amusing happening that took place at the opening.

Jean Boggs was welcoming the guests and when she came to Alec, she paid him a particularly gracious tribute as one of Canada's leading painters. The audience burst into spontaneous applause. Alec had not heard what Jean had said, but when he saw everybody applauding enthusiastically, he joined in. Whereupon Mary Jackman, who was sitting next to him, turned and put her mouth to his ear, saying in a stage whisper that was heard all across the hall: "But Alec, they are applauding *you*." Alec grinned and stopped applauding. The crowd burst into another round of applause.

Photographer John Evans, who was watching the proceedings, caught the mood of the moment in a shot taken just as Mary Jackman had finished her stage whisper. Alec took the whole episode as good fun; he could always laugh at himself. Even with his health deteriorating seriously, his spirit remained.

CHAPTER 15

Harris and Lismer on Jackson

When I began collecting the works of the Group of Seven, seven out of the ten who had been members were still alive — A.J. Casson, Lemoine Fitzgerald, Lawren S. Harris, Edwin Holgate, A.Y. Jackson, Arthur Lismer, and Fred Varley. I was able to meet all of them except Fitzgerald, some of them becoming friends, some good acquaintances. Three of the members had died earlier, J.E.H. MacDonald in 1932, Franklin Carmichael in 1945, and Frank Johnston in 1949. I was also in touch with members of the families of those I didn't meet in person.

I asked those I met about Alec. Some remarks were humourous, while others showed great affection. A brief conversation I had with Lawren Harris and some lengthy discussions with Arthur Lismer about Alec* are particularly interesting.

In February 1962 the Royal Commission of Health Services was holding hearings in Vancouver. Being there, I took the opportunity to see Lawren Harris again. He was alone; his wife, Bess, had gone shopping.

I invited Lawren and Bess to Alec's eightieth birthday party, scheduled at our Ottawa home on May 5, 1962, and Lawren said he'd be there, his doctor permitting. Toward the end of our discussion, I put two questions to him that seemed to startle him: "Did you and Alec compete while you were members of the Group of Seven? Did the question of 'leadership' ever come up?" Then he smiled. "You *are* curious," he said.

Harris's first comments were about Alec's move from Montreal to Toronto and the interest he had taken in Alec, as a person and as a painter. Then he added that I would know all about that period because both he and Alec had talked about it, and a great deal had been written. He continued (and I want to emphasize that these are not the words Harris used, but only the gist of our conversation), "The

---

*I also asked other artists for their views, and some of these are reported elsewhere. See for example the comments of Charles Comfort (pp. 59ff, 130 ff.), Henri Masson (pp. 126ff.), and Andre Biéler (pp. 216ff.).

Group has always been reported as having no leader.* We were all equal members who had a common vision**, and we believed in the spirit of Canada. I was asked to set down for that first exhibition of ours what we were all trying to do. What I did was to put into words how we all felt. Some people have described this as 'leadership.' That is a matter of semantics. But I can tell you, when it came to painting Jackson had no peer. I used to say to him that I was following him, but he would not accept it."

I was uncertain how to interpret what Harris had said. When I returned to Ottawa, I found a sentence in a letter from Harris, written on January 14, 1955, that Alec quoted in his book *A Painter's Country*: "You were the real force and inspiration that led all of us into a modern conception which suited this country."[193] This seemed to me to be a much clearer indication that he acknowledged Alec's leadership in the Group than I had been able to glean from our conversation.

Three months after I'd talked to Harris, we had another utterance from him that could be interpreted in two different ways. Harris could not attend Alec's eightieth birthday party because of his frail health, and so he sent the following telegram on May 5, 1962:

> Heartiest congratulations on your eightieth birthday from us both. It is amazing to think that anybody has lived that long. No matter how I try you will be leading and I trailing. Good luck and both of our blessings. Lawren and Bess.

Some weeks later, after the excitement of the party had subsided, I asked Alec what he thought of the Harris telegram. "Harris just wanted me to feel happy at my birthday party," he replied. "I've heard that phrase about giving 'leadership' before, but I don't take those Harris remarks seriously.***He is a great painter who believes in freedom of expression and in change. Just as he embarked on a new course, as we all did, in 1913 and 1914, he turned to abstract work in the late twenties. I have never changed. I guess I'm in a rut,**** but I like what I'm doing."

I asked Harris's son, Lawren Phillips, what he thought his father meant in speaking of Alec as "leading." He paused and said: "My

---

*This point has frequently been repeated in the literature, including Alec's writings.[194]

**He had used this phrase in writing the foreword for the catalogue of the 1920 Group of Seven Exhibition.

***In another context Alec acknowledged, "Without Harris there would have been no Group of Seven. He provided the stimulus; it was he who encouraged us always to take the bolder course, to find new trails."[195]

****This was one of Alec's stock phrases.

father was three years younger than Alec. The mention in the telegram of Alec leading refers to the age difference, not to painting. My father never claimed that he was the leader of the Group in an artistic sense. But, in fact, he was the driving force behind the Group. He had invited Alec and others to join because he felt a need for the stimulation that comes from cross-fertilization of ideas from artists with similar visions. As for Alec, my father had a high regard for him, both as a man and as a painter. His remark about Alec leading the other members of the Group into a modern conception that suited this country reflected his thinking. He genuinely meant it."

The younger Harris's comments were in line with the observations that an eminent British art critic, Percy M. Turner, had made in 1922 when he saw an exhibition of works by the Group. He described the members as a group of "radical artists" with "no leader" but with A. Y. Jackson in the role of "chef d'école."[196]

While Alec never spelled it out specifically, he himself seems to have felt that Harris lacked some of the qualities that make for artistic leadership. Looking at his work in the twenties, he wrote: "Harris paints a world that is not related to humanity, a world without passion or emotion."[197] Alec believed that such feelings are essential if others are to be inspired. On another occasion, Alec described Harris as a "traveller with his eyes on some far-off goal who no longer sees what is around him. I don't feel that way about life."[198] Here again that interesting contrast: Alec the realist and homespun philosopher, Harris the dreamer and mystic.

Some people who knew the members of the Group of Seven well have held that if there were a leader in the Group, that person was Harris. One person who appeared to have the view was Florence Maud Brown, the widow of Eric Brown, director of the National Gallery between 1910 and 1939. When she gave the main address on the occasion of the opening of the Group of Seven Exhibition at the National Gallery of Canada in Ottawa on June 18, 1970, Mrs. Brown said, "Probably Lawren Harris led the Group in discarding the current conventions."[199] Art historians are likely to debate the question of leadership in the Group of Seven for a long time. Was it Harris or Jackson who led? Or did they both provide leadership, each in his own way? The current view is that there was no leader; there is the further possibility that several members with leadership qualities contributed to artistic advancement and the fight for public recognition. At some stage it might be useful to set out what we mean by "leadership" in an art movement so that we will have more objective criteria than we have at present to examine this phase in Canada's art history.

I was in Montreal for a week in April 1962. During that time I saw Arthur Lismer twice in his office at the Montreal Museum of Fine Arts and I took the opportunity to ask him what he thought of Alec as a man and as a painter. At first Lismer wouldn't take my question seriously, but after some urging he asked me to wait a few minutes. He rummaged through his papers (I was never able to decide which filing system was worse, Alec's or Lismer's) and finally produced his 1955 sketchbook. In it there were two of his drawings depicting Alec as a clown.*

"When I did these drawings," Lismer said, "I had to make a choice. Should I portray Alex as a bear or as a clown? I was tempted to draw him as a bear.** He's clumsy and he shuffles his feet. But then I thought of drawing him as a clown because it was a better reflection of his personality rather than his physical appearance. Alex can be really funny. It's a natural fun that comes easily to him, not the kind I make up." (But a month later he was kidding Alec about not being funny.)

I went on trying to get serious answers from Lismer — but with no success. Like Alec, he could be stubborn. Finally, Lismer said, "If you really want to know how I feel about Jackson, I'll find you some notes I wrote about him many years ago. You can read them, and next time you visit me, we can talk about it." It took a quarter of an hour of hunting, but Lismer persevered, and he finally found the notes, which I took away with me. Later on he gave me permission to keep them.

The notes were the text of an address Lismer had given on January 30, 1942, when he was the main speaker at a dinner for Alec at the Art Gallery of Toronto.***Alec was being honoured by his friends as an artist and as one who was being elevated to the status of Doctor of Laws by Queen's University (his first honorary degree, with many more to follow). John Lyle, RCA, president of the gallery, acted as chairman of the dinner, and two hundred fellow artists, friends, and well-wishers joined in a happy and uproarious evening, which Lismer described as "memorable." *Canadian Landscape*, a National Film Board colour documentary about Alec as an artist and showing representative works of his, had its premiere in Toronto that night.

The manuscript was long — twenty-seven pages, typed double-

---

*"A.Y. Jackson as Clown, I" 1955, pencil drawing, 9⅝ by 7⅞ inches (24.5 cm by 20.0 cm), initialled lower left and "A.Y. Jackson as Clown II" 1955, ink and wash drawing, 9⅝ by 7⅞ inches (24.5 cm by 20.0 cm), initialled lower left. We purchased the two drawings later on. ". . . Clown II" is reproduced here on page 181.

**Lismer liked drawing animals.

***Arthur Lismer was at that time educational supervisor of the Art Association of Montreal.

Arthur Lismer, *A. Y. Jackson as Clown, II*

spaced, with corrections in ink in Lismer's handwriting. There were also handwritten comments in the margin pencilled in by somebody else. Apparently, Lismer had had some advice before delivering the address, and the comments were noted on the original manuscript. In addition, there were three typed pages preceding the text. The cover page read: "Any references to persons, places and events in the following pages may be fictitious, but are definitely intentional and no apologies are offered..." (typical Lismer humour). Above, in red pencil in Lismer's handwriting was "Return to A. Lismer." The second page carried the title of the address, "Dedication to the Spirit of the Old Group of Seven." The third page was the foreword, describing the occasion at which the speech was being given.

This manuscript had been among a pile of old papers. The cover page had turned grey, and the paper felt as though it hadn't been handled for at least two decades. The bundle was held together by a knotted string.

This speech in praise of Alec covered so many topics providing new insights into the man, and the manuscript inspired so many questions (which I later took up with Lismer) that I could not possibly discuss them all. I have therefore chosen three main subjects, which I discussed with Lismer on my second visit that week. The first is Alec's relationship with Tom Thomson. Lismer's speech read:

Comparing Jackson with Thomson (which is perhaps unfair to either), Thomson was the voyager, the discoverer, a little pop-eyed with wonder mixed with surprise and awe, that the colours and brushes in his grasp could give even in so brief a manner some quality of nature that he saw... Thomson sees visions and dreams, his paintings are his visions made articulate. He is not a primitive, he is an intuitive mystic; he felt nature, adored her, crept into the woods and as paint was the only medium in which he was articulate, he painted, and his canvases live in the Canadian mind and in the Canadian mold and for those who needed such a revealer, he was themselves made articulate.

And in another passage Lismer made the point that as exhilarating as Thomson colours were in his later canvases, Alec's paintings remained unsurpassed in their totality of artistic appeal and intimate understanding of the Canadian character:

The other element, of colour — here is where A. Y. is supreme. In my jealous moments I could call him a prevaricator — because I can't see it — and fortunately few others can achieve it — as in this respect he is inimitable. But for pure enjoyment this painter of Canada in technicolour is a master. I know there are stranger colours and deeper richness in many of Thomson's canvases, but for form *plus* colour, in rhapsody and in sobriety, in season and in tune, and place, Jackson's sketches, particularly, express a reality and a conviction that he has grasped a whole stretch of lakeland or winter landscape with its symbol of convincing wholeness, and has made of the colour itself a form of adoration and revelation of Canadian character. The landscape painter *has* to compose — to boil down, as it were, his own optical impression to diminutive proportions. A. Y. retains the quality and identity of the whole. His sketch becomes the unit, as it were, from which nature took its theme.

On my second visit I told Lismer that I'd once asked Alec about his relationship with Tom Thomson; Alec had explained that Thomson had had no training and little experience when he met him, and he had seen little good art. When Thomson first saw *The Edge of the Maple Wood*, he said to Alec, "This is the first Canadian picture I have ever seen."* Alec taught Thomson composition and the use of colours. He learned quickly. The six weeks they spent together in Algonquin Park appear to have opened new vistas for Thomson, as became apparent from his later paintings — brilliant in colour and composition. Thomson learned also from some of the other members of the Group, particularly Harris and MacDonald. Conversely, Alec later paid tribute to Thomson in his book: "His [Thomson's] contribution to the movement that eventually found expression in the Group cannot be measured."[200] When we were celebrating his eighty-third birthday, Alec said, "Thomson was one of the greatest people I ever met and one of the most modest. [He] did not have much experience and he knew the country and I didn't. We became close friends."

Lismer confirmed that there was a strong creative urge in Thomson but that he needed help articulating it. Some of the colours of Thomson's later canvases may have been more brilliant than Alec's, but Alec's paintings were more Canadian than those of any in the group, and that included Thomson.

These passages, taken from the manuscript, reveal what Lismer had been trying to tell me: "In the Canadian picture, Jackson is definitely the Canadian, impatient at any other who cannot see what it means to be Canadian and living, here and now, in a land unsurpassed and still growing — just like A. Y. himself . . . He has set a standard of high achievement. It is for others who follow to bring into his setting all those aspects of human occupancy that reveal the dimmer side of man . ."

---

*This is a direct quotation from my notes of a conversation with Alec.

The second area of my reactions prompted by the Lismer speech was Alec's relationship with Harris. Lismer noted how different the two men were. Alec was the realist; he knew perfection was unattainable — but an artist could have a good honest try at it. He was no dreamer but a true painter who kept searching all his life. He wore his hat with a cocky slant as if to say, "I am A. Y., and I know what I'm doing." Harris was a mystic. He was looking for what he called infinity in space and peace for all men. He was an original thinker, and he knew better than most how to express his thoughts. This is how Lismer described Harris in his manuscript:

Harris is the man of dynamic action; he has ideas for everything and finds their solution in argument and cosmic speculation. He believes in the *illusion* of earth, the unreality of existence and the permanence of change — change of heart, change of mind, and action — but always with a purpose .to find a sort of perfection in living to prepare for a supreme perfection in a life beyond the senses and bodily existence. So *his* trees and houses and lakes and clouds are part of an ordered unfolding plan — incomplete, imperfect — but creating endlessly new forms. He moves with them, sees in a big and noble manner their relation to idea and creative purpose. It was inevitable that he should symbolize rather than represent; his abstractions are not modern in the painter's way — nor Freudian, nor expressionistic; they represent exquisite balance and movement, cosmic, slow, and spacious.

"The two," Lismer said, "were good friends. They respected each other. Jackson would sometimes shake his head when some of the Harris ideas seemed far-fetched. If Jackson was arguing, he preferred to do so on the ground and not in the sky — that was the Harris territory. Jackson's vision was as great as Harris's, but at times they moved on different planes."

When I turned to the third question, how Lismer himself felt about Alec, he replied, "We are very good friends. You shouldn't ask me any questions about Alec; I'm a biased witness. All I had to say is in that speech of mine — you have a copy. It was given twenty years ago, and I have forgotten most of the things I said about him at that time."

I therefore tried the strategy of reading aloud a passage from the manuscript: "I think it is true that all the members of that Group acknowledged that Alec Jackson* was a prime inspiration and perhaps the most consistent in following out the beliefs and convictions of the Group's ideas."

---

*Note that Lismer says "Alec," not "Alex."

"Is that your way of saying that Jackson provided leadership to the Group?" I asked. "In an inspirational sense, yes; in a practical way, no," he replied.

People had called Alec a genius, I continued. What did Lismer say to that?

Picasso was perhaps the greatest artist of the twentieth century, he replied, and people called him a genius. If there were such a thing as a Canadian genius, Jackson would probably be one. "But," Lismer said, "I don't like the word. It is easily applied and doesn't mean very much." (He also made that point in his manuscript.)

I then quoted to Lismer this passage from his speech:

> An artist can do many things in the course of his career of work, but two are typical of most artists. He can change repeatedly in idea, in design and in subject, like Picasso who commences and terminates many movements and styles in his own personal and changing attitude, or he can progress intelligently in consistent stages, mellowing gracefully with the years, and achieving not so much a triumph — a tour de force — as giving evidence of a progressive development of a carefully considered life plan in his art. In other words, he develops a talent, records his environment and times, and pushes his medium along a chosen road toward a definite goal. Such an artist is A. Y. Jackson.

"Now that's better," he commented. "What Jackson achieved was the result of hard work and his willingness to grow and move on. He was the restless type who couldn't sit still. I could never keep up with him. He didn't wait for inspirations to come to him. He would search out the land, and that was his inspiration." He was saying again what he'd said years before in the manuscript: "Jackson goes out after his material and he changes his scene and that's why — or one of the reasons — his canvases have variety, change of design, season, colour, weather, and place."

I kept questioning — how it was, for instance, that the stories Alec had been telling about Canadian art for the previous two decasdes had so much popular appeal that he had more requests to lecture and make guest appearances than he could accept. When Alec talked about Canadian art, Lismer explained, he spoke the language of his listeners. He understood the people to whom his paintings were designed to say something. He painted "*their*" landscape — not just what he himself saw, but also what he thought others saw in the landscape. This was another side of Alec's expressive personality. It was, as Lismer had explained previously, "his ability to integrate his interests and to absorb the interests of others. Whether they are loggers, miners, students of all ages, Eskimos, or dwellers in cities. In his way, he is a beneficient spreader of good fellowship. Not having any taint of the generally accepted bohemian or conventional idea of the professional artist, he finds himself in company with all kinds of people, talking their language and sharing their lives."[201]

Of all the nice things Lismer had to say about Alec, there was one sentence that Alec described as "the most precious of all." (In referring to it Alec noted, "I'll end up by embarrasing myself.") The statement: "Jackson has done more than any other writer or artist to bind us to our own environment, to make us vitally aware of the significance, beauty, and character of the land."[202] Alec said of Lismer's words: "He shouldn't have done it, but I love every word of it."[203]

I asked Lismer whether Jackson had asked him to quit his job at the Montreal Museum of Fine Arts to devote his full time to painting. He replied, "Yes, several times in the past decade. But when I once said that I liked teaching art, particularly to children, as much as he liked painting, the subject was never again raised." He continued, "I have a drawing somewhere showing Alec meeting some young students in Montreal. You know, Alec likes children, but he doesn't take enough time to get to know them. I wonder whether he would have had enough patience if he had had children of his own."

After some searching, Lismer produced the drawing (see page 187) showing Alec walking purposefully and apparently bent on passing quickly by as a group of six young girls look expectantly at him.* I asked Lismer when he did the drawing; he wasn't sure. It was probably 1940.

I had many a talk with Lismer over the years, but I never knew him to be as eloquent and enthusiastic as when the subject was Alec. Most of the time, in fact, I found it difficult to make Lismer talk seriously. He would try to be funny, sometimes naturally, sometimes in a contrived way. But on the few occasions when Lismer did talk seriously and substantively, he had a lot to say. Under a personality that portrayed superficiality was a character of depth. It was this depth that Alec appreciated, and he took Lismer's "funny" ways in his stride.

The concluding passage of Lismer's tribute to Alec, taken from the manuscript, reveals Lismer in a non-joking mien: "Tonight we honour him for his skill, his tenacity, his sturdy championing of his native land, for which he has striven by voice in defence of his faith. He has fought for it on the battlefield; he has painted, voyaged, and portaged over many trails and in many varied parts of this Canada. But by his personality and his genius, he has brought new and lasting life to Canadian art, new experience to others, and prestige and honour to his country."

---

*This drawing is now in the Ontario Heritage Foundation Firestone Art Collection.

Arthur Lismer, *Mr. Jackson Visits the Children in Montreal*

Lismer may not have liked to use the word "genius," but he found it the most telling one that he could think of to describe Alec's work as an artist. What I found so interesting in talking to Lismer about Alec was that, joking apart, he stressed the positive aspects. At no time did he suggest that Alec kept plodding along, repeating the same theme over and over again. Alec believed in change, certainly, but change had little effect on Alec. He was always a believer in "Canada first." Lismer, like Alec, believed that it was important for Canadian painters to break away from the traditions of England, France, and the rest of Western Europe. This, in fact, was one of the main themes of the whole Group of Seven during the twenties and early thirties. But after the Second World War, Alec and Lismer drifted apart in their ideology. Alec kept doing the same thing while Lismer was calling for new goals in Canadian art. He felt that painters should break out of the narrow bounds of nationalism, taking into account "the great complexity and growing internationalism of contemporary life."[204]

I once asked Lawren P. Harris to give me his impression of Alec's view of himself and to compare it with the self-views of Arthur Lismer and Lawren S. Harris. He replied, "Alec did not take himself seriously, but he took his work seriously. Lismer did not take himself or his work seriously. My father took both himself and his work very seriously."

Three more different people are hard to imagine. Still, they were driven for many years by a common spirit.

CHAPTER 16
Alec and the Diplomats

During the decade of the fifties, when I was economic adviser to the Minister of Trade and Commerce, I was regularly invited to the Embassy of the Soviet Union on their country's national day and on other occasions. I remained on the embassy list of invitees after I left the government service to teach at the University of Ottawa.

In 1962 Isobel and I met Ivan F. Shpedko, who had recently come to Canada as Soviet ambassador, and his wife, Anna. He stayed in Canada for about six and a half years, longer than any previous Soviet ambassador, in part because he was involved in the preparations for the Soviet contribution to Expo '67 in Montreal, with the proceedings during the fair, and the winding-up afterward. (His wife eventually left for Moscow earlier than he because of poor health.)

We shared a love of paintings, and both he and his wife were interested in learning more about Canadian art. At one of the receptions at the embassy, we promised to introduce the Shpedkos to Alec, and we did so at the next party at our house. After dinner we asked Alec whether he wanted to take some of the guests to the Jackson Room, and several people went upstairs with him, including the ambassador and his wife. Most of them returned after ten minutes, but Alec and Shpedko remained there for some time. When Shpedko returned, he took me aside and mentioned how much he admired Alec's work. It reminded him of landscapes at home, and he mentioned a Russian painter (whose name I have forgotten) who had painted in a similar style. He asked me whether Alec would accept an invitation to the embassy, and I replied that he probably would. Since Alec did not drive a car, we agreed to pick him up at his home on MacLaren Street, to take him to the embassy, and return him home. From this introduction there developed, over the next five years or so, an unusual friendship among a Soviet foreign affairs career official, an artist, and a university professor.

I should say a few words about the Shpedkos. Ivan was stocky, heavy-set, slow-walking, careful in conversation (his English improved considerably during his long stay in Canada), and had bright eyes that seemed to be searching for something not apparent at first glance. His speech was soft, masking a powerful intellect. He smiled rarely, but when he did, his whole face lit up. He had been born in the Ukraine, and he looked to us typically Russian.

His wife, Anna, was a beautiful woman, a little taller than her husband. She had kept her slim figure (though she had a daughter, Tatiana, finishing her education in Moscow), walked with easy grace, and, unlike her husband, had a ready smile. She was good natured and easygoing. She was proud to have been born in Leningrad, where greater value seems to be placed on culture than in most of the other Russian cities. As we got to know the Shpedkos better, we sometimes heard her tease her husband about how anyone coming from the Ukraine could know anything about culture. Ivan would smile at his wife's sense of humour and reply, "Not everybody can come from Leningrad."

During these years Alec became quite friendly with the ambassador, and went to two or three receptions a year at the Soviet embassy (he was invited more frequently, but was often out of town). He was always accompanied by Isobel or me, most of the time by both of us. Our custom was to introduce him to a few people and then to leave him alone. Alec was never at a loss for words. He enjoyed himself thoroughly.

The world-famous Russian cellist Mstislav Leopoldovich Rostropovich was coming to Ottawa. The Soviet ambassador organized a musicale to be held at the embassy, and he invited Isobel, Alec, and me to attend.

When I called for Alec at his studio before the performance, I asked him whether he liked music. To him, music was like painting. If it were well performed, it could help people explore and enjoy new visions of beauty they might not have realized existed. It was something that could give people a lift — take them out of the doldrums of everyday living by joining the artist, the composer, and the performer in a flight of fancy into the unknown. Though I do not remember the specific phrases he used, I remember that Alec grew quite lyrical on the subject. He added that the Russians had produced many fine musicians, and was looking forward to the performance.

I asked whether he was planning to use his hearing aid at the concert. He didn't like using it — besides, he said he was not sure where he had put it, and, in any event, the batteries weren't working. I offered to buy new batteries, but Alec just smiled sheepishly. "Never mind," he said. (I was not the only one who tried. When Betty Kirk suggested that Alec use the hearing aid, he retorted, "You try it." She did, and never asked him again.)

Alec and I found seats in the first row, and Isobel sat at the back of the embassy reception hall to get a better overall impression of what

189

turned out to be an exceptionally fine, though short, performance. Afterward, the ambassador introduced Alec to Rostropovich, and the two, with Isobel and Shpedko, had an animated conversation. There were refreshments, and Alec joined in a toast with vodka to the genial cellist from the Soviet Union.

Alec said later he enjoyed the musicale thoroughly, although I am not sure how much he actually heard. When I told the story about the hearing aid to Ralph Burton, he mentioned that he had had a similar experience with Alec, who had protested then that the batteries "cost too much." This remark could be interpreted as Alec's way of being funny, but to me his reluctance to use his hearing aid reflected something else. Alec was hard of hearing for most of his life, and the condition became worse as he grew older. True, he did not like to be bothered by trivia or mechanical contraptions, but he seemed to have developed a philosophy to deal with the affliction. What was important people would make an effort to make him hear; the rest was unimportant.

In May 1965, the Department of External Affairs announced that two officials of the Soviet embassy in Ottawa had been asked to leave Canada for "activities incompatible with their official status." Apparently, these two diplomats had obtained from a Canadian civil servant information and documents that would aid in the performance of "economic intelligence tasks."

It turned out that the Canadian official was a Vancouver postal clerk named George Spencer, who had been paid by the two Russians for documents that could have been purchased from the Government Printing Office and/or the Dominion Bureau of Statistics. Even the Minister of Justice admitted in the House of Commons that the information in question was of a kind available to anyone.

Isobel, Alec, and I were invited to the Soviet embassy on June 3. Alec was out of town. As the crowd thinned and Ambassador Shpedko mingled with his guests, he took me aside. He was quite upset about the so-called spy affair, and he would not accept my dismissal of the matter as a storm in a teacup. For the previous three years he had been labouring hard to improve Soviet-Canadian relations; now this silly affair had ruined what good had been achieved. The problem was that the forces of goodwill were up against the forces of suspicion and distrust. What could an ambassador do, being a little cog in a big government machine? What could a little university professor do, I retorted, or a little painter, if Alec had been with us? "Well, Mr. Jackson is a great painter," the ambassador replied, smiling a little. "He stands far above the little people," he added with admiration in his voice, and I said I'd pass this comment on to Alec.

190

When Alec returned to Ottawa, I told him about my talk with the ambassador. Alec's reaction was typical and in some respect quite similar to the sentiments expressed by Shpedko. "If the Canadian and Russian people were left alone, everything would work out. Little people understand each other and get along fine."

I know Alec's feeling about this matter. It was all the fault of politicians and bureaucrats, who were "them"; the little people were "us," and he would never have thought of excluding himself from that community. As for politicians and bureaucrats, they were confirmed troublemakers, whether they were of the Canadian or the foreign variety.

Discussion was underway in the mid-sixties to extend cultural relations between Canada and the USSR, and Shpedko and I talked about a possible showing of works of the Group of Seven in the Soviet Union. Shpedko had by that time become knowledgeable about the Group of Seven, and he admired many of their paintings.

I approached the National Gallery with the idea and was told that the gallery had already made commitments for foreign showings for the next two years. A Group of Seven show would take another two years of preparation, and budgetary restraints were another hindrance.

Disappointed, I mentioned the matter to Samuel Zacks, a good friend from Toronto then visiting us. He and his wife, Ayala, were leading collectors of art in Canada — mainly French impressionists along with some good Canadian works. Sam was on his way to Moscow and Leningrad to inquire about the possibility of a North American show of some of the leading works from the Hermitage Collection. (He was ten years ahead of his time, for such an exhibition did not arrive until the bicentennial celebrations of 1976 in the United States, visiting Winnipeg and Montreal as well before returning to Leningrad. Sam did not live to see his aspiration realized.) I raised the question with him of a Group of Seven show in the Soviet Union, and he said he would discuss the possibility with the senior official he expected to see at the Ministry of Cultural Affairs. When he returned, he told us that the official he consulted had heard of the Group of Seven and his ministry would be prepared to consider any concrete exhibition proposal.

I reported the Zacks conversation to my gallery contacts. This time, I was told that the gallery was not sure it was in the national interest to send a Group of Seven exhibition to the Soviet Union. It would be a somewhat one-sided and dated show. Why not an exhibition of modern Canadian artists?

This was not a particularly helpful answer from Alec's and my point of view. A short time later, I met Paul Martin, then Secretary of

State for External Affairs. I'd known Martin since the days when he had been parliamentary assistant to the Minister of Labour in 1943, and we had always gotten along well. I told him about the difficulties I was having and asked whether there was anything he could do. He replied that as this was a matter that concerned the arts, the National Gallery was best equipped to handle it.

I had kept Alec informed as the discussions proceeded. At one stage, when things were looking up, Alec mentioned that if a Group of Seven show for the USSR were organized, he would like to go along. I asked him whether such a trip would not be too strenuous for him but he replied, "If I can go to the Arctic, I can go to Moscow." Isobel and I said that if he would go, we would go too.

As the news about a possible exhibition became more discouraging, we hesitated to tell Alec about it. My wife suggested that we use what we call the Mackenzie King technique: when it is not essential to do something now, put it off. So the subject was not discussed. But a couple of months later Alec brought the question up and I had to tell him the truth.

His first reaction was to blame the National Gallery, which he said was "always pushing the new fellows. Some of that modern stuff isn't worth the canvas it's painted on." In spite of his usual regard for abstract art, Alec occasionally lashed out at it in anger. I agreed with him to the extent that there was room for both kinds, and that we should expect the National Gallery to have a balanced view on the subject of exhibitions.

We could not know that two years later the gallery would ask one of its senior curators, Dennis Reid, to organize a major retrospective exhibition of the Group of Seven, to be opened on the fiftieth anniversary of the Group's first show in Toronto in 1920. Reid worked for two years and did an outstanding job.

The news I brought Alec meant the end of his dream of visiting Moscow and being present at an opening of a Group of Seven exhibition there, but he was a good trooper. After the first anger faded away he remarked, "It was a good try. You can't win 'em all."

It took eleven years, but the project finally did materialize, with the initiative taken by the McMichaels and the Ontario Government. A fine selection of the works of the Group of Seven and Tom Thomson from the McMichael Canadian Collection was sent to tour the Soviet Union and other European countries in 1976 and 1977.

In the spring of 1966, Shpedko asked me whether the Soviet government could acquire a large Jackson canvas. I replied that as far as I knew, Alec had no large canvases of his own work in his possession — nor a small painting, for that matter. I volunteered to ask him whether over the summer and fall he could paint a large canvas to meet this request.

Alec said he would consider it, and said he would charge $750. I reported this to the Soviet ambassador, who said that $750 in foreign exchange was a lot of money for his country. He would, however, forward this suggestion with his recommendation to the foreign ministry in Moscow, and he would let me know.

I heard nothing for several months, then, late in the fall of that year, Anatoly A. Doilnitsyn, responsible for cultural affairs in the embassy, phoned me. He was very apologetic about what he was to tell me, saying that he was calling on behalf of the ambassador; he took about five minutes to get to the point. It appeared that the ministry in Moscow had turned down the request to spend $750 for a Canadian painting, even by as famous an artist as Jackson, because of the great scarcity of foreign exchange for non-essential purchases. Culture is important, the Soviet official explained, but wheat and machinery were even more important. Nevertheless, he continued, the ambassador had received permission to spend one hundred dollars. Could a small painting perhaps be obtained?

Alec was a little disappointed: he would have liked a large canvas of his to go to Moscow. He agreed to sell one of his sketches for one hundred dollars to the Soviet embassy — but couldn't find one. His cupboards were bare.

The matter was now of some urgency; word had come indicating that the ambassador might return to Moscow early in the new year. I offered to let Alec choose from the sketches I had obtained from him the previous year. He picked one entitled *Barns, Sugarbush, Brownsburg, Quebec* painted in April 1965 on a regular 10½ by 13½ inch panel. He promised to replace it in the spring when he came back from his next sketching trip, and he did. On January 21, 1967, the cultural secretary called at our house to pick up Alec's painting. He paid one hundred dollars, in cash, and we turned the money over to Alec.

Isobel and I had been wanting to present the Shpedkos with a farewell gift. We decided to use the occasion of the cultural secretary's visit to pass on our gift to Ivan and Anna. Our present, appropriately inscribed, was A. J. Casson's *Near Barry's Bay, Hopefield Road*, which he had painted in 1964 on a panel measuring 12 by 14½ inches.

We mentioned to Cass, who had met the Soviet ambassador on a previous visit to Ottawa, that a painting of his, in addition to one by Alec, was going to Moscow. He was pleased and so was Alec. As it turned out, this painting of Alec's went to the residence of the Soviet ambassador in Rockcliffe Park, but Alec never knew.

There had been a change of plans, and Ivan Shpedko was advised

193

that his stay in Ottawa would be extended until after Expo '67. Those were very busy days for the ambassador, and we saw little of him. Alec, Isobel, and I were invited to visit the Soviet pavilion at Expo and to attend a performance of the Bolshoi Ballet Company. Alec had other plans, but Isobel and I did go, and were very much impressed by several of the pavilions, including the American, the Russian, and the Czech.

The ambassador invited the two of us to a supper party with some of the dancers after the performance. There were many Russian dishes (I had difficulty with their borsch), plenty to drink, music and dancing.

Two ballerinas sat at our table. The ambassador asked one of them to dance with him, and he suggested that I dance with the other. I am not shy, but when he saw me hesitate he said, "She won't bite." Then he said something in Russian to the young lady, and she laughed. I learned later that he had translated his remark to me and asked her to dance with me.

She got up, and before I knew it, we were whirling around the dance floor. I had never danced with a ballerina before. She held me firmly, and she was leading: it was an unaccustomed sensation for a man. The dance felt like floating on air, and I was amazed by her combination of gracefulness and strength. She did not speak English and I did not speak Russian. The only work I knew was *spasibo* (thank you) and I repeated it several times.

Back at the table, while Isobel danced with one of the male dancers, I asked Shpedko to translate two questions to my dancing partner. The first was, "How is it that a classical ballerina is so well versed in the modern dancing current in North America?" She replied that she and the other girls did some modern dancing at home in their spare time, just for fun, though their ballet master frowned on it, and it was done when he was not around.

Shpedko had mentioned to me previously that the ballerina with whom I had danced was married, and the troupe had been on tour for several weeks. That night had been their last performance in North America, and in a day or two the dancers would be returning to Moscow. This led to my second question, "What will you be doing when you return to Moscow?" After she answered the question in Russian, both she and the ambassador burst into laughter. Shpedko translated for the ballerina, "I shall have a holiday. My husband is also taking a holiday. He has bought some food and drink. We lock the door to our apartment, we take the phone off the hook, and we don't leave the place for a week."

It was getting late, and Shpedko said he was sorry Alec could not have joined us. He mentioned that he expected to return to Moscow after he had attended to various matters after the Expo closing, and — could he ask a favour? The Jackson painting that had been purchased belonged to the Soviet government; he wondered if Alec would sell him another sketch, one he could own personally? It would be great, he intimated, to have paintings from two leading members of the Group of Seven in his modest apartment in Moscow. I promised to pass on his request. And so when Alec returned to Ottawa from his summer travels, I told him about our evening with the Soviet ambassador and the Bolshoi ballet group. When I came to the story about locking the door for a week, he remarked with a chuckle, "The Russians know how to live."

Alec was sympathetic to the ambassador's desire to take a sketch home with him as a memento of their acquaintance and a remembrance of the time he spent in Ottawa, which, with some brief exceptions, had been happy days. When he came back late that fall, he brought one quite strong sketch with him. He had it framed and said to me that he would charge the ambassador only one hundred dollars, absorbing the cost of the framing himself.

When the sketch was ready, I phoned the cultural secretary, who told me that the ambassador wished to call on Alec to pay his respects, and that the secretary would accompany him. Alec later told me how jolly the conversation with the ambassador had been, with Shpedko expressing regrets that the efforts to bring a Group of Seven exhibition to the Soviet Union had failed and that Alec's visit to Moscow had not materialized.

The ambassador had brought him a bottle of brown vodka (the special kind reserved for diplomats abroad and bigwigs at home) and a record. Since Alec did not drink vodka and did not listen to records, I presume he later gave them away. The secretary paid the one hundred dollars, again in cash, and Alec bade farewell to his visitors.

A. E. (Ed) Ritchie, Under-Secretary of State for External Affairs, was appointed Canadian ambassador to the United States in 1966. The Canadian government owned a stately ambassadorial residence in Washington — 2825 Rock Creek Drive North West (a stone's throw away from Massachusetts Avenue, a neighbourhood that housed many diplomatic residences). The building had been acquired in 1927 for close to half a million dollars, and was spacious and well-appointed, with adequate facilities for entertaining and a competent staff to help the ambassador and his lady. There was only one drawback — it lacked paintings and other works of art.

The Department of External Affairs had a fairly large stock of paintings, and the decisions on art works was left to the incoming ambassador and his wife. The department's collection consisted mainly of modern Canadian abstract paintings, some by artists who had already made a name for themselves, but most by young artists just coming along. None of the works appealed to the Ritchies.

Ed and Gwen Ritchie, due to take up their new posting, mentioned to Isobel their predicament in choosing Canadian works of art. The two women agreed to suggest to their respective husbands that the Firestones lend the Ritchies, for the duration of their stay in Washington, two canvases, one by A. Y. Jackson and the other by A. J. Casson. And so it was.

The two chosen were Alec's *Lake Rouvière* (painted in 1961), reproduced on page 197, and Cass's *Clearing after the Rain, Late October — Lake Kamaniskeg*, painted in 1964. (Both paintings are now in the Ontario Heritage Foundation Firestone Art Collection.) Once the decision was taken, the arrangements for crating, shipment, and insurance were quickly made. The paintings were gingerly loaded onto an RCAF flight September 21, 1966, from Ottawa to Washington, and were whisked in the ambassador's limousine from airport to residence. One was hung in the drawing room, the other in the dining room, for greatest exposure. Ed Ritchie noted in a letter to me: "One of the incidental advantages in getting the paintings down here that early, is that it would be possible to have them already hanging in the residence at the time of Mitchell Sharp's visit [Sharp was then Secretary of State for External Affairs] when we shall be having a dinner in his honour for some distinguished financial representatives of various countries, including Secretary Fowler."

When I told them about the arrangements, both Alec and Cass were greatly pleased. I suggested to Alec that it might be helpful to the ambassador and his wife if they had more information about his painting. Alec agreed, but said it would take too long to write it up. My notes covering that conversation on September 20, 1966 describe the experiences that led to his painting *Lake Rouvière* in September 1959.

During the summer and early fall of 1959, I went on a five-week sketching trip to the western Arctic. I made my headquarters at a camp in the vicinity of Great Bear Lake in the Northwest Territories. I was wandering about the countryside sketching the stark wilderness that has become known as the barren land. But what people in the more developed parts of Canada do not realize is the bewildering beauty of the Arctic — the strong contrasts in colour and topography, the uniqueness of a clear sky that lends a crispness to contours that cannot be observed in the more southern regions of Canada.

Lake Rouvière

Thanks to the courtesy of Eldorado Mining and Refining Limited, which operates a mine at Port Radium, located on the east side of the McTavish Arm of Great Bear Lake, a small company plane equipped with floats flew my two companions and myself to Lake Rouvière, some sixty miles south of Coppermine, well within the Arctic Circle.

Coppermine is a tiny settlement, mainly Eskimos, with an RCMP station, a Hudson's Bay trading post, a weather and radio station, a school, government health centre, and two missions (Anglican and Roman Catholic). This is a friendly community where visitors are rare and most welcome, where Eskimos come to trade the meagre results of their hunting and trapping efforts, selling hides to the Hudson's Bay Company to obtain enough cash to meet some of the basic necessities of life. Eskimos do not know any other way of making a living but to fish and hunt the whale, the caribou, the polar bear, and the white fox. The line between survival and starvation is thin — a bad fishing and hunting season can bring havoc to both young and old. No other region more than the North drives home the reality of the saying that it is only the fittest who survive the struggle for life.

Still, all the Eskimos I have met in the western Arctic have had a ready smile and a childlike curiosity that extended even to my paintings. They would watch me paint but would be too shy to ask questions. What a difference! When I paint at Georgian Bay, hardly an hour passes that somebody does not look over my shoulder and ask me about the painting — and in many instances inquire whether I would consider selling the sketch before it is dry.

But even in the western Arctic there appears to be a growing interest in Canadian paintings. Though I worked hard, painting two and sometimes three sketches a day, I was able to bring back only a few sketches. The rest were bought by all kinds of people, from a school teacher to a clerk at the Bay, from a geologist in the field to a technician at the weather station.

To come back to the Eskimos and to show how friendly they are — when landing at Lake Rouvière, I was reminded of the story of how some twenty years earlier two Catholic priests were murdered by Eskimos. The motive was starvation. So when the pilot brought us down at Lake Rouvière for a week's stay, we were reassured by his smile and his promise to be back in a week's time to pick us up.

We were cut off from everybody. We had a radio, but it was the only means to keep in touch with civilization, and we had a fire to keep us warm. There we were — myself, the professional painter whose desire to explore the vast expanse of Canada, and particularly the unconquered Arctic, was undimmed, though I had passed the age of three score and ten, with my friend Maurice Haycock, a mineralogist by profession and a part-time painter by choice, and his assistant, Pinard.

We put up our tent, stowed away our supplies, and then went out looking for sites: the scenery to paint, the reflection of the sky on the water, the mix of living and dead matter, the shrubbery and the rocks, the dwarf trees and the dark crevices in the ground, the berry bushes and the deadwood strewn where it fell, some of it some fifty years ago.

There is one thing plentiful in the western Arctic besides snow and ice, and that is firewood, for there is very little time for dead trees to rot. The summer lasts two months, July and August, and the fall one month. Spring is only known as a date on the calendar. The freezing of the lakes may start before the summer is out but surely before the fall has had time to shower the countryside with a mantle of brilliant colours — red, yellow, and purple.

We arrived at Lake Rouvière on September 9, 1959, and stayed till September 16. The small lakes in the area were already frozen over.

Lake Rouvière, which is fairly large (about three miles long and two miles wide), was beginning to freeze up and would be completely frozen by the end of September.

For a country that is reputedly treeless, with contours that are generally flat, the western Arctic presents a remarkably rewarding region for a painter to explore and to interpret in form and colour. There were quite a few small spruce trees growing along the shores of lakes and rivers, of which there are many — too bad a painter spends so much time painting, for the country is a fisherman's paradise. Then there are dwarf birch trees, willows, and huckleberry bushes. They all add a soft green touch during the brief summer period to what otherwise might be considered a forbidding and lonely wasteland of rock, muskeg, and water, covered by snow and ice nine or ten months out of the year. And there are also the mountains, usually a distance away, not too high. They represent a welcome contrast to the rolling countryside and they add definition to the landscape.

We had wonderful weather during our week's stay at Lake Rouvière. The days were clear, bright, sunny — remarkably little wind and few cloud formations. The nights were cold, with temperatures below freezing.

The weather was invigorating, the company congenial and the landscapes a challenge to a painter's ability to capture it in its quicksilvery beauty. I worked every day from about 7:30 a.m. to 5:30 p.m., with a brief break for lunch. I painted a total of about fifteen sketches during the week. The sketches were painted on plywood panels, 10½ by 13½ inches, which I had treated previously with a thin coating of orange shellac so as to minimize warping.

I liked one or two sketches particularly well and brought them home. I painted this canvas, *Lake Rouvière*, late that fall from the sketch I had done in the western Arctic.

When Alec had finished dictating the notes to me, I remarked that he was not only a great painter but also had the makings of a fine poet and imaginative writer. Alec just smiled. There was no comment. I asked whether he was pleased that a painting of his was going to the Canadian ambassador for his stay of three to four years in Washington, and he said he approved, but when I asked if he had a message for the ambassador, he only chuckled. "If you are in a mood to write," he replied, "you might as well take this down."

I am particularly pleased that Professor and Mrs. Firestone are making available to Mr. and Mrs. A. E. Ritchie this painting of mine, *Lake Rouvière*, to be hung in their official residence in Washington. I believe that the arts are another means of communicating directly ideas and sentiments among people of different nations, and that beauty and form, as caught by the creative artist, whether portrayed in abstract or representative form, knows no boundaries. Perhaps this canvas will show to our American friends and others visiting the Ritchie residence that there is beauty and excitement to be found in Canada's northern "barren" lands.

Well put, and how true! Alec had an admirably clear and polished way of expressing himself, a notable accomplishment for a person who had gone to school for only six years. I once commented on Alec's extensive vocabulary to Dr. Starrs, and he told me he'd asked Alec to explain his excellent command of the English language, and that Alec had replied he'd studied the dictionary.

Alec's painting was seen by several thousand visitors to the ambassador's residence in Washington between 1966 and 1970, and was not only admired but contributed in its way to that better understanding "among people of different nations" that was one of Alec's firm objectives.

CHAPTER 17

Supply and Demand, Prices and the Inevitable Taxes

Alec claimed he painted fifteen to eighteen canvases a year — true enough about larger pieces but, if some smaller works are included, the number probably was twenty-five or more a year. In a good year, he might also be left with more than a hundred sketches after destroying those he rejected. When he returned from his trip to Baffin Island in 1965, Alec said in an interview with Dennis Foley that during the two-month trip he'd done "100-odd sketches," from which he planned to "complete 20 to 25 canvases."[205] The figure for the number of canvases in this case is about right, but the number of sketches may be a little on the high side.

On a good day of an outing trip, Alec would usually paint two sketches, and the figure given to Foley suggests an average of three sketches a day or better. There is, however, evidence that when Alec was really in the mood, he could do up to four sketches a day, so one hundred sketches a year (net) may be on the low side. Whatever the number, it rarely detracted from the quality of his work. Moreover, most of the sketches I saw from the Baffin Island trip were vibrant and stronger than I'd seen in years.[206]

At Alec's eighty-third birthday party, I reported that during the period he had been active as a professional painter he had painted approximately five thousand sketches and had destroyed close to a thousand, so that there remained in the possession of galleries, institutions, dealers, and private collections something more than four thousand sketches. Alec also estimated that the number of canvases which survived after he had weeded out those not up to standard numbered about a thousand.* (I checked all these figures with Alec before mentioning them and he also read over and corrected the notes I was using.) Since he painted for another two and a half years after the birthday party, the numbers given here are conservative — so it's no

---

*When Alec gave me these figures, he mentioned that he might have been underestimating his output in earlier statements (see, for example, his statement in a 1959 interview in which he mentioned that he might have done "more than 2,000 outdoor sketches" and "about 600 oil paintings on canvas and thrown 100 in the fire."[207]

wonder some of Alec's Group of Seven colleagues called him the most productive member of their small circle. He also had the longest span of creative life — about sixty years as a professional painter.

These six decades beginning in 1908 can be divided into three periods, from a supply-and-demand point of view. The first three decades were ones in which the excess of supply over demand for Alec's paintings was such that he was prompted to make the ironic comment (as many other artists have said of their own work) that he had the largest collection of A.Y. Jackson paintings anywhere. The next decade and a half were years of significant increase in demand, and there was a trend towards a balance between the supply of paintings Alec still owned and the sales of works. By the late fifties, he had almost entirely disposed of the inventory he had built up over the previous forty-five years. Thereafter, future demand could only be met from new production.* In the last decade and a half of his productive life, Alec's output, his advancing age notwithstanding, remained fairly unchanged. His health was remarkably good, and his desire to paint as strong as ever. Nevertheless, because of the higher value put on his works, the demand exceeded the supply by a considerable margin, and chaotic market conditions ensued.

To some extent this situation resulted from Alec's idiosyncrasies; it was also the outcome, however, of the fragmentation of the Canadian art market.

Alec believed that his paintings should be within the reach of as many Canadians as possible, and he was reluctant to raise prices. Also, because he was so good-natured and so impatient with business, his prices differed from one buyer to another. He also gave works away (as he did to help several small galleries build up collections of his paintings**) and sold works at nominal prices.***

The Canadian art market after the Second World War was a conglomerate of regional markets functioning at different levels. The main centres were Toronto and Montreal, with a Vancouver market appearing in the more recent period. The market worked through the main commercial galleries, some small dealers (many of whom were marginal operators, with new commercial outlets being set up every year while others were going out of business), and sub-dealers, people

---

*Contrasting the situation in the sixties, when all his work was sold frequently before it was completed, with the situation before the war, Alec observed, "I used to have hundreds of paintings around and wouldn't be able to sell a sketch a month."[208]

**He gave nine oil paintings to the Greater Victoria Art Gallery, for example.[209]

***In 1964, Alec sold thirty-one drawings, representative of his life's work, to the Art Collection Society of Kingston, which in turn donated the drawings to the Agnes Etherington Art Centre, associated with Queen's University.[210]

with small overhead who would either undersell established commercial galleries or sell at higher prices when the opportunity to do so arose.

There were also the art auctions: one major auction house operated in each of the two major cities, and many smaller auctioneering firms were active across the country. Jackson dealt mainly with well-established commercial galleries, but in some cases sub-dealers had access to him. He also sold directly to the public.

As demand continued to exceed supply, public pressure for Alec's canvases and sketches increased by leaps and bounds, and his output could not keep pace. New public galleries were being built, and every time these galleries acquired one of Alec's works, the supply on the open market was reduced. One would have expected higher prices to ensue, reaching a level that would have restored the balance between supply and demand, but in this instance, changing price levels were not allowed to play the role of balancing the two sides of the scale. For one thing, Alec for a long time refused to raise the prices he charged for his paintings.

Again, Alec's dealers could have raised the prices several times over for any of his paintings they had for sale. Few dared, however. They knew Alec would hear about it, and knew he'd frown on their "profiteering." To keep the supply flowing, they kept prices of new works considerably below what the "market" price would have been, that is, prices set as a result of transactions between a willing seller and a willing buyer.

People who could not get an A. Y. Jackson painting from Alec's regular dealers were sometimes able to buy a sketch from a small gallery or a sub-dealer, usually paying a higher price than the regular dealers were charging. Prices were also sometimes higher at public auctions where people went because they expected to find bargains.

All during the years Alec lived in Manotick and in Ottawa, I tried to teach him certain principles of economics. We discussed two subjects on a number of occasions, Gross National Product and the law of supply and demand.

I explained to Alec what GNP and national income meant — I had been giving a course on National Income Analysis at the University of Ottawa — and that Canada, with her growing affluence, could well afford to spend a greater proportion of GNP on cultural pursuits, including support for the fine arts. Alec agreed, and adopted the concept.*

---

*"It is high time Canada began to spend a decent proportion of her national income on art," he said, for example, in his comments when participating in a panel discussion organized by the Gallery Association of Ottawa on December 2, 1958.[211]

On the subject of supply and demand and the working of the price system, I was less effective in making a dent in Alec's thinking. He said this kind of economics did not apply to him; it applied to people who wanted to make money, and money was not important to him. He had done with little for so many years that his later success and wide public acceptance did not change him. On several occasions I tried to persuade him to raise his prices, but Alec wouldn't budge.

Once, when he returned from a painting trip, he had brought back for us a particularly good sketch, which I admired greatly. "I'll pay you one hundred dollars for this sketch," I said. I made out a cheque and put it on the table.

"But the price is sixty dollars," he said, smiling.

"I like that sketch very much, but if you won't accept the higher price, I don't know what to do. Honestly, I find it difficult to take it at the old price," I said, moving reluctantly toward the door.

Alec looked at me with amused eyes "All right," he said. "But that means I'll have to charge everybody else higher prices."

"It's about time," I replied, and we shook hands on it. About eighteen months after that conversation I tried to persuade Alec to raise his prices again, but I didn't succeed.

Henri Masson, a fellow artist who believed in the law of supply and demand, once asked Alec why he wouldn't raise his prices. When Alec said he didn't need more money, Masson asked whether he would consider endowing an A. Y. Jackson Foundation whose funds could assist struggling artists or promising Fine Art students. To this Alec replied, "Too much trouble." He wanted an uncomplicated life. Setting up a foundation would have taken valuable time away from painting. In his later years, if Alec had a choice between time and money, time would invariably win out.

Given that the law of supply and demand and the price system were not allowed to work, the market for Alec's works was bound to be chaotic. To make things more difficult, the claim was being made that certain dealers were putting some of Alec's works away on the assumption that when market forces were allowed to have their full play, prices would rise dramatically. Whether that was true or not, prices did rise substantially after his incapacity and, later, his death. Sketches of the sort I bought two decades before for between sixty and one hundred dollars have been selling in the three-thousand-to-five-thousand-dollar range at commercial galleries, with even wider swings in prices at public auctions.

On April 8, 1970, a Jackson canvas painted in 1961 and measuring 25 by 32 inches and a 10½ by 13½ inch sketch done in 1950, both of fair quality, were sold by Sothebys at public auction for $4,600 and $3,400 respectively.[212] The canvas sold below and the sketch a little above the price a purchaser would have had to pay a regular art deal-er. At the same auction, one of Alec's drawings measuring 8⅜ by 10⅞ inches, done in 1939, and of good quality, sold for $580,[213] more than double the price these works fetched at the first commercial sale of drawings in Toronto in 1962.

Five and a half years later, the same auction house sold a 25 by 32 inch canvas painted in 1928, of very good quality, for $23,000.[214] It is one of the canvases Alec did after he returned from his first Arctic trip, and could probably have been brought from Alec in 1928 for $400. Allowing for inflation, the relative price would have been about $1,500 in 1975. The figures suggest an appreciation for high-quality work of about fifteen times the original price, after allowing for the effects of inflation, over a period of close to half a century.

But not all Jackson works fared as well. Another canvas of the same size, painted in 1945 and of fair quality, brought $10,000.[215] One of Alec's sketches in the standard size, done in 1960 and also of fair qual-ity, sold in 1975 for $2,600, less than a similar sketch had fetched in 1970.[216] At the same auction another sketch, probably done in 1946, of good quality, sold for $4,500, almost double the price of the first sketch.[217] Quality and buyer preference could make a great deal of difference in the auction price at which Alec's works were selling.

While Alec was still painting, selling of his works at public auctions was sporadic. The number of his paintings on the market after he became inactive increased substantially, as individuals were attracted by the higher prices to sell works from their collections either at public auction or to dealers. Alec did not think highly of public auctions, but they did not seem to bother him.

On several occasions we discussed his feelings about commercial art dealers and the galleries that handled his works. He was a little scepti-cal about them, in part because of his earliest experiences in Mont-real. After Alec had returned to Canada from France in 1910, he entrusted a Montreal dealer with a few of his paintings. The dealer sold some, but when Alec came to him to get his share of the money, he was told that expenses equalled proceeds. Alec wrote later: "It was a bitterly disappointing time." [218]

He said that in the twenties commercial art galleries would not touch his sketches and canvases. In the middle decades of his career, his main customer was the National Gallery of Canada, which became a significant buyer beginning in 1939. Alec paid particular tribute to two of its directors, Eric Brown and H. O. (Harry) McCur-ry.

Although there was a little more general interest in the thirties, those were hard days in Canada. Few people could afford to buy paintings. After the Second World War, as demand for Jackson's

205

works picked up noticeably, dealers became more interested in his paintings. He mentioned Blair Lang as the one dealer in Toronto who had appreciated his paintings long before he became so popular. Lang had shown great discernment and probably had the largest stock of Alec's early works. He appeared to be less interested in more current work. His stock was particularly helpful to people like myself who had not begun to collect Canadian art until after World War II and could not have known Alec when he was a young man. A few pieces in our collection came from this dealer, though the bulk of it, both early and recent works, came directly from Alec, with a few pieces coming from his sister Catherine.

Art dealers in Montreal constituted the main market for Alec's work. From the fifties on, they would buy anything Alec sent them. The purchase was a fairly safe bet because the dealers knew Alec's insistence on quality. He had destroyed many sketches, plus some canvases he considered not up to par. Hence, what Alec sent them was what he considered accceptable.

Because the dealers could not meet the popular clamour for Alec's works, they used various ploys to get Alec to sell them more paintings: letters, phone calls, telegrams, mailed cheques that constituted prepayment for works to be shipped later. (Alec was always nagged by a sense of moral obligation when he had accepted prepayment, as he frequently told me.)

Some dealers used a soft-sell approach; some were more aggressive. One dealer offered to buy all of Alec's production for the rest of his life and wanted to sign a binding contract to that effect. Alec was to be allowed to change his prices from time to time. "The sky is the limit," the dealer in question said, according to Alec.

But Alec was more susceptible to the soft sell, and he turned down the offer. "Money isn't everything," he remarked piously, adding, "I like my paintings to be across the country." By and large, he kept a healthy distance away from his dealers and continued to sell a fair number of works directly to individuals. On occasion, Alec also accepted commissions or agreed to paint a canvas based on one of his sketches supplied by owners.

I was among those to whom Alec sold direct. He wanted to help me build up a representative collection of his works, and we had an understanding that he would try to keep a sketch for me when he returned from most of his painting trips. If this was not possible, he would bring me a drawing or two. The fact that some buyers on occasion would resell his works did not deter Alec from selling directly. In fact, he liked doing it. It brought him together with people. Still, selling direct was often a mixed blessing. In his later years, three problems in particular plagued him: he was overwhelmed by people

206

wanting to buy his works; he was a poor bookkeeper; and he ran into trouble with the tax authorities.

Many people became increasingly anxious to buy paintings directly from Alec because the supply in the open market was so limited. Most of them were strangers he had never met and requests to buy his works took every form, including personal visits. These were sometimes irksome, though I do not recall any occasion when Alec really complained in earnest. He seemed to be amused most of the time.

Potential buyers would inquire about buying a sketch, and Alec would say that he had none for sale. Then they would ask when was he going on his next sketching trip and when would he be back? For a while, Alec answered such questions. But then he would find (and this applied to his Ottawa days) one or two persons sitting on the steps of 192 MacLaren Street on the day of his return. They would ask to buy a sketch and they usually got one. So Alec found it was safest to say that he wasn't sure.

People would sometimes drop by unannounced, and when Alec said he had no sketches left except the one from which he was currently painting a canvas, they would begin to poke around. Alec was somewhat careless about putting his sketches away, and usually when a caller found one, if it did not have a potential recipient's name on the back, he would let himself be persuaded to sell it to the "finder."

Eventually, in sheer self-defence, Alec became more sophisticated. I remember one occasion when he said that he could have sold the sketch he had kept for me five times over. "Where did you hide it this time?" I asked. He grinned and pointed under the bed. I bent down and pulled out what looked like an old suitcase. Inside, under some paraphernalia, was the sketch. Another good hiding place was Alec's high wardrobe, the top of which could only be reached if one stood on a chair.

Some prospective buyers asked Alec to put their names on a waiting list. He had no waiting list, he told them, but if the caller would be patient, he would try to remember him or her. Some of those who persisted might — two or three years later — get a sketch.

In a few instances, when visits to 192 MacLaren Street brought no result, persistent "searchers" would ask where Alec was going on his next sketching trip and where he was staying. They would drive out, sometimes making a journey of several hours to find him, wanting to buy one of his sketches, still wet. One person, not from Ottawa, who was an amateur painter and also a sub-dealer even arranged to go on painting trips with Alec. He did the driving and looked after the expenses; Alec rarely returned from these sketching trips with more than two or three sketches, though he might have painted a dozen or more.

What was so amazing about Alec was that he took all these little episodes with a grin and a wave of his hand, as if to say "It doesn't matter."

He liked to cook for himself and didn't mind washing dishes, looking after his laundry, and doing chores around his apartment and studio. But there were two things he considered a real bother — answering letters that concerned business, and bookkeeping.

He used a drawer (later a box) to keep invoices for art supplies, receipts for expenses connected with sketching trips, an occasional framing bill, statements and accounts with commercial galleries and trust companies, income tax notices, correspondence, and similar items. Not only did he not keep books, but he had no adequate count of the number of sketches and canvases he had painted the previous year. In a way, this was understandable because of his habit of destroying some paintings and giving away others. The number of paintings he sold therefore reflected neither the number of paintings he'd done nor the number remaining after the weeding-out process.

Dealers paid Alec by cheque; people who bought directly from him sometimes paid cash. He would put this money in his painting trousers and there it might stay for weeks. (He did not use a wallet. As far as I know, he did not own one.) When he finally took the money out of his painting trousers, he put it into his going-out pants without making note of amount or circumstances. He then used the cash for household items, art supplies, or sketching-trip expenses. More often than not, he failed to ask for receipts, so that his expenses connected with his painting work must have been significantly understated.

Cheques remained uncashed for months; some of them became stale-dated. From time to time, I would warn him about depositing the cheques when I saw them piling up. After urging him for several years to be more careful, I began to notice fewer of them accumulating, and I assumed that he had acquired more businesslike habits. I should have known better. After Alec moved to Kleinburg and his niece Naomi and Dr. Starrs were cleaning out his apartment-studio, they found tucked away in his books a number of cheques, some stale-dated, and twenty and one hundred dollar bills that he had put away for safekeeping and forgotten.

Once a year, as the date for filing an income tax return was nearing, Alec would take a box full of papers bearing on his last year's work to the trust company to have his return prepared. The trust company people questioned Alec a little, but they soon realized that they were on their own in preparing the return. How they did it, I will never know. Done it was, however, and Alec had peace for many years. He seemed to have found the perfect bookkeeping method — keeping no records — until he had visits from two tax inspectors, that is, one from the federal government, the other from the Ontario government.

One day when I had finished work a little early, I phoned him and asked whether I could drop in for a brief chat. He really preferred that I didn't come, he said; he was not in the mood to talk to anyone. If he were troubled, he might wish to talk it over with a friend — perhaps I could help him. He reluctantly agreed.

When I arrived at his studio he barely said hello to me. He sat in his living room mumbling, "Those damn ——, those damn ——," I couldn't quite make out what he was talking about. I'd never seen him so cross.

"*Who* are the damn so and sos?" I asked. He didn't reply but just kept mumbling, so I sat in my favourite rocking chair and waited quietly. Suddenly, he looked up and said sheepishly, "I had a visit today from the tax inspector, the federal one." And then the story came out.

He had received a phone call from someone in the Department of National Revenue (Income Tax), asking whether he could see him. The gentleman was very polite and said that it was just a routine inquiry. He had been to the trust company, and their people had shown him the receipts and financial documentation. He had asked to see Alec's books and they had referred him to "the taxpayer." Alec told the investigator that he had no special account books, and explained how he accumulated the papers relating to income and expenditures and then turned them over to the trust company once a year. The official then asked Alec how he could be sure that all his income had been declared and all allowable expenses had been deducted. Alec admitted that the figures were approximate, whereupon the investigator asked how many paintings Alec had done annually during the last few years, what prices he received for each painting, who his major buyers were, and other relevant questions. Alec's answers must have been somewhat disconcerting to the precision-oriented official, for he concluded with a (friendly) lecture on the duty each taxpayer had to make *full* disclosures. To do that, Alec should be keeping books, he cautioned. Alec said he'd replied that he was getting on in years and that keeping books would take time away from painting, which he considered his main aim in life.

The official was evidently rather sympathetic, seeing Alec's sincerity and the consternation his visit had aroused. He left, saying that the matter would be looked into, and if Alec heard no more about it, he should consider the inquiry completed. I suggested to Alec that the trust company could keep his books for him, but I don't think he took me seriously. Alec just didn't like figures.*

---

*Alec said of himself that when he attended Prince Albert Public School in Montreal (until he was twelve), "except for mathematics, I was one of the outstanding pupils there." [219]

As Alec accompanied me to the door I heard him mutter, "Those damn bureaucrats." That was the word I hadn't been able to hear when I arrived.

As I was driving home, I was thinking about the conversation. I knew that Alec had a phobia about bureaucrats. He thought they were individuals who had nothing better to do than meddle in other people's affairs. Several times he had remarked that from his reading of the newspapers he found the world getting worse, not better. I concluded that Alec's experience that day must have convinced him more than ever of the gulf that existed between "them," the bureaucrats and the politicians they served, and "us," the little people.

Everything was quiet for a while, but then Alec's income tax difficulties increased. George Loranger, who at that time was working at the Dresdnere Gallery in Toronto, persuaded Alec to make fifty of his pencil or pen-and-ink drawings available to the gallery for exhibition and sale. This was done; the drawings were matted and nicely framed, and they went on sale in 1962 priced at between $200 and $250 each, two to three times the price that Alec was then charging for his oil sketches. The exhibition was a sell-out.*

Alec could not believe that people would pay such prices for mere "notes." On one occasion after this exhibition, Alec remarked, "I guess you were right when you said to me that my works were seriously underpriced."

"Will you change your prices?" I asked him.

"No," he replied. "Why should I?" This remark confirmed what I already knew about Alec's attitudes: painting came first. Money was useful, but the amounts did not matter as long as the necessities of life and work were covered and some was left over for what he called his "old age."

Well, the amounts *did* matter to the income tax people, and in due course Alec received a supplementary assessment on the money earned from the Dresdnere Gallery sales. The Canada Permanent Trust Company, which handled Alec's financial affairs, suggested that he set out in a memorandum the background that led to the sale. This upset Alec again. When he called me about it, I went to see him. With a little help, he composed a memorandum. He asked me to have it typed, and a few days later he took the typed copy to the trust company. The information was passed on to the Department of National Revenue, but the income tax people stuck to their assessment. Although the trust company suggested an appeal to the Income Tax Appeal Board, Alec had had enough aggravation and he paid up.

---

*In 1964 there was a second exhibition and sale, this time of forty drawings with prices of three hundred dollars and up at the same gallery, again a sell-out.

Incidentally, the Department of National Revenue showed the respect it had for Alec by addressing him in their correspondence as "Doctor A. Y. Jackson" (referring to his honorary degree). I know a number of Ph.D.s whom the Department of National Revenue has never addressed as "Doctor."

Alec had a visit from another tax inspector, this time from the Ontario Department of Revenue, who was concerned with collection of sales tax. That visit was quite disconcerting for Alec, though it was a less traumatic experience than the visit from the federal income tax official. The Ontario government had introduced a sales tax of 3 per cent effective September 1, 1961. Several months passed, and I had no opportunity of discussing with Alec the applicability of the sales tax provisions to what he was doing because we were busy planning his eightieth birthday party.

Early in 1962, when I saw Alec alone in his studio, I brought the matter up. No sales tax was payable if Alec sold his paintings to a commercial gallery, because the gallery would charge the sales tax to the buyer of the painting and then remit it to the government. But according to the law, when Alec sold paintings directly, he was required to collect sales tax, fill out forms, and remit the tax payable to the Ontario Department of Revenue. Alec said that one of the dealers had explained this to him previously, but he would *not* give up selling directly, he would *not* collect sales tax, and he would *not* fill out any damn government forms.

He got rather annoyed — I do not know whether with the government or with me — when I mentioned that anyone selling items subject to sales tax was considered to be an agent acting for the Crown in collecting the tax at the time of the sale. He was not going to be any damn Crown agent, he retorted, raising his voice (a rare happening). When I pointed out that the Ontario Department of Revenue would sooner or later come after him and that he would be required to have a vendor's licence, he just shrugged his shoulders.

After that discussion, I added the sales tax to any purchase I made; Alec accepted it with great reluctance. The only point he found difficult to oppose was my statement, "It is the law." This is not to suggest that Alec was not a great respecter of the law. Far from it. He was meticulously honest and genuinely honourable. But he believed, as Dickens said in *Oliver Twist*, and I am paraphrasing, the law can also be a ass.

Although one would think that after the years of poverty money would have begun to be really important to Alec, on the whole it never was. He could, however, be annoyed when he thought he had been overcharged for something. But people were much more likely to

211

hear him say that painting was fun and he shouldn't be paid for it.[220]

In due course, Alec had a visit from an inspector asking for his records — sales receipts, sales tax charged — and vendor's licence. Alec could not provide all the documents or satisfactory answers, and as a result he received an assesment for sales tax on the basis of "assumed" sales. The government continued to use this system. When I asked Alec how he felt about it, he said that he was nearly annoyed enough to give his paintings away, considering all the bother he had with the government.

Alec's priorities were painting, first; then family, friends, and people generally; third, travelling, seeing all parts of Canada, and having that feeling of being close to the land; and finally, chores — all the mundane things necessary to everyday living. Among chores, bookkeeping and looking after tax matters were at the lowest level. It was a very individualistic philosophy of life.

I occasionally tried to soften Alec's critical attitudes toward politicians and bureaucrats. Once I paraphrased Churchill's dictum that a democratic government is really a highly unsatisfactory type of government but all other forms are worse. To this, Alec replied, "But does it have to be *that* bad?"

CHAPTER 18
The Eighty-fifth Birthday Party

Alec was going to be eighty-five on the third of October in 1967, Canada's centennial year, the year of Expo '67 in Montreal. He was in a mood to celebrate.

Although his body was no longer as strong as his fun-loving spirit (for age was beginning to take its toll), he was all in favour of having a birthday party at our house if it were held early enough in the year. He was to have another birthday party in Toronto in the fall.

Alec wanted a date in May before he went on his sketching trips, as we had done for his eightieth birthday party. He mentioned Saturday, May 27, and offered to draw up the guest list.

Alec's list for an early-evening buffet supper included about forty family and friends. He was disappointed at the response: about a quarter could not come. Two artists to whom Alec felt particularly close, A. J. Casson and Charles Comfort, had other commitments on that date. Dr. Starrs and Dr. Jeffries and their wives were going to be out of town. Robert and Signe McMichael, with whom Alec had become friends in the meantime, also sent their regrets.

Still, there were half a dozen members of Alec's immediate family and a good number of friends who could come. They helped Alec realize how many people genuinely cared for him. Painter friends, and their wives, at the party were André Biéler, Henri Masson, Ralph Burton, and Maurice Haycock. Hubert Rogers, the portrait painter who'd bought Alec's Manotick studio-house, also came.

Alec was particularly keen to have his good friend Betty Kirk from Buckingham, Quebec, present. He also asked to have the Putnams, who had been so kind to him when he was painting in the Grenville area, invited. Isobel and I invited some other friends as well, so that about fifty people came to pay tribute to Alec on this occasion — a milestone in his productive career as an artist and a turning-point in the full life he had led. We could not know then that this was the last birthday we would celebrate with Alec with him in full possession of his physical and mental faculties.

I consulted Alec about the two main speakers at the birthday party, and he concurred in the choice of André Biéler and Dr. William Dale.

213

He also agreed that we should tape the proceedings of the party, including his reply, as we had done on his eighty-third birthday.

André Biéler was fourteen years younger than Alec. Born in Switzerland in 1896, he came to Canada at the age of twelve and, like Alec, he enlisted in 1915 and was wounded in 1916. After the war he studied art in the United States, Switzerland, and Paris. When the Group of Seven was holding its first exhibition in 1920, Biéler was studying at the Department of Fine Arts of Stetson University in De Land, Florida, and attending the Art Students' League at Woodstock, New York. Returning to Canada in 1926, greatly enriched by his study and learning experiences in Europe and very much inspired by the work of Paul Cézanne, Biéler settled on the Ile d'Orléans in the lower St. Lawrence region. In 1930, he moved to Montreal, where he continued to paint as a member of that loose circle of friends known as the Beaver Hall Hill Group. In 1936 he commenced teaching art at Queen's University in Kingston, Ontario, becoming the head of the Fine Arts department and director of the Agnes Etherington Art Centre, two positions he held until 1963, when he retired as professor emeritus and resumed painting on a full-time basis.* Biéler's works have been shown in major exhibitions in Canada and in many cities abroad, including Paris, London, Warsaw, New York, Chicago, San Francisco, and Rio de Janeiro. They can be found in the collections of most of Canada's public galleries.

As fine an artist and art teacher as Biéler was, one of his greatest contributions was his concern for the loneliness of artists in Canada and his energetic efforts to rouse them from lethargy to rally to a common cause. Biéler was the source of inspiration for and an energetic organizer of the Queen's University Conference of Canadian Artists in 1941, later called the Kingston Conference.**

Biéler had a lot in common with Alec. Both had started professionally by painting the Quebec landscape, the small villages, the churches, the barns, the fields, the rivers. Biéler then branched out

---

*In the same year, the Agnes Etherington Art Centre mounted a Biéler retrospective exhibition showing 115 of his works including, for the first time, seven of his sculptures. (In 1970, the same gallery organized a fifty-year retrospective comprising sixty-five of Biéler's works and circulated it to Charlottetown, Montreal, Windsor, London, Hamilton, St. Catharines, Kingston, Oshawa, Stratford, and Winnipeg.)

**This was an important event, "the first chance for many artists to meet each other, to discuss the position of the artist in society, and to talk about their methods of expression and technique in workshop sessions. As Robert Ayre has written, '[the] ideas and energies generated on the campus of Queen's culminated in the Canadian Arts Council, the Brief Concerning the Cultural Aspects of Canadian Reconstruction, presented to the House of Commons Special Committee on Reconstruction and Re-Establishment in 1944, the Royal Commission on National Development in the Arts, Letters and Sciences (the Massey Commission) and the Canada Council.' Biéler himself became the first National President of the Federation of Canadian Artists, a new organization which grew directly out of the Conference."[221]

into figurative, genre, and mural painting, experimenting also in a semi-abstract and abstract vein. Gradually the Cézanne influence passed, and Biéler turned to painting in bold and vivid colours employed with great subtlety. It was more like the approach of Van Gogh, for whom he, like Alec, had great admiration. In his later years, Biéler returned to painting the Quebec landscape, and we have one of his works of that period, *Procession, Ste-Famille, Ile d'Orleans* (1970), both the original watercolour sketch and his oil painting.[222]

Biéler, who had known Alec since the twenties and saw him frequently on his trips to Montreal, joined the Canadian Group of Painters (of which Alec was a founding member) in 1933. They were good friends and liked to tease each other, and both enjoyed reminiscing and telling stories. Also like Alec, he would sometimes wander off the track when unfolding what he thought was an amusing tale. In the end, he would either forget what he was driving at or take a great amount of time in coming to the intended point.

They differed in painting style, brush work, and willingness to venture into new forms of expression.[223] Biéler was closely identified in his work with people, and it gave him real pleasure to be painting the human figure,[224] either alone or as part of a farm, market, or church scene.[225] He married his charming wife, Jeannette, in 1931, and Alec was very fond of her. Biéler was expected to offer some comments at the birthday party on Alec as a fellow artist.

The second speaker, Dr. William S. A. Dale, would look at Alec's contribution from the perspective of the Canadian art scene. Dale, born in 1921, an art historian with a Ph.D. from Harvard University, was the deputy director and, at the time of Alec's birthday party, the acting director of the National Gallery of Canada in the period between the departure of Charles Comfort and the arrival of Jean Boggs. He and his wife, Jane, had been married in 1952. He had started his professional career as a curator at the National Gallery of Canada, moving later to the Art Gallery of Toronto as a curator and the Vancouver Art Gallery as director, and returning to the National Gallery of Canada as assistant director in 1961.

Dr. Dale had lectured in art history at Carleton University and had written many articles for art journals. Shortly after Alec's eighty-fifth birthday party, he left the National Gallery of Canada to become chairman of the Fine Arts Department at the University of Western Ontario. Realizing that the resources available at the university were limited, he undertook as one of his objectives to build up a "teaching collection," including good works by minor artists of various periods. These teaching aids would help students acquire an understanding of the techniques and styles pursued at different times and in different regions.

When I reported to Alec what kind of comments he could expect from the two speakers, he replied, "Both could say that my work is 'old hat,' but then, André Biéler and I like old hats — and Bill Dale can find a place for *this* old hat in his art history." It would be hard to imagine a greater contrast between two speakers, one a warm and emotional humanist, and the other a careful and precise scholar; one almost effortlessly being beautifully subjective and the other, having done his homework, determined to be meaningfully objective by understating the case.

Although not as vigorous in health and firm in stride as he had been at earlier birthday parties, Alec arrived in high spirits. He had brought Isobel a corsage, which he tendered her with élan and affection. With a shy smile he said, "To my gracious hostess," and was warmly embraced.

By 7:30 most guests had arrived, and there was a lot of happy banter, reminiscing, and some poking of fun at Alec, which he took in good part, though responding more slowly than he ususally did. After drinks, dinner, and wine, with the cutting of the birthday cake and champagne still to come, several of the ladies assembled around the piano with my wife playing. She had adapted the words of the song "Hello, Dolly" to "Hello, Alec, well hello, Alec/It's so nice to have you back where you belong..." After leading a chorus of the song, on behalf of all assembled she wished Alec a very happy birthday, adding, "I just adore you." Alec, whose complexion was quite pink by that time, promptly turned red. He thanked her warmly with a smile.

Before introducing the speakers, I mentioned all the letters and telegrams Alec had received on this "pre-run," the first instalment of his birthday celebrations. I also informed our guests that our Jackson Room had been expanded from an exhibition of Alec's paintings to a small Jackson museum through the addition of various memorabilia — including those well-worn snowshoes, his discarded painting hat, and his old sketch box. There were also numerous photographs of Alec, along with books and publications, and his original design of a Canadian flag — items that added to Alec the painter another dimension: Alec, the man. Isobel interjected that she had asked our younger son, Peter, then ten years old, what he like best in the Jackson Room, and Peter had replied, "The old hat." To this I added that our son was in good company because the hat was Alec's favourite item too.

Following a brief introduction, seventy-one-year-old André Biéler rose with great agility to take the floor. He gripped the microphone of the tape recorder with a firm hand and looked at the expectant faces of his audience with an impish smile. His notes, written on cards, seemed to get mixed up and he started to improvise. This, in part, may account for some of the digressions and the length of his talk.

He had made some inquiries about life in Montreal in the early 1880s, had dug up Alec's birth announcement from the Montreal *Witness*, and animatedly offered comments about customs, fashions, the arts, economics, and international conditions prevailing at that time. The point was, apparently, that Alec was the product of a generation barely out of the woods; to me, the implication was that it was a miracle that Alec had turned out as he had — a great painter, handicaps and hindrances notwithstanding.

Biéler finished with a tribute to the "very distinguished style of painting" Alec achieved early in his career. Alec had not been one of those who took hints from the Barbizon school of painting, modifying them "to a little degree to our own environment." Instead he had effectively "interpreted the mood of our landscape, no matter what the latitude." His inspiration had always been renewed by nature rather than by schools or art movements. Concluding his speech in French, Biéler referred to Alec as the painter who, more than anyone else, had attempted to portray the true spirit of Quebec, painting its spring landscape with vivid colours and bold brush strokes.

William Dale, looking ten years younger than his age, then rose to speak. His face was serious with only an occasional suggestion of a smile; his delivery was precise and eloquent. He spoke from notes, which he checked intermittently.

My first contact with A. Y. was that of an art-historian-in-training. I was an undergraduate at the University of Toronto. Doctor Comfort, in the course of his duties as an instructor in studio work in the Fine Arts course, took his students, myself included, to the Studio Building, that famous landmark in the history of art. There we visited the studio of A. Y. And there he was, himself, the real fellow. Now this was quite a thrill in those days, in 1940, a long way back for me. But as time went on, I made a strange discovery about the history of Canadian art and particularly about A. Y. — and that is that time does not seem to make a great deal of difference.

This evening, I would like to say something about the history of Canadian art and how I see Alex Jackson fitting into it.... When we are talking about Canadian art, we are talking about three hundred years, as will become apparent when the National Gallery of Canada opens its exhibit, *A Pageant of Canada*, next fall. That is not a great deal, particularly when one remembers that A. Y. Jackson himself can account for at least a quarter of that period....

The reflections of European styles persisted in Canada until the end of the nineteenth century. Early in the twentieth century there was a searching for something different. But the first really national style emerged only with the Group of Seven.

[Recently,] I was reading a letter . . . written to a Mrs. Bowman in Edmonton, in 1933, at the time when the Canadian Group of Painters had been formed and had its first exhibition. It was written by A. Y. In the letter, he reviewed the achievements of the Group of Seven, and he did it justly and in a balanced way, without trying to pretend that they achieved more than they did. At the same time, in the particularly generous vein which is so very characteristic of Alec, he wrote: Younger people are coming along and we have to be fair to them. They are going to push us off the stage. But we have got to look at their work and accept it, just as our work has had to be accepted in time.

It is my belief that the successors of A. Y. and the Group of Seven have had a much easier road to follow. They have not had the battle with the critics — and perhaps this has been their undoing. Perhaps they have had too much encouragement, too much promotion on the part of their dealers. Time alone will tell. That generosity of A. Y., as far back as 1933, was characteristic of him. It is still characteristic of the man today. . . .

I think if one is talking about Canadian art in art history (perhaps it is true of all art history), we have to update our approach. We are no longer concerned with narrating a sequence of events, one after the other. History, and particularly the history of art, because of the eternal presence of the works of art themselves, is much more something which is renewing itself all the time. . . . There are cycles in taste. Unfortunately, our public galleries are the victims of those cycles of taste. Perhaps art historians must begin to think in terms of permanent values. Permanent problems or questions come up in art during all ages. What really separates us from the art of the cave man or from fifteenth-century Florence? Not very much, really — not as much as historians would like to pretend, because the human quality is what survives.

Now Alex Jackson, in the history of Canadian art, what is he? He is not simply an event at one time. We have the living man here with us, and yet fifty years ago that man was alive too, and he was taking part in what was happening in the Canadian art scene. It is not simply a matter of survival, although we are very happy that Alex is with us today. It is because the works themselves survive. They carry on the spirit, the human spirit of the painter who created them.

218

I think it is very appropriate that we should be celebrating A. Y.'s birthday in the spring, because his art, like the man himself, is ever young and ever green. If I were to chose a symbol for A. Y. today, I think it would be the pine tree. A. Y., we salute you.

Alec used the occasion of his reply to review the first thirty-eight year of his life. He spoke for about forty minutes, saying that he could not talk about his whole life because "that would take a long time, and probably put you all to sleep."

He described what made him become a painter, and induced him to paint the way he did, by answers to six questions. Selections from Alec's remarks, taken from the tape, provide a sense of Alec's informal yet crisp style of speaking. Alec had already mentioned some of the events in *A Painter's Country*, such as the move from Montreal to Toronto, but I have included some of them because Alec considered them milestones in his life. There are also some minor discrepancies in wording between what he said at the party and his remarks on other occasions, which I have noted.

When had he first thought of becoming an artist? It was when he was working at Bishop Engraving as an office boy. "I was always fond of drawing, but not always intelligent drawing. I used to make copies of Henri Julien's drawings in the *Montreal Star*. I used to make hand drawings; that was before the photoengraving. All the drawings had to be drawn with pen in order to be able to reproduce them. I used to copy these things when I wasn't running messages, and one day the boss saw me and liked my drawings, so I moved to the art department.

"Well, the art department, the last thing about it was art. I was making labels, beer labels; we used to make labels for corn meal and barrel labels. I had several years of that kind of thing. The only thing to relieve [the monotony] was my boss, the chap who worked with me, a chap named Arthur Nantel.* He was a French-Canadian, a most remarkable person. He had no education and had a salary of $15 a week; [he was] one of the best-read men I have ever run across. He used to go up to the Fraser Institute [a Montreal library] to get books. He used to read philosophy; he used to read biography and history — a most amazing chap. He got me in the way of reading. I started reading books on art and on all kinds of things. I waded through Ruskin's *Modern Painters*, and that was the first beginning of when I ever thought of being an artist."

---

*Alec used the word "boss" sometimes to refer to Nantel, sometimes to the manager of the company. For example, "The boss, seeing these drawings one day, decided to put me in the art department where I became assistant to Arthur Nantel, a most fortunate arrangement for me."[226]

When had he first thought of giving up commercial art and becoming a professional artist? Alec seems to have made up his mind to become a full-time painter after returning to Montreal from his visit to England, France, and Holland with his brother Harry, in 1905. "We went over to the Continent and met some of the artists there. Clarence Gagnon was there, and Eddie Boyd. We went to all the museums. We got as far as Rotterdam. It began to widen my range of experience. After I got back, well, then I began to think about not doing any more of this commercial stuff."

When and where did he spend the happiest days of his life? "Nineteen-seven, that was the year that I went to Europe to study. And I went to Julian's. I didn't know much, but it was a school where they had students from all over the world. There were Russians and Germans and Italians and South Americans and Japanese and all kinds of people. The training wasn't anything very much, but it was worthwhile watching the other students work, and the standard was very high, too. Well, anyway [that was what] I went to Julian's for. I worked all day long for six months. I began to learn something about drawing, anyway.

"At that time, France was a wonderful place, 1907. You never thought about war; people were friendly. I don't think I was ever cheated out of a franc all the time I was over there. I think that [those were] perhaps the happiest days of my life, when I was a student over in France."

When did he start to paint in the style of the French impressionists, and who among them influenced him most? "I came back home. I needed some more money. . . . The only way you could get it — there weren't any scholarships then — [was to come] back to Montreal. First I went out to the Eastern Townships, and I did a little bit of painting to try out what I had learned over in France. I painted a canvas which is known as *The Edge of the Maple Wood*. Then I went back and did commercial work for the rest of the year and saved up enough money and went back to France again. I stayed over in Europe for another two years.

"I came back in 1913. That was another memorable year, because when I got back to Montreal, I found out that my pictures were not selling. Of course, I was very much interested in the French impressionists, particularly Sisley and Pissarro, and I guess my work kind of resembled theirs. In Montreal they had no use for French impressionsits, and they used to describe Cézanne as a *farceur* and that kind of thing. . . . When I came back I found that I couldn't make a living there. Nobody wanted my work. I was a French impressionist, and that finished me."*

---

*In 1954, Alec wrote that he was very much impressed with the work of Claude

220

When and how did he change from being a Quebec painter to become a Canadian painter? It was 1913, and, Alec said: "I had hanging over me this feeling of giving it all up and going over to the States. [Eddie] Boyd and [William] Clapp and [Fred] Hutchison had all gone off to the States.... I [was about] to do the same thing [when] I got a letter from a chap named MacDonald, and he said 'Have you still got a painting that you painted about three years ago called *The Edge of the Maple Wood*?' It had gone up to Toronto after I had gone back to Europe. So he said, 'If you have it, there is a young artist by the name of Lawren Harris who would like to buy it.' I wrote back and told him I had everything I had ever painted, and so I still had it. He said to send it down. Well, it was through that that I decided that I would go and see these people, anyway, who wanted to meet me. So 1913 was another very definite date in my career....

"[In the summer of 1913] I got to Georgian Bay. That was amazing country.... I always felt it was a place that the *bon dieu* had made when he was on a holiday, just for fun....

"One day a motorboat came in, just nosed up on the sand beach, and a chap got out and introduced himself as Dr. MacCallum. I had heard of him. He wanted to see my work. Well, I showed him some of the things I had been doing. He like them. We had quite a chat.... Then he said, 'What are you going to do when you leave here?' So I said that I would probably go down to the States, the way all the young Canadians were doing.

" 'Well,' he said, 'Canadian art is never going to get anywhere if you young fellows all go off to the States. We've got to have our young fellows here who love their own country and who paint it. Lawren Harris and I are putting up a studio building,' he said, 'of about six studios, and you take one of those studios and I'll guarantee your expenses for a year.'

"Well, I pretty near fell out of the boat being so excited.... I got down to Toronto all right.

"I met all the boys, and a lot of excitement. They wanted to see my work. Then one day, Dr. MacCallum arrived with a nice-looking

Monet and Camille Pissarro after browsing through the Chicago Art Gallery in 1906. "It was the first time I had been able to study the French impressionists at leisure — the school led by Monet and Pissarro. They influenced me deeply and for the first time I saw what could be done with landscape."[227] It might be appropriate to note that Camille Pissarro, whom Alec admired greatly, was mainly a landscape painter, though he also painted some exquisite still lifes and a few portraits. He insisted on going on sketching trips each year to vary his subjects. He has been described as a man of great humility, wisdom, kindness, profound interest in others, homespun human philosophy, and unselfishness. The question arises whether Alec was influenced not only by Pissarro's painting style, which he readily acknowledged, but also by his personal traits. The similarities are so striking as to make it difficult to attribute them all to coincidence.

chap. We were all very much taken with him, and he introduced him as Tom Thomson.... MacCallum was trying to persuade him to chuck his commercial art. He was a commercial artist, too. Just become a painter. He said he'd guarantee [Thomson's] expenses for a year if [he'd] chuck [his] commercial art altogether. So he persuaded [Thomson] to chuck his commercial art, and we took a studio together in this new building.... That was the end of 1913, [and] that [is] another date that is in my mind."

When and how was he told that the Group of Seven had been "formed" and that he was a member? It was February, 1920. "I thought I'd go up to Georgian Bay in the wintertime. I'd been there in the summer, of course, but never in the wintertime. So I went up to Penetang. I had my snowshoes with me [and] I stayed there for two and a half months.... I did a whole lot of interesting things as the ice was going out... Eventually the ice went out, and I got back to Toronto. First thing they told me when I got back to Toronto was that we'd formed the Group of Seven and 'you're one of them.' "*

At this point, Alec, who had been quite lucid all through his talk, showed signs of being very tired. When he reached the year 1920, having covered the first two-fifths of his life span, he observed that so many things had happened since then that it was difficult for him to remember all the events, where they occurred and when. He ended with the words, "Anyway, I can't sort them all out, so I won't try. Goodbye."

Everyone was astounded by Alec's *tour de force*. Allister Grosart rose spontaneously to comment on Alec's "fantastic, detailed memory of these great events in our cultural history," and it was several minutes before all the congratulatory noises subsided.

Alec looked absolutely drained from the effort; we had expected some brief comments, not a detailed speech. I took him away from the crowd, and we spent a short period alone in my study. Seeing how worn out he was, I asked him whether he would like to stay with us overnight. He said he preferred to go back to his apartment.

Since none of the guests showed any sign of leaving even as it neared midnight, I asked Kay Ryan, who had her car and driver waiting for her, whether she could take Alec home while Isobel and I stayed with our guests. She agreed, and Alec was willing. I asked her to be good enough to accompany Alec up the four steps to the door of his apartment. I was concerned that he might stumble in his fatigued

---

*The phrase "Group of Seven" was used before Alec's return to Toronto by Lismer when he wrote about the forthcoming exhibition demonstrating "the 'spirit' of painting in Canada." He stressed the common link among its members: " 'Group of Seven' is the idea."[228]

condition, and when I saw Kay later on she mentioned that Alec had leaned very heavily against her as they climbed the steps up to the porch.

Alec had left quietly, and few people noticed his departure. The party went on until after one o'clock. I reflected sadly on human nature: here we had met to honour a great Canadian artist — he gave us his best, but it was soon forgotten. His departure was hardly noticed.

Would he be remembered after he passed away? And if so, will it be because of his painting, because of the great human being he was, or the combination? As time goes on, his paintings live, but Alec the man drifts into the shadows of history. The process of forgetting the man is already underway. The building at 192 MacLaren Street where Alec painted between 1962 and 1968 has already been torn down. Will that also be the fate of his former studio-house in Manotick — or will it be possible to preserve it as a heritage house and as a Jackson museum?

CHAPTER 19
A.Y. — The Man

Alec was a perfectionist when it came to his painting; in his personal life his attitudes were more pragmatic. He felt deeply and keenly about certain things and certain issues, but his way of expressing his feelings was usually in a minor key, moderate in language and apt to play down the point he was trying to make. When on occasion Alec was emphatic, it meant roused feelings.

He was rarely angry, but he was likely to get quite worked up when fundamental issues were involved. It stemmed from his innate integrity and high moral values. He was proud of his country and he loved nature. He was generous with his time in helping younger artists, and he was happy to see his paintings available to the public from Atlantic to Pacific. He did not feel that people were taking advantage of him when in his later years they came to him directly to buy works at prices considerably below market value. He liked being with people; he was gregarious and outgoing. He responded warmly to most of those who sought his company, to the young and the old. Even in his advanced years, Alec was young at heart and remarkably energetic, capable of outdoing people thirty years his junior in outdoor activities.

When he heard complimentary things being said about him, Alec sometimes blushed, embarrassed. He could take justified criticism in his stride. It was not that he didn't care what people said to him or about him — he did — but his positive outlook let him concentrate on what he considered essential. He did not let other things bother him much.

A comment, on his eighty-third birthday, succinctly captures his sense of values: "Life is a great big joke, I think ... I don't seem to be able to be miserable." Not taking oneself too seriously, he implied, wards off a lot of self-caused misery.

Alec was a master at self-deprecation, and frequently indulged. Over the years it became a distinct characteristic of his personality. Most people described this as innate modesty, but I believe it went deeper. He had a strong personality, and he knew what he wanted. He'd learned over the years that he could realize his objectives, the things he considered to be really important, with less wear and tear, if he used a soft approach rather than wilful assertions.

He was a self-reliant man who preferred to look after himself, though he was not averse on his last sketching trips to having others do chores for him or drive him to painting sites. Nor did he object to others helping him in such mundane matters as cleaning up his place, moving from one locality to another, or arranging parties at his studio.

Alec was not a particularly religious person, but in his later years it made him feel good to be among people on Sunday morning. When he was at Kleinburg there was a young nurse whom he liked, and she took him to Sunday Mass.

He strove singlemindedly for excellence in his art. When he was not satisfied with a canvas, he worked on it, even if it took him many months, until he felt that it was "right." If the canvas refused to meet his standards, he would destroy it. If he considered his sketch panels unsatisfactory, he scraped off the paint and used the panels again. Sometimes he just painted on the other side of the panel and put an X through the original painting. He did the same with his drawings (or artist's notes): he destroyed many of these or simply put an X over them.

Alec was a landscape painter all his life. He endorsed progress in styles and forms of art, and he supported abstract art even though he did not practise it himself. What mattered was that the quality be high.

I heard a number of art critics observe that Alec's paintings grew progressively weaker as he moved into his seventies and his eighties. Alec did not quite agree; he felt that when circumstances were right, his sketches continued to be strong and his canvases were as carefully planned and meticulously executed as ever. He commented to me on this criticism several times and spelled out his thoughts in an interview given to I. Norman Smith. When Smith asked Alec whether he had become "a better painter" with advancing age or whether he felt he had lowered his standards, Alec replied: "No, I hope not. No, I think it is just that I've learned a little. I have a surer guess as to what is going to make a picture."[229]

Alec was always regarded as an independent painter, strong in his convictions about what was good art and what was not. As a rule, he painted only what he wanted to paint, though there were exceptions. He had many arguments with his critics in the earlier days, and he seemed to enjoy joining battle with letters to newspapers or an ornery remark or two when he was making a speech.

On the other hand, Alec listened gladly to constructive criticism from his painter friends, and sometimes he even took account of what the public said about his work. When his Quebec winter scenes began to be popular in the thirties and people expected to find certain motifs in them, they got what they wanted. Alec wrote from St-Urbain, Quebec, in early 1933: "At twenty-five sketches, the halfway mark, I will let up a little. I am putting little red sleighs in most of them as a concession to public demand." Then he added, as if embarrassed by making this concession: "I really should put dog sleighs in as that is the chief means of locomotion here."[230]

In all the years I knew Alec, I never saw him seriously distressed. He mourned when some dear friend passed away; he was sympathetic when other people faced illness, marital problems, financial difficulties, or that professional death of most painters, neglect and indifference; but I never heard him utter the word "depressed."

A number of artists I knew had gone through periods of depression because wives or husbands, sweethearts, art critics, art galleries, or art dealers had created emotional shock. I wondered what made Alec's outlook so positive that he went through life unwaveringly and apparently unperturbed by stressful circumstances that he, like anyone else, must have faced. Many of the stories Alec told show that he had had difficulties and hardships, but he seemed to be able to take adversity — and good fortune when it finally came — in his stride.

Once, when I was alone with Alec, I asked him about this. "I don't have the pressures some other people have," he replied, "a wife, a family. Nor do I care much about money, as some others do. And then, it is also a matter of attitude. I don't let little things bother me. If people stopped to think, they would realize that there are so many things in life that are not worth fretting about. I can get angry when I think something is important — a matter of principle, a question of morality — but, as a rule, I stick to things I know best, and I try not to get involved in matters that don't mean much to me."

Alec clearly had confidence in himself and in his own judgement as to what was important and what was not. It contributed to his inner strength. He did not avoid confrontation about the important things; indeed, he would rise to the occasion like a young warrior in his early days and like an elder statesman in his later years. He could argue with family and friends alike. He could throw down the gauntlet before politicians, the media, and all kinds of people connected with the art world. But in the end, arguments were quickly forgotten. He was not the man to bear a grudge for any length of time.

There were some people with whom he had little patience: politicians, who he felt could not be trusted; tax-gatherers, whom he considered to be bureaucratic meddlers and fusspots who did not treat people with the dignity they deserved (though he recognized that taxes had to be paid); art critics, some of whom in his opinion did not know what they were talking about; gallery officials who were pompous and more concerned with their own importance than with Canadian art; and people who asked what he considered stupid questions. Most of the time, though, Alec was able to take all these things in his stride.

He could also be very considerate. For example, when Lawren Harris's son, Lawren P. Harris, visited the studio in Manotick, Alec pointed to a big chest of drawers and said, "This is your dad's. I got it from him. When I'm gone, I'll leave it to you." Two decades later, after Alec's death, the younger Harris was notified by the trust company looking after the Jackson estate that Alec had left him the chest of drawers, which they would ship to his home in Sackville, N.B.*

I have talked earlier about Alec's liking for parties. During the period we knew him, whenever he attended a party he was the centre of attention. He responded freely by telling stories or amusing yarns, usually about what he had done in the distant past rather than the previous week or month. As his memory began to dim, it became easier to remember what happened years back than events more recent.

He was a great storyteller, and had a bank of stories to tell (anyone who has read his *A Painter's Country* will be acquainted with his style). Until his serious illness in April 1968, he had rarely been sick. He had led an active life as an artist, as a traveller, as a student of human nature, as a lover of his country, and as a homespun philosopher. He had a lot to say, and he said what he had to say with skill, sincerity, and with humour. He had his own style, with many Jacksonian phrases that another person might have had trouble coining, but that flowed from his lips easily. His chuckle added colour to his storytelling, and it would fill in some of the breaks when he paused. Alec's manner of speaking was spontaneous, and there was nothing stilted about it — so much so that he sometimes gave the impression he was talking off the top of his head — but this did little to detract from the point he was trying to make.

In his seventies and even more in his eighties, however, Alec's storytelling ran into difficulties. He had trouble remembering dates and figures. He once said, "I get the years all mixed up; if you can get within ten years, this is all right." He became increasingly long-winded, straying from the subject and at times unable to remember the point he was trying to make.

In the years I knew Alec, people enjoyed listening to his stories both because he was a Canadian artist of great repute — an elder states-

---

*Alec's niece Naomi subsequently offered to trade the chest of drawers for a framed drawing by Alec. Lawren Harris accepted, and the chest remained with the Jackson family.

man of the art world — and because of the way he told them. He was not without some criticism, however. It was noted that he was relying more on storytelling than on engaging people in two-way conversations. In part, this was a result of his deafness, which grew worse in later years. It also had someting to do with his sense of values. Alec was polite, but he found small-talk a bore, and this impatience may be the basis for some criticisms about the way Alec talked to people in his later years.

A case of diphtheria when he was nine years old left him slightly deaf. (Most people I have talked to thought this was the result of his war service or that it developed in his middle years, but this was not the case. The condition did, however, become worse with the passage of time.) Although Alec resisted pressure to get a hearing aid in his sixties, at the age of seventy-two he succumbed and bought a battery-operated set.[231] He avoided using it whenever possible.

At times, he found his deafness helpful. On occasions when he did not want to get involved, he would give the impression of not having heard what was said. As time went on, I began to notice this. His eyes showed a particular twinkle. When I saw this twinkle, I would smile. Alec too would smile, and nothing would be said.

As Alec's ability to hear worsened, he found it easier to communicate with stories than to engage in a give-and-take conversation. He would respond, however, if the speaker looked at him directly and spoke up loud and clear. People who mumbled or spoke too quickly found it difficult to conduct a conversation with Alec lasting longer than exchanges of a few sentences. People who preferred two-way conversations and not monologues, as Alec's stories were occasionally described, sometimes asked whether he was not egocentric, more interested in himself than in the world around him. Even his jokes playing down self-importance did not still the criticism.

When asked specific questions, Alec would usually answer cheerfully and with humour, small-talk sometimes excepted, and then he'd try to move the conversation in the direction of one of his stories. As he proceeded, he would watch the level of interest — and when he noticed interest flagging, he would suddenly stop and admit with a wry smile, "I guess I've told that story before."

He acquired a reputation of living in the past, but that was only partially true. He was also a man of the future, and often mentioned the many things he still wanted to do. If one idea did not work out, never mind; there were other challenges.

Unlike his contemporaries, Alec did not live for the day. He lived for tomorrow. Alec exemplified Charles F. Kettering's saying, "We should all be concerned about the future because we will have to spend the rest of our lives there." He was always happy to share his past with others; most of his thoughts about the future he kept to himself.

His forward-looking attitude is illustrated by this story. At some time in 1958, I had browsed through a large batch of Alec's drawings, almost all of them landscapes covering his sketching trips from one end of the country to the other and up to the Arctic. I inquired whether I could purchase some of them. Alec replied that he preferred to hold on to them for a while, explaining, "I am keeping them for my old age [he was seventy-six at that time] — I can use them when I am too old to go on sketching trips, say, at the age of eighty-five or ninety." Laughing, I said that I thought he would go on painting outdoors as long as he could walk, and Alec agreed.

Some two years after we had this discussion, Alec changed his mind about keeping the drawings. Over a period of eight years, I acquired some two hundred drawings from him. These drawings, with their notes by the artist, constitute a helpful source of reference material spanning the sixty-year period 1908-1967.

A year or so later, Alec told me that he was thinking of collaborating with his niece Naomi in putting about one hundred of his drawings together in a volume, in which Naomi would write the text and he would do the introduction. This most welcome project faced a number of ups and downs during the ensuing years. If it had not been for Naomi's perseverance and hard work, the book would not have seen the light of day. Alec was happy with the quality of reproduction of the drawings, and mentioned it to me on several occasions. He helped in the selection of the drawings, but he did not devote as much time to the project as he might have because he was so preoccupied with his painting, travelling, and lecturing. I asked Alec several times whether he had done the draft for the introduction to the volume and I offered to comment on it. "I'll do it when I get around to it," he'd say. He never did. In the end, it was Naomi who wrote a brief foreword for *A. Y.'s Canada*.

Enthusiastic about this project, and with Alec's concurrence, I got in touch with the Undersecretary of State for External Affairs to suggest having a copy of the book available in each of the forty major Canadian missions abroad. I indicated that Alec would be prepared to autograph the copies to give this special distribution a personal touch. The Department of External Affairs considered the matter and finally purchased twenty copies, claiming the need for economy.

The book was published in 1968, and a launching ceremony was held in Kleinburg on November 1. Alec and Naomi sent me a copy, autographed by both of them. The book went into a second printing and sold ten thousand copies, a highly respectable number for a Canadian art publication in those days.

Naomi summed up beautifully what the drawings meant to Alec: "Spontaneous, unstylized, masterly, an act and not an object, A. Y.'s drawings reveal how he takes possession of his subject, gives it his own characteristic imprint, and then puts it aside, to gather a rich patina in the sketch-bag and to lie maybe for years in a casual heap in the studio — rich record of life and land."[232]

Though Alec could obviously get enthusiastic about a project, that did not necessarily mean he'd see it through. He recognized that sometimes circumstances beyond his control made it difficult for him to keep his promise. Then too, there were occasions when he just plain changed his mind, and when he did, his tactic was to say nothing but to stall. Anyone perceptive would soon realize what he was up to.

Some people were critical of Alec for other reasons. They considered him stubborn and impatient and capable of holding grudges for a long time if someone crossed him. He had certain prejudices, and he could be scornful about "academic" painters and "young" artists who made exaggerated claims. He made sarcastic remarks about "experts" (curators, art critics, and reviewers) who tried to "stuff meaningless art down people's throats." One of his favourite phrases was, "What the 'experts' will say does not matter."*

Alec scoffed at acclaim, but deep down he throve on the nice things people said about him. Although he seemed modest, there were times he liked to show off, such as at a gathering in Kleinburg where he demonstrated how strong a swimmer he was in his eighties.

He pretended not to like publicity and the recognition he received in his later years, and seemed to care little about all the honorary degrees that were bestowed upon him and the awards that came his way. This was a myth, for he was really not averse to most of the adulation and the fuss people were making over him. In fact, he at times encouraged such reactions, even though subtly, by dropping hints, and would volunteer to sit on juries, give press interviews, or make speeches all over the country. This was not the way to minimize publicity. I do not want to be hard on him, but anyone who looked carefully could not help but notice a good deal of vanity in his personality.

Anne McDougall, who has reviewed in detail the correspondence between Alec and his good friend Anne Savage, suggests that "another side of the painter emerges in these private letters. It is that of a warm-hearted man, capable of great loyalty, a man with very tough

---

*For example, in a letter he wrote to Franklin Arbuckle dated June 13, 1965.

convictions but very little vanity. He is a steady flame in the lives of his friends."[233] I do not quite agree with the judgment "very little vanity."

Alec was pretty good at stressing the humble side of his personality, and there was a goodly amount of humility in his character. But there was another side of him as well. Whether we call it vanity or self-assertion is a matter of semantics. Alec knew he was a very good painter, and he felt it did no harm for others to know it as well. This characteristic is understandable, for Alec had to be strong and believe in himself to survive the many lean years before he received wide recognition. He was a complex human being, and there was more to him than the man who emerged easily in his conversations or writings.

On several occasions, I remonstrated with him: all this travelling and speech-making took too much time and kept him from painting, which was his first love. To this he replied, "But people want me to talk."

When I retorted, "Alec, how about saying no once in a while?" his response was "I don't like saying no if I can help it."

This was one of Alec's problems, this reluctance to say no. He genuinely cared for people, and most of the time he was willing to oblige them, sometimes at a significant cost to himself. His escapes from these pressures were his sketching trips, where he felt he was his own man, and closest to his friend, nature.

There might have been a kind of inverted snobbery in the way he treated some of his honours. The trappings seemed to mean little to him. In 1962, for example, he received the Canada Council Medal, which was made of pressed bronze. One day a guest visiting his studio lit a cigarette and looked around for an ashtray, but none was to be found even though Alec smoked. He picked up the medal and said, "Here, use this." Alec was made C.M.G. (Commander of the Order of St. Michael and St. George), a Commonwealth award, in 1946. Governor-General Viscount Alexander made the presentation of a badge, a seven-armed cross in gold and white enamel, attached to a handsome inch-and-a-half wide blue-and-red striped ribbon, to be worn around the neck. When Alec was asked whether he planned to use it, he replied with a serious face, "Certainly, I'll put it on when I go swimming."

All of which confirms Alec's saying, "Artists are a queer lot."

There was also his rather careful way with his money — a laudable quality if not taken too far. Many of Alec's friends teased him about being a tightwad. An example is the occasion when Alec painted with Franklin Arbuckle in Ste-Adèle and St-Sauveur in March 1957. They shared Arbuckle's bottle of rye over several evenings. When the bottle was finished and Alec made no move to replace it, Arbuckle bought another. When that one had been consumed, Alec asked his friend whether he was planning to buy another one. It did not occur to him to make a contribution to the friendly and modest evening drink. I asked Arbuckle, who told me the story, whether he had in fact bought another bottle, and he said he had. He admitted that he was a little peeved about Alec's stinginess but nevertheless felt that it was part of his friend's nature, and he was willing to accept him the way he was. Then Arbuckle added, laughingly, "I had planned to buy two of Alec's sketches, which he was selling for sixty dollars each. But then I said to myself, 'If he is that tight with his money, to hell with it.' I didn't buy the sketches. Now I feel that I cut off my nose to spite my face."

Alec was not a well-organized person. He knew what he wanted, but he wasn't very good at working out the necessary arrangements. Hence, most of his life and, certainly during the years I knew him, much of what he did was improvised and on the spur of the moment. He looked ahead with the optimistic belief that "tomorrow will take care of itself." He was not a planner, and many of his great excursions and important encounters happened by chance and not by design. His nature was bohemian in that tidiness was a nuisance to him and he drove some of his lady-friends to distraction with his "I don't care" attitude. Some of them who could take his traits in their stride described Alec's way of life as "quaint." What they may not have realized was that Alec was a born non-conformist.

He was physically and mentally the robust outdoor type. He loved to explore unknown country on sketching trips, to brave the rigours of cold weather, heavy snowfalls, and rainstorms. Neither mosquitoes, blackflies, impassable portages, steep mountain trails, nor trackless wilderness country hundreds of miles from civilization deterred him. These were challenges, and he accepted them readily. Even when he was in his eighties he wanted to be his own self-sufficient man and insisted on doing camp chores. He felt well able to cope with hardships, and was for most of his life a man in excellent health and of resolute mind. He had the physical and spiritual strength that comes to people who have a particularly close bond with nature. The land and Canada, the country he loved, were the prime inspirations for his creative style and he would paint that challenging landscape with vigorous strokes and in bold colours. He once wrote: "I'm as husky as a piano mover and if I can sublimate my physical energies and turn them into art it should not be weakly stuff."[234]

He wrote to Anne Savage in March 1931: "I'm one of these rough birds from the big open spaces and me and Fred Banting we just say 'hell' when the north wind blows."[235] Thirty years later, when Alec was eighty years old and out sketching in the winter with Betty Kirk, he would climb the farm fences, carrying his ruck-sack filled with painting equipment on his back, with an ease that astounded his companion. "He did what a man half his age couldn't do. I had a hard time keeping up with him. He was an extremely energetic person." Betty said.

Sometimes, Alec poked fun at his own strength and endurance. For example, in writing to his friend and fellow Group member J. E. H. MacDonald from Baie-St-Paul in January 1924 — he was then forty-one years old — he spoke of bones that "get set and brittle. In most cases, the brain gets into the same state."[236] He repeated versions of this remark for decades to come. Early on he would say such things with a touch of irony, but in later years, although he was still trying to be funny, a certain sadness crept into his voice, followed by a shrug of the shoulders, as if to say: "It can't be helped, so I don't care."

Painting nature became Alec's mistress, faithful to his last days, always beckoning, continuously challenging, and endlessly endearing. Because he never married, nature became a source of comfort to him when he needed it. "Nature is my friend," he said. "You are not lonely with a friend."

In his political beliefs when I knew him, Alec was conservative, with a small *c*. He believed in the virtues of hard work, thrift, and individualism. The state served people best if it left them alone, within reason. He acknowledged that government had a role in helping the poor, the unemployed, the sick, and in supporting worthwhile causes, such as the arts, in Canada. "But the trouble is," he once observed, "politicians don't know when to stop. Some handouts are fine, but too many can ruin the country." Not only that, but politicians made a mess if they got too involved in business affairs.

I teased Alec, saying that for a man who had been described as a rebel this was quite a change. With tongue in cheek, I asked him whether he didn't believe in progress in social and economic affairs as well as in the arts.

"Yes, I do," he replied, and he recalled that during the thirties depression he, like many others, had doubts about whether the capitalist system could survive. He had written in a letter on October 26, 1932: "The present capitalist era is putting itself out of business and we will soon have a swell new world."[237] But looking back, he thought the free-enterprise system, with some modifications, was still the best in an imperfect world.

Alec was proud to be Canadian, and genuinely believed in the oneness of Canada. He did not distinguish between English- and French-

Canadians. To him Canada was one country, one people with a common destiny and a culturally exciting future. He was imbued with a conviction that he and other artists could contribute significantly to making the Canadian people more aware of their heritage and the beauty and vitality of their country. "It is remarkable that with such little encouragement Canadian artists have accomplished so much," he observed,[238] but more was needed to "create a climate in which the arts will flourish," necessary if Canadians wanted to work out their "own national destiny."[239]

To Alec, the Canadian artist was not only a creative person who forged his or her own future, he or she also had a social responsibility: "We need artists to reveal to us the beauty of our heritage, and the adventures and the struggle and the heroism that have gone into making Canada."[240]

Until his early eighties Alec loved writing letters. He wrote them to friends and acquaintances, to colleagues and art galleries, to newspaper editors, and to some ladies he greatly cherished. One of these ladies, Anne Savage, received three hundred or so letters from him over a forty-year period. They were found after she died, and extracts from a number of them were published by her niece Anne McDougall.

Alec's style was brisk and to the point, his prose simple and straightforward. Most of the time the content was factual, though on occasion he included some comments — facetious, funny, challenging, or critical. When he was annoyed, a touch of his feelings could be detected in his letters, but they were never cynical, and where possible, they were positively oriented.

Although most of the letters seem to be casual efforts, in fact, they have behind them a high intellect, great perceptiveness, and innate honesty. In one instance I would qualify the word "perceptiveness": Alec's letters to Anne Savage seem to have had something to do with creating doubts in her mind that were not helpful to Alec's matrimonial intentions. It is not generally known that deep down Alec was really a romantic. He could write from the heart if he was so inclined. It did not happen often, but when it did, even his close friends could be amazed by his ardour, as in one letter to Anne Savage written in 1933: "I should come dashing in from the western plains and sweep you off your feet because you're a darling."[241]

When words failed him — and that was rare — he would chose a poem or quotation that reflected his sentiments. It was difficult, as far as I know, for him to verbalize strong feelings, but others did it for him. Thus during his courting of Anne Savage, he sent her a letter on October 31, 1931, commenting on her feelings about rebellion, resignation, and humility, and saying: "I don't think the *bon dieu* worries much about our attitudes." Enclosed with the letter were some lines from a poem* by the British poet laureate of the day, John Masefield:

And all their passionate hearts are dust
And dust the great idea that burned
In various flames of love and lust
Till the world's brain was turned.

God moving darkly in men's brains
Using their passions as his tool
Brings freedom with a tyrant's chains
And wisdom with the fool.

Blindly and bloodily we drift
Our interests clog our hearts with dreams
God make my brooding mind a rift
Through which a meaning gleams.[242]

Some of the letters reproduced in this book illustrate Alec's style. Writing came easily to him, and he liked doing it when he thought it worthwhile. In his later years, he became less inclined to reply to the avalanche of mail he was receiving, and he was particularly reluctant to write business letters. But for the rest, as his good friend Yvonne Housser says, "he was a great letter writer."

Alec liked women and he appealed strongly to many of them. Some called him a ladies' man; others said he had charisma. Even when I knew Alec in his later years, his personal magnetism still seemed to be effective in his relations with women — and that included reactions from women of all ages, from the curious glances of teenagers to the bolder looks of their older sisters, to the encouraging overtures of women in their thirties and forties, to the friendly nods of matrons.

Two questions concerning Alec's relations with women have to do with his personality. What made Alec so attractive to women? And what was there in Alec's attitude toward life and in his priorities that kept him from sweeping some lady he was courting off her feet, into matrimony? In spite of many pleasant opportunities to marry between age thirty and age eighty, Alec remained a bachelor all his life. The comments I offer here are based in part on personal observation and in part on conversations with his friends.

Alec was not a particularly good-looking man. He lost much of his hair fairly early, tended to develop a paunch, and became increasingly

---

*The Tragedy of Pompey the Great, a poetic drama written in 1910.

235

hard of hearing as he grew older, but he had other physical and spiritual qualities that appealed to women. He was robust and strong, the healthy outdoor type, his face usually a weather-beaten brown and shining cherublike, with twinkling eyes and a ready smile. Here was a man with a devil-may-care attitude, reckless, easygoing, the pioneering type, ever ready to tackle the wilderness and brave the elements.

At the same time, he had real personal magnetism and a kind of elusiveness that in itself constituted a challenge to any red-blooded woman. There was an aura of ardent romanticism around him. And further, women liked his gentleness and the courtesy and respect he showed them — except for those who annoyed him with small-talk and silly questions. He was entertaining with his stories and letters. In his later years, his fame as a painter grew, honours were bestowed upon him until he became a living legend, and people frequently stood in awe of him. Yet he was still the same Alec, unassuming most of the time, with the ladies and children his preferred admirers.

Anyone who reviews Alec's efforts to court ladies with whom he thought he was in love and reads his letters will discover a curious duality in his personality. Once he had entered his forties he began to be more aware of loneliness and to feel that a good wife would be better for him than a dozen adoring women friends. But either he couldn't settle on one woman because of his demanding standards, or more likely he had another love with higher priority, his desire to paint, to remain free as the birds winging their way north in the summer and south in the winter. His urge to be a truly Canadian painter in his knowledge and interpretation of the whole country was an overriding consideration with Alec, but there were times when his desire to marry was so strong that he thought he was willing to make the necessary promises he realized were essential if his was to be a successful marriage.

In any event, on those occasions when his desire to have a particular woman for his wife was strong enough for him to make the necessary sacrifices, he could not persuade the lady he was courting that he really meant what he said. He convinced himself, but not the few people who really mattered to him. Alec seemed to face a permanent psychological block. Who could be sure that he was serious? Some of his lady friends tell me that he was relieved when his marriage attempts came to nothing and he found he could continue with his free-wheeling ways. I am inclined to think differently. I believe that Alec meant what he said — he just didn't say it convincingly enough.

He was not the idealized human being that legends are likely to portray, nor was he by nature a person who would turn the other cheek when hurt or riled. He was not just Mr. Nice Guy, the way many people remember him; he had all the imperfections and the frailties that characterize humanity and reflect individuality. On the whole, he was a good and dedicated man, sincere and highly principled. He was understood and loved by most people who met him, though not by all. But then, who is?

CHAPTER 20
Stricken by Illness

It was becoming noticeable in the spring of 1967 that Alec's health was deteriorating. He still insisted on continuing his regular mode of life, however, going on sketching trips, accepting lecturing assignments that involved strenuous journeys, making regular trips to Toronto to see his friends, going to parties and exhibitions, frequently staying up late, and getting up early in the morning every day. As far as Alec was concerned, age might take its toll, but he was not prepared to change his lifestyle or alter his habit of living alone.

He had had some minor health problems in 1962 and 1963, mainly connected with his diabetic condition and some infections. Fortunately, his diabetes was a mild kind that required only some change in his eating habits, giving up drinking ginger ale with his rye (he continued drinking rye), and taking his pills regularly.

Lawren Harris, who found Alec a sporadic letter writer, had asked me to let him know occasionally how Alec was getting along. I quote from three letters I wrote to Harris:

October 22, 1962: "My wife and I have just returned from the Civic Hospital, where we visited A. Y. Jackson. He is presently undergoing some tests for diabetes. He is otherwise in good health and in excellent spirits. We are all hopeful that his condition is not very serious and that he will soon be able to leave the hospital."

December 18, 1962: "The diabetes does not seem to bother Alec very much. The only thing he says he misses is some bacon in the morning. He is allowed an occasional drink and he is in good cheer."

September 19, 1963: "Alec has just returned from the hospital himself. He spent a week there. He has an infection of the bone in the middle finger of his left hand. He has been making progress slowly. He has received a heavy penicillin treatment which has sapped his strength. However, he is otherwise cheerful and is talking about going on a two- or three-week sketching trip later this month."

It was in 1965 that we began to notice old age finally catching up with Alec. He tired more easily, fell asleep during meals or speeches, and was subject to more colds and other minor ailments than former-ly. Early in November 1965, Alec became quite ill. Since his friend Edwin Holgate was very much concerned, I kept him up to date. On December 11 I wrote to him:

[Alec] had an infection of the inner ear, with extreme dizziness and other discomforts. He stayed in the hospital for about ten days. As soon as we heard about his illness we contacted his doctor, who advised us that Alec responded well to treatment. We visited Alec daily in the hospital and he recovered quickly.

The doctor advised Alec to cut down on his many extracurricular activities. I mentioned to him what you, dear Edwin, had said to me: "When will Alec take it easier?" Alec replied: "I have too much fun in doing what I am doing." However, after he left the hospital Alec confided to me that he would listen to his doctor's advice and would turn down many of the invitations he was getting to go out for social engagements and to make speeches.

We had Alec at our house for luncheon last weekend. He feels bet-ter and he is taking it easier. He started to paint again, a little at a time rather than working all day as he used to do.

In another letter to Holgate on January 8, 1966, I wrote: "We had Alec Jackson and Charles Comfort join us for a New Year's Party. Alec had a good time but he tires more easily than he used to and we made sure that he went to bed by midnight."

At his eighty-fifth birthday party in 1967, Alec tired early in the evening and he had a dizzy spell. Taking him into my studio to rest, I opened the window until he regained his composure. I asked him whether he had ever felt dizzy before, and he admitted that he had occasionally. When I asked him whether he had told Dr. Starrs, he said he thought he had, but there was no reason to be concerned — it was nothing that a good night's sleep and a sketching trip couldn't cure. I gained the distinct impression that by laughing off his condi-tion, Alec was leading the conversation away from his health. He had been well for so long that he still looked at ill health as an annoyance, something to be gotten over quickly, so that he could continue with important work.

During the ensuing months when I visited Alec in his studio, I noticed that he sometimes held on to a chair, a table or the mantle-piece. He had not done this a year earlier. I asked him whether he had ever fainted, and he said he "might have." But again he was reluctant to talk about it.

Naomi Groves told me that she too had noticed a change in Alec's health, and was concerned. Dr. Starrs had told her that Alec's symptoms were part of the aging process. Hardening of the arteries could momentarily diminish the blood supply to the brain, which would bring on a dizzy or faint sensation. Naomi said she was visiting Alec more frequently. I began to do the same, and I phoned him often when he was in town, particularly as the winter of 1967 approached.

Late in February, 1968, with the break-up of the ice, Alec went on a sketching trip with Ralph Burton in the Rippon, Papineauville, Thurso, and Buckingham area of Quebec. Betty Kirk went with Alec and Ralph on some of the sketching excursions. The last sketch Alec painted was done at Notre Dame de la Salette, about four miles east of Buckingham on one of the back roads. This, incidentally, was the sketch Alec used when he laboriously painted his last canvas.

When Alec was home from this sketching trip, he reported that he had brought us a sketch (it was *Water's Edge, Duhamel, Que.*). His voice sounded strange over the telephone; he had a cold, he explained.

I went early to the studio that Saturday morning, to find Alec coughing and not looking very well. He showed me the sketch he had kept for us, which needed to be finished at the corners and signed, dated, and titled. Alec did not feel up to finishing the sketch and he asked me to put my name on the back. He said he would add the finishing touches the next week. He never did.* I paid Alec for the sketch, and he told me about the sketching trip. The conversation turned to Nancy Greene, for whom Alec had conceived a great affection.**

His continued coughing and sore throat made his voice erratic. When he got up, he leaned heavily against the chair. He was quite pale, and I thought he might faint. I offered to phone Dr. Starrs, but Alec wouldn't hear of it. He sat down again, and in a few minutes his colour returned and he said he felt better. I left Alec that morning feeling quite uneasy about him.

I visited him several times during March. Gradually, he seemed to be in better health, and I asked him to lunch on April 13, if he felt up to it. Alec accepted, and that Saturday was the last time he was at our home after visiting fairly regularly for meals and parties for thirteen

---

*He signed the back of the sketch in the hospital several weeks later.

**Nancy Greene was one of the greatest skiers Canada had ever produced. A member of the Olympic ski team at sixteen, she won the World Cup in 1967 and 1968. In February 1968, at twenty-four, she won the Gold Medal in the Ladies' Giant Salom at the Winter Olympic Games in Grenoble. Alec followed her sporting achievements with keen interest. To him, she was doing for her country what he also was trying to do: making Canadians aware of and proud of their country in the way she knew best. In achieving world acclaim as a sportswoman, she was putting Canada on the map.

years. He became curious who else would be there. I told him that the Austrian ambassador, Franz Leitner, and his wife, Inge, would be coming. (He was one of the few people who could out-talk Alec, who found that accomplishment very amusing.) There would also be three young women: Madeleine Gobeil and Marie-Louise Funke, both members of the faculty at Carleton University, and our daughter Catherine, home for the weekend from McGill University.

The day came, and the guests gathered. The ambassador held forth about Austria's struggle to regain independence after the Second World War and the trials of a small nation occupied until 1955 by the USSR, the United States, and the United Kingdom. Alec praised the Austrians for their courage and perseverance, and referred to their great contributions to European culture.

We also had quite a discussion about Pierre Elliott Trudeau, then Minister of Justice in the Pearson government, who had just been chosen leader of the Liberal Party. Madeleine Gobeil, who had been a close friend of Trudeau's for years, forecast that he would be a strong force in Canada's future. Alec, a frequent critic of the weak leadership of the then current Liberal government, retorted that it was time Canada had a "good" government. Alec's notion of good government may not have coincided with that of Pierre Trudeau, but in the presence of Madeleine's enthusiasm, Alec, in his gentlemanly way, conceded that Trudeau should be given a chance to prove what he could do.

Alec then launched into an animated discussion with Marie-Louise Funke on art history, in particular about how it was possible to retain objectivity in the light of conflicting evidence. He found time to talk to Catherine in French about her studies in French literature at McGill and her coming year at the University of Aix-en-Provence, telling her about his experiences when he went to the Académie Julian in Paris.

I was amazed — here was Alec, at eighty-five, participating actively in a diverse and demanding conversation. I had heard people say that his mental faculties were fading, but on that day he was alert and at his charming best. I had the impression of a tired giant rising once more to show that there was still some of the old strength left.

Although he was not feeling very well — he was again suffering from a cold — Alec would not allow this to interfere with his enjoyment. Except for the coughing he got through the meal quite well, but I noticed that his face became puffy and he appeared to have difficulty keeping his eyes open. It was plain that his strength was giving out toward the end of the luncheon. I took him home sooner than I would have ordinarily, followed him into the apartment, and suggested that I should perhaps stay with him until he was settled in bed. But Alec just shook his head and said good-bye. He wanted to be alone. I left with a heavy heart and forebodings for the future.

At home again, I discussed Alec's health with Isobel and we agreed that the time had come for us to try to persuade Alec to have someone stay with him full time. This would not be an easy task. We reviewed various lines of persuasion, including talks with Naomi and Dr. Starrs. But events moved swiftly, too swiftly to put our good intentions into effect.

Two days later, Monday, April 15, Alec had an invitation to come with us to a reception at the Soviet embassy. I asked him whether he wouldn't prefer to stay home, but he said he wanted to go. We found him more drawn than ever when we picked him up.

Next day, Isobel met Alec on Elgin Street. His face looked haggard and he was still coughing, but he told her that he was planning to go to Toronto for a day, taking the early morning bus, which for Alec meant five or six o'clock. Isobel pleaded with him to put off the trip and get over his cold before going on with his regular activities — a schedule most people half his age couldn't match. But Alec just smiled about Isobel's concern and said he could manage.

On the phone that evening, he promised me he would take good care of himself. He had an important date on April 26, he said, when he was to be made a Companion of the Order of Canada at an investiture at Government House. What was to him even more important, he was going to have a chance to meet a young woman he had greatly admired for years, champion skier Nancy Greene, who was also to receive an award. Somehow, I felt reassured, for his enthusiasm was heartwarming.

I phoned Alec again several times later during the next week but could not find him in. On April 23, Dr. Starrs phoned to say that Alec had suffered what appeared to be a stroke.

As I learned afterward, Naomi, who had a key to Alec's studio, dropped in on the afternoon of April 22 and had found Alec lying on the floor. She immediately called Robert Starrs, who lived only a block away. Within five minutes, the doctor arrived, and he and Naomi moved Alec to bed, where he examined him.

Alec had apparently fainted and had hurt his head in the fall. His heartbeat was irregular, but there was no indication that anything more serious had happened. Dr. Starrs felt that Alec should either be moved to a hospital or be kept under observation at the home of friends or family. He phoned Ralph Burton, who suggested that Alec be brought to his house to stay with him and his wife for a few days, until he felt better. Dr. Starrs and Naomi took Alec to the Burtons' and stayed with him until he was comfortably settled in bed.

The next day, Lovedy Burton, off work to watch over Alec, found his condition deteriorating noticeably. He lost consciousness, and when he regained it, he appeared confused. She phoned Dr. Starrs, who had Alec taken by ambulance to the Ottawa Civic Hospital.

Late that afternoon, Alec lost consciousness, and his condition was preliminarily diagnosed as a stroke. His left side was paralysed, and he had lapsed into a coma. It could not be established at once whether the stroke was caused by an intracerebral hemorrhage, a localized blood clot, or an embolus. If hemorrhage was the cause, it was likely to be fatal, but if it was a blood clot, there was a chance for survival. Surgical intervention was also a possibility. He remained in a coma for three days, and as they passed the prospects dimmed.

Dr. James H. B. Hilton, Dr. Edward A. Atack, a neurologist, and Dr. Howard J. Bagnall, a neurosurgeon, were brought in for consultation. Extensive tests followed, and a brain scan showed a subdural hematoma. The explanation was that one or more of the blood vessels in the dura, the brain covering, had been injured when Alec fell, and blood slowly oozing from the damaged vessels was increasing pressure on the brain. The condition would be fatal unless the accumulation of blood, and thus the pressure on the brain, were removed. Even if that part of the operation were successful, there was a great likelihood that residual brain damage would remain and a neurological deficit consisting of paralysis of muscles and aphasia (inability to speak) would continue.

On April 26, there was a consultation among the four doctors and Alec's three nieces, Naomi Groves, Ton Hamilton, and Geneva Petrie. The surgeon recommended surgery as the sensible thing to do. Dr. Starrs, who feared residual brain damage, was the most cautious of the four physicians. In the end, the decison was left up to the three nieces. Their unanimous verdict was to operate. The surgery took place the next day and was termed successful.

Friday, April 26 was a particularly onerous day for Naomi. Not only did she have to take part in making a life-or-death decision affecting Alec but she also had to represent her uncle at the investiture at Government House. When she had an opportunity to meet Nancy Greene at the reception that followed presentation of the awards, Naomi told her and her mother of Alec's admiration for Nancy's achievements and what she had done for Canada. It was sad that his ill health kept Alec from the evening he had so looked forward to.

The Greenes shared Naomi's feelings. She promised to let them know if Alec's condition improved and to ask the doctor whether the two of them might visit Alec in the hospital. After the success of the operation on Saturday, Dr. Starrs did give permission for Nancy, her mother, and Naomi to visit Alec briefly on Sunday. He warned them, however, that there was no assurance that Alec would regain consciousness during the visit or that his faculties of recognition and communication would be functioning.

Why Alec's doctor would permit two strangers to visit a patient recovering from major surgery so soon after the operation is simply explained: Dr. Starrs was well aware of Alec's feeling for the young champion, and he felt that Nancy's visit, ill as he was, could have therapeutic value.

When the three visitors arrived, Alec was unconscious. Dr. Starrs bent and repeated several times in Alec's ear that Nancy Greene was here to see him. Lo and behold, Alec regained consciousness. He looked at Nancy long and searchingly, and then the halting speech came out: "What a lovely child." Although some of his words were blurred, Alec, according to Dr. Starrs, was brighter during this brief visit than he was anytime in the ensuing three days. Alec's parting words to Nancy repeated his familiar statement, "I would have loved to have you as my daughter."

When Nancy married Al Raine a year later, Alec was in Kleinburg. Hearing about the wedding, he asked that one of his sketches be sent as a gift to the young woman of whom he was so fond.

It was a full four days after the operation before the first signs that he was mending appeared. Dr. Starrs phoned us to say that Alec would live, but that he would never be the same. Alec was partially paralysed and his speech was impaired.

No visitors, except family, were allowed. Alec had private nurses around the clock during the critical period. A few more days passed, then we were given permission, as close friends, to visit. The visit was scheduled to be short, but it lasted longer than expected because of an unforeseen occurrence.

We were on Alec's floor at the Civic Hospital but still about fifteen doors away from his room when we heard a commotion down the hall. Isobel said it sounded like Alec's voice. It was. At first we could not hear any words, just the raised voices of Alec and a woman, apparently the nurse. As we came closer to the room, we heard the nurse say in a firm and authoritative voice, "You go back to bed, Mr. Jackson." Then came "No, *no*," from Alec, followed by some words we could not understand. As we came to the open door of the room, we could hear Alec loud and clear: "Getting up, getting up . . ." The two voices of the nurse and patient blended together at a high pitch, with each trying to outdo the other: "Getting up!" and "No, you go back to bed, you hear me!"

As we entered the room, we saw a sight we will never forget. There was Alec in his hospital gown, his thin legs sticking out, with one foot on the floor and his body stretched over the bed. The nurse had her arms around his chest, trying to pull him back into bed. Her cheeks were flushed, her hair was dishevelled, and her white uniform was rumpled. Alec was glaring at her angrily, shouting mainly incomprehensible words. He was obviously putting up a fight; in spite of his recent surgery and advanced age, he was more than a handful for what appeared to be a capable nurse of middle age. As we came in, Alec turned to look at us, and the struggle temporarily subsided. "Are you friends of Mr. Jackson?" The nurse queried, and when Isobel said yes, she continued, "Can you please help me calm him down? I'm trying to get him back to bed. He is under strict orders to stay in bed until the doctor comes."

Isobel put her arms around Alec and kissed him on the cheek, and with the nurse's help he went back to bed. As Isobel tucked him in, he continued to mutter to himself, but the commotion was over. The nurse, having regained her composure, asked whether we would stay with Alec while she straightened her hair and uniform. Turning to Alec, she admonished, "You be good, Mr. Jackson, while I'm out of the room."

It was very difficult to understand his words. He was pale, his face drawn and much thinner than when we had last seen him. When I shook his hand, his grip was weak. There was no smile, just sad, sad eyes. We were obviously talking to a very sick man. He was still excited from the hassle he had had with his nurse.

Isobel, sitting on the edge of the bed and making soothing sounds, kept an arm around his shoulder as he leaned against her, and gradually he calmed down. Nothing of consequence was said for the first few minutes, but then we came back to what had caused the commotion. Although we understood only about every third word of what he was saying, we got the message. He had announced to the nurse that morning that he was feeling better, that he was going to get up, that he wanted his clothes, and that he wanted to go home.

The nurse, who had heard similar requests before, tried to soothe and humour him by suggesting he wait for the doctor to come, when the matter could be discussed. But Alec was having none of that. He kept calling for his trousers. When the nurse finally said he couldn't have them because the doctor had ordered him to stay in bed, he had tried to get up to get his clothes himself.

Alec was sure he was well enough to leave the hospital and go home to 192 MacLaren. He pleaded with us to get his clothes and rescue him from this "damn place" and from this "damn woman." Isobel urged that he stay where he was to get well as quickly as possible: the nurse was only trying to help him. I asked Alec why he didn't like the hospital and why he didn't like the nurse. He replied, "I can't stay cooped up in this place. And the nurse — she fusses so much. I cannot *stand* fussy women."

There it was. He was intelligent enough to know that the stay in hospital was essential for him, at least for a while, but after his independent outdoor life for seventy years, it was more than he could take to have to stay indoors, dependent on a female keeper.

While we were listening to all this — and it took some time because of Alec's speech impediment and difficulty in hearing — the nurse had returned, and sat quietly in the corner listening to our discussion. We were able to reassure and pacify Alec by promising to phone Dr. Starrs and asking him to visit Alec. Perhaps he would give Alec permission to begin walking around the hospital grounds or go for drives. As soon as he regained his strength the question of what he would do next could be discussed.

We departed, greatly distressed, with tears in our eyes. Not only were we sad to leave him, but it was plain also that our old friend was facing an uncertain future.

Dr. Starrs arranged with Ralph Burton to take Alec for occasional drives in his car to break the monotony of the hospital stay. Alec badgered Burton, too, with insistent demands to be returned to his apartment. The question of finding a long-term solution to the problem of Alec's declining years became more and more urgent.

CHAPTER 21

The Last Six Years

Medical skill had snatched Alec back as he faced death — but his left arm was paralysed, and so was the left side of his face. His mental faculties had been impaired by the three-day coma. It was a sadly ironic fate for the man who had often told us that he hoped to live to one hundred in full possession of his faculties. He had dreaded the thought of having other people make decisions for him.

When his stay at the Civic Hospital in Ottawa was coming to an end, the family consulted Dr. Starrs about the kind of custodial arrangements that could be made for Alec. Four possibilities were considered.

The first was to take Alec back to 192 MacLaren Street and employ a full-time housekeeper to look after him. Dr. Starrs believed this would not be satisfactory because Alec had suffered residual brain damage, and would be subject to loss of memory, fainting spells, and possibly irrational behaviour, which made constant nursing care necessary.

Second, Alex might stay with a member of his family with a nurse in attendance. But none of his nieces was in a position to take on this responsibility.

A third possibility was to put Alec into a nursing home, where he could have both medical and nursing care. One trouble with this solution was that Alec might be a "difficult" patient; there was also the distinct possibility that he would object violently to the arrangement. In fact, it might have been almost impossible to keep Alec in such a home, for he was fiercely independent. A city nursing home, furthermore, would not have made outings to paint possible, despite their therapeutic value. Even though he was physically handicapped, he did expect to take up painting again. The fact was that he was unable to work at a professional level after his operation, but his will demanded that he keep on applying paint to a panel, no matter what the result. Regrettably, he had lost his skill, and his ability to judge what constituted good painting was impaired.

The fourth possibility was to accept the invitation of Robert (Bob) and Signe McMichael for Alec to move to Kleinburg, to stay there for the rest of his days. The original invitation had been made when the McMichaels offered Alec a place in Kleinburg if and when he wanted to retire. They would look after him like family. At that time Alec's reply had been that he had no intention of retiring: he loved painting, and he expected to continue at it as long as his health held out.*

When Bob McMichael heard that Alec had recovered but would live on in an impaired condition, he repeated the offer he and his wife had made to look after Alec if he would come to Kleinburg. Dr. Starrs made it clear to the McMichaels that they would be taking on a major responsibility. Like anyone else who might take responsibility for Alec, they would have to cope with both the partial paralysis and the effects of brain damage. He also told them that Alec would need constant care from either professional or practical nurses. This, then, would be not only a labour of love but also a substantial financial responsibility. To their great credit, the McMichaels reiterated their willingness to take care of Alec, whatever the costs.

At that stage, it was not known to the family that Alec had built up fairly large financial resources during the previous ten years. As it turned out, he had adequate funds of his own to look after his expenses during the last six years of his life. This was one artist, at least, who did not end his days dependent on public or family charity.

Alec's nieces were slow in coming to a decision, as they weighed all these options with compassionate deliberation. They knew that it was Alec's wish, which he expressed whenever lucid, to return to 192 MacLaren Street. Perhaps the most important consideration was that if Alec were not in a controlled environment, he might try to assert himself by walking out, perhaps to his own harm. In the end, with the McMichaels willing and Dr. Starrs recommending it, the family agreed to move Alec to Kleinburg.

Although at first Alec protested that he wanted to go back to his apartment, they were able to persuade him that the move to the country would make it much easier for him to go sketching. Further, many visitors came to see the McMichael collection, and Alec could meet some of them if he wished to. He would have his own quarters. He would be alone (except for his nurse) or he could have company, depending on how he felt. On the assurance that he could paint to his heart's content and meet many young people in Kleinburg, he consented.

Bob McMichael was a successful businessman who had retired early. Both he and his wife, Signe, loved Canadian art, particularly the

---

*Two years earlier, an inquisitive reporter had asked Alec how much longer he planned to keep on painting (Alec was eighty-three at the time). He replied, "I'd like to do a good sketch and then drop over dead. That would suit me all right." The reporter commented: "It is worthwhile to note that he said 'sketch' and not 'painting.' Because in doing a sketch, he would be in the outdoors he loved so much."[243]

works of the Group of Seven, Tom Thomson, and some of their contemporaries, As they had no children they decided to devote the remainder of their lives to building a collection of Canadian art that could be exhibited in a rural setting and made available to large groups of viewers.

In 1952, Bob McMichael had purchased ten acres of gently sloping, partly forested land, on the outskirts of Kleinburg, then a village of two hundred people, twenty miles north of Toronto. Two years later the McMichaels built a four-room house of stone and square-hewn century-old timbers there. They called the place *Tapo wingo*, an Indian word meaning Place of Joy. Their love of the land enabled them to identify readily with the works of Thomson and the Group of Seven. Between 1953 and 1960, they acquired about fifty paintings; by 1965, the number had grown to over two hundred. In 1964, at the age of forty-three, McMichael had assumed full-time direction of the McMichael Collection of Art.

When there was no more room in their home for all the works on exhibit, they built several galleries. They also arranged to have the Tom Thomson shack that had been located at the back of the Studio Building in Toronto taken down and re-erected on the property. In 1965, the McMichaels donated their works of art and their property to the Crown through the Province of Ontario.* The government of Ontario, in turn, created the six-hundred-acre McMichael Conservation Area and undertook to maintain the buildings and the grounds in perpetuity and to expand the facilities when necessary. Bob and Signe McMichael became unpaid curators. The name is now the McMichael Canadian Collection because it includes (besides Thomson and The Group of Seven) works by J. W. Morrice, Maurice Cullen, Emily Carr, David Milne, Albert Robinson, Randolph Hewton, and Clarence Gagnon, and representative works of native Indian and Eskimo cultures. The collection has been seen since it opened in 1965 by hundreds of thousands of people, many of them "young people."[244]

On a fine warm day in June, 1968, Dr. Starrs, his wife Rita, Naomi, Bob McMichael (who had come up from Kleinburg), and a nurse went to collect Alec at the Civic Hospital. Alec was dressed in pyjamas, slippers, and a hat. The six piled into the car, with Dr. Starrs driving. Naomi assured Alec that his sketch box, paints, brushes, and other artist's paraphernalia were going with them, so that he could take up painting whenever he felt like it.

---

*The initial impetus for the collection came from the works acquired by the McMichaels. Since 1965, it has grown enormously, mainly through gifts from collectors, artists, and public-spirited citizens. By 1970, it exceeded six hundred items housed in more than an acre of gallery space, and there were about a thousand items in the late seventies.

The trip to Toronto and from there to Kleinburg was uneventful. Alec was brought to his quarters and after a while was shown the swimming pool, one of the comforts of quality living that was a characteristic of the McMichael establishment. Alec was encouraged to use the pool and did so, with enjoyment, as his sense of humour slowly returned. Dr. Starrs turned Alec over to the medical care of Dr. Peter Granger, who lived not far from the McMichaels. Thus began the last episode in Alec's life.

After he was settled in, Alec frequently painted outdoors, always accompanied by his nurse and occasionally by his loyal friend Casson, or by other artists. But it was more daubing than painting. Bob McMichael issued strict instructions that none of these last efforts of Alec's should leave the premises, the understanding being that the panels would be destroyed.*

Thirteen years before, Alec had moved to the Ottawa area a hale and hearty man with a firm stride, a searching eye, and a keen mind, bent on proving that getting older means getting better. He left an invalid, broken in health and in mind.

After his move to Kleinburg, we missed his cheerfulness, his impish sense of humour, that chuckle, and his so-familiar tales. Isobel and I often talked about him. When his eighty-sixth birthday came round on October 3, 1968, we sent him the following wire: "Dear Alec. We are thinking of you as the most unforgettable person in our lives. Many happy returns. Love, Isobel and Jack."

When I saw Alec next at the opening of the MacCallum-Jackson donation at the National Gallery on January 23, 1969, I asked him whether he had received our birthday telegram. He said he couldn't remember. He looked at me with sad and searching eyes, a sombre expression on his face, as if to say, "See what old age can do to you!" He said nothing, but just shook his head. His eyelids dropped and he shuffled on.

Late in the summer of 1969, I was talking to Cass Casson on the phone. he told me that he and his wife were planning to visit Alec at the McMichaels'. It was several years since we had seen the McMichael place and we had heard that several galleries and many new paintings had been added. A visit would also mean that we could see Alec again. We went to Toronto, and the Cassons drove us to Kleinburg.

Alec was resting when we arrived. We chatted with the McMichaels, saw the new buildings, and admired the paintings. Then we had a brief talk with Alec. He was sitting in a chair, with a practical nurse nearby. We were told that he had had a fall and needed constant care.

---

*One of them, a canvas, survives in the possession of Betty Kirk.

Isobel told Alec all about our children and what they were doing — Brenda and Catherine graduating from university, Bruce finishing his engineering studies at McGill, and Peter finishing public school and going to summer camp at Ahmek. The only question Alec asked was whether Peter still enjoyed Algonquin Park. When Isobel said yes, he nodded and smiled a little, remarking, "A great place. I'd like to go there again."

At that point the nurse excused herself for a few minutes. I asked, "Alec, are you happy here?

He looked around, and then shook his head. When I asked him why, he replied, "Too many women."

"But the women are trying to help you," Isobel said soothingly.

Alec unhappily shook his head again, and this time said, "Too many people." At this point, the woman attendant returned, and the conversation ended.

On the way back to Ottawa Isobel and I discussed these two remarks of Alec's. We knew from our experience with him at the Civic Hospital that he could not stand being cooped up and fussed over by women. It was "un-Jackson-like" to be dependent on women; it was something to fight against. The A. Y. spark was still there, but he had neither the physical nor the mental strength to assert his will.

Others who visited Alec in Kleinburg told us conflicting stories. To some Alec said that he was being kept a "prisoner," and he pleaded with them to take him away. To others he said that he was pleased to be able to go out sketching and to meet so many young people who wanted his autograph. Barker Fairley, one of Alec's oldest friends, visited him in Kleinburg and told me that he thought Alec was happy there. Yvonne McKague Housser, who had known Alec for over half a century, saw him in Kleinburg several times. She remarked how sad she was to observe "a childishness creeping over Alec." But there were two positive features to his stay there — he liked giving autographs because it reassured him that people still cared about him and his work, and he was happy being outdoors and doing some sketching. It was really daubing, however, and he knew it. On one occasion, he brought back a sketch and showed it to Yvonne, who had been waiting for him at the main gallery. "Not quite good enough," Alec remarked, and Yvonne nodded. The two friends looked at each other ruefully and understood. Nature had struck him a cruel blow when it took away his creative strength.

Even during these trying days of impaired health, Alec's sense of humour would occasionally surface, as the following story told to me by Betty Parkes of St. Thomas, Ontario, illustrates. She was visiting Kleinburg and bought Alec's book. When she saw him sitting alone, with his attendant at his side, watching people go by, she went up and asked whether he would autograph the book. She mentioned she was from St. Thomas but doubted whether Alec had ever heard of the place.

To this Alec replied: "I certainly do. My mother came from St. Thomas. Her name was Young." He then autographed the book signing "Young." He deliberated for a short time, crossed out Young and changed it to A. Y. Jackson. He added with a little smile: "I made a mistake, just as mother did when she had me."

It was charged by some that Alec was being put "on show" and "exploited." Alec seemed quite content with his hosts and his nurse at times. At others, he was very difficult and grouchy. His moods changed frequently. I once asked Dr. Starrs whether there was a rational explantion for what appeared to be constantly changing behaviour and conflicting emotions. Dr. Starrs made the general observation that it was typical for an aging person to become confused at times, to be forgetful, to be angry and unreasonable at one moment only to become pleasant and peaceful without further fuss the next. The situation would be worse in a case where there was residual brain damage and where hardening of the arteries would interfere with normal thinking and feeling.

This medical explanation is acceptable to anyone who has watched the decline of an old person whose mental faculties have begun to fail. In Alec's case, I think there was also a traumatic element that he perhaps recognized in his lucid periods: the abrupt descent to utter dependence of a proud and self-reliant man. Would the alternative, to have been allowed to die peacefully, have been better? If the dilemma arose for me, I would hope for the second choice.

I never returned to Kleinburg to see Alec. In that supervised environment, no matter how necessary it was, there was little opportunity to renew the close bonds of friendship with the old easy-going, intimate exchanges. Besides, there were periods when Alec did not recognize his friends or, if he did, could not respond to them. The idea of his being on show made me unhappy. I could not go along with the claim that he was "Artist in Residence" [245] at Kleinburg. He was a sick old man who needed compassion and unobtrusive care. Feeling about him as I did, it was impossible for me not to be sad about the circumstances in which Alec was to live out his last years. Yet the die had been cast, and there was little that continuing visits could contribute to his well-being.

I do want to pay a special tribute to two couples who were faithful friends to the end. Cass and Margaret Casson visited Alec as often as they could. Cass also gave the McMichaels useful advice about ways to make Alec's remaining days more bearable. His visits must have been bright spots in Alec's life. Bob and Signe McMichael took on a task that many people would not assume for a father or mother. In spite of some trying experiences, they treated Alec with affection and understanding. Whether Alec fully understood their care and friendship in his declining years I do not know. But it was freely given and should be recorded.

We saw Alec for the last time in Ottawa in June 18, 1970. He was guest of honour at the opening of the exhibition at the National Gallery celebrating the fiftieth anniversary of the first Group of Seven show. Alan Jarvis and Charles Comfort, former directors of the gallery, were also present. The exhibition, organized by Dennis Reid, consisted of over two hundred paintings, oils and watercolours, by the Group of Seven and Tom Thomson. Of these, more than fifty were A. Y. Jacksons (oil canvases and sketches done between 1909 and 1935 and a watercolour done in 1905). Reid had prepared a scholarly and well-documented catalogue. The main speaker was the widow of Eric Brown, who reminded the audience of the risks to his career her husband took by supporting those rebellious young painters in the twenties.

Alec, accompanied by his nurse, walked slowly to the podium, his face flushed. Jean Sutherland Boggs, director of the gallery, paid him a special tribute. Smiling sheepishly, he sat down as the crowd burst into spontaneous and extended applause. After the proceedings were over he was surrounded by well-wishers. Slowly, accompanied by Signe McMichael and the nurse, Alec made his way out of the crowd. After a while Isobel and I had an opportunity to talk to him briefly. Isobel gave him a kiss and asked how he was. "Fine," he replied, but his face was redder than usual, and he looked bewildered as more people approached. A smile appeared almost automatically as he shook one hand after another. To me his motions looked mechanical. He seemed resigned, and not as frail as he had the year before.

I wondered whether Alec recognized what he saw. The twinkle in his eyes was gone. He shook my hand weakly, nodded, and closed his eyes for a moment. Then, without a word, he moved on. I doubt very much that he understood the speeches or what people said to him as he was led firmly through the crowd by the two women. He may well have wondered what all the commotion was about.

For the later years of his stay in Kleinburg, Alec was confined to a wheelchair. He spent the last eight months in a nursing home at Pine Grove, near Kleinburg. When his mind was focusing, Alec remained positive in spirit. Hazel Devereux, who had looked after him when he was painting in her part of the country, visited him at the nursing home in March, 1974. As she tells the story, Alec expressed concern about her health. When she replied, 'A. Y., I'm worried about you," Alec retorted, "Don't worry about me. I'm going to live to be a hundred." Three weeks later he was dead.

Alec died quietly on the morning of Friday, April 5, 1974, in his ninety-second year. He was buried on the grounds of the McMichael Canadian Collection next to three other members of the Group of Seven, Harris, Lismer, and Varley. His grave is covered with large Algoma boulders surrounded by evergreens.

To Alec, the beauty of the land was his life. In death, he became part of that land.

Appendices

WORKS BY A. Y. JACKSON
MENTIONED IN THE TEXT

Works reproduced in the text are marked with an asterisk.

1. *The Red Maple*, 1914, oil on canvas, 79.4 x 97.2 cm (31¼ x 38¼ in.), signed and dated lower right. The National Gallery of Canada.
2. *The Edge of the Maple Wood*, 1910, oil on canvas, 57.2 x 66.0 cm (22½ x 26 in.), signed and dated lower right. The National Gallery of Canada.
3. *Night, Georgian Bay*, 1913, oil on canvas, 53.3 x 64.8 cm (21 x 25½ in.), signed and dated lower left. The National Gallery of Canada.
4. *Sand Dunes at Cucq*, 1912, oil on canvas, 52.7 x 64.1 cm (20¾ x 25¼ in.), signed lower right. The National Gallery of Canada.
5. *The Freddy Channel*, 1920, oil on canvas, 53.3 x 66.0 cm (21 x 26 in.), signed lower right. Estate of Charles Band.
6. *A Quebec Village*, 1921, oil on canvas, 54.0 x 66.0 cm (21¼ x 26 in.), signed lower left. The National Gallery of Canada.
7. *Early Spring, Georgian Bay*, 1920, oil on canvas, 54.0 x 66.0 cm (21¼ x 26 in.), signed and dated lower left. The National Gallery of Canada.
8. *Morning after Sleet*, 1913, oil on canvas, 64.1 x 79.4 cm (25¼ x 31¼ in.), signed and dated lower left. The National Gallery of Canada.
9. *November*, ca.1922, oil on canvas, 81.9 x 101.9 cm (32¼ x 40⅛ in.), signed lower left. The National Gallery of Canada.
10. *Cacouna, the Winter Road*, 1921, oil on canvas, 52.1 x 61.9 cm (20½ x 24⅜ in.), signed and dated lower left. There is a dispute about the title. It is registered as "Winter Moonlight," with a notation that it was printed in "Cacouna on the south shore of St. Lawrence." The painting is on extended loan from the National Gallery of Canada with the Kitchener-Waterloo Art Gallery.
11. *Maples, Early Spring*, 1915, oil on canvas, 63.5 x 81.3 cm (25 x 32 in.), signed lower right. Sarnia Public Library and Art Gallery, Sarnia, Ontario.
12. *Early Spring, Quebec*, ca. 1923, oil on canvas, 54.0 x 66.7 cm (21¼ x 26¼ in.), signed lower left. The National Gallery of Canada.
13. *Northern Lake*, 1928, oil on canvas, 82.6 x 127.0 cm (32½ x 50 in.), signed lower left. The National Gallery of Canada.
14. *North Shore, Baffin Island*, 1928, oil on canvas, 53.3 x 66.0 cm (21 x 26 in.), signed lower right. East York Board of Education, East York Collegiate Institute.
15. *Barns*, ca. 1926, oil on canvas, 81.6 x 102.0 cm (32⅛ x 40 3/16 in.), signed lower left centre. Art Gallery of Ontario.
16. *The "Beothic" at the Bache Post, Ellesmere Island*, ca. 1928, oil on canvas, 81.3 x 101.6 cm (32 x 40 in.), signed lower left. The National Gallery of Canada.
17. *Winter, Charlevoix County*, ca. 1932-33, oil on canvas, 63.5 x 81.3 cm (25 x 32 in.), signed lower left centre. Art Gallery of Ontario.
18. *Terre Sauvage*, 1913, oil on canvas, 127.0 x 152.4 cm (50 x 60 in.), signed and dated lower right. The National Gallery of Canada.

19. *Springtime in Picardy*, 1918, oil on canvas, 65.1 x 77.5 cm (25⅝ x 30½ in.), signed and dated lower right. Art Gallery of Ontario.
20. *Kingsmere*, 1963, pencil drawing on paper, 22.9 x 30.5 cm (9 x 12 in.), signed, dated, and title lower right. The Ontario Heritage Foundation Firestone Art Collection.
21. *Portrait of O.J.F.*, 1963, pencil drawing on paper, 22.9 x 30.5 cm (9 x 12 in.), initialled and dated lower right. The Ontario Heritage Foundation Firestone Art Collection.*
22. *Self Portrait*, 1963, pencil drawing on paper, 22.9 x 30.5 cm (9 x 12 in.), initialled and dated lower right. The Ontario Heritage Foundation Firestone Art Collection.*
23. *Gentians*, 1920s, painting exhibited at the O.S.A. Exhibition, 1924, and mentioned by Hector Charlesworth in *Saturday Night*, 12 November 1924. No other details are available and would be welcomed from anyone with further information.
24. *Pickerel Weed, Split Rock Island, Georgian Bay*, 1965, oil on canvas, 97.2 x 127.6 cm (38¼ x 50¼ in.), signed lower left, signed, dated, and title verso. The Ontario Heritage Foundation Firestone Art Collection.*
25. *Pickerel Weed, Georgian Bay*, 1930s, oil on panel, 26.7 x 34.3 cm (10½ x 13½ in.), signed lower left. The National Gallery of Canada.
26. *Massey Home, Port Hope*, 1934, oil on panel, 26.7 x 34.3 cm (10½ x 13½ in.), signed lower right. Estate of Vincent Massey.
27. *Indian Church at Brantford, Ont.*, 1963, oil on panel, 21.6 x 26.7 cm (8½ x 10½ in.), signed lower right, signed, dated, and title verso. The Ontario Heritage Foundation Firestone Art Collection.
28. *Portrait of Pte. J.C. Kerr*, 1917, oil on canvas, 101.6 x 76.2 cm (40 x 30 in.), unsigned. The National Gallery of Canada.
29. *Portrait of Lt. Robert Shankland, V.C.C.*, 1918, oil on canvas, 104.1 x 33.7 cm (41 x 30¼ in.), signed lower left. The National Gallery of Canada.
30. *Coy-Sgt-Major Robert Hanna, V.C.C.*, 1918, oil on canvas, 101.6 x 76.2 cm (40 x 30 in.), signed and dated lower left. The National Gallery of Canada.
31. *September Mountains*, 1958, pencil drawing on paper, 21.6 x 27.9 cm (8½ x 11 in.), signed, dated, and title lower middle. The Ontario Heritage Foundation Firestone Art Collection.*
32. *Manotick Evening*, 1956, pencil drawing on paper, 21.3 x 27.9 cm (8⅜ x 11 in.), signed, dated, and title lower right. The Ontario Heritage Foundation Firestone Art Collection.*
33. *Church at Etaples, Pas de Calais, 1908*, oil on panel, 24.1 x 18.4 cm (9½ x 7¼ in.), signed lower right, signed, dated, and title verso. The Ontario Heritage Foundation Firestone Art Collection.
34. *Church of Jerusalem, Bruges, Belgium*, 1908, oil on panel, 22.2 x 16.5 cm (8¾ x 6½ in.), signed lower right, signed, dated and title verso. The Ontario Heritage Foundation Firestone Art Collection.
35. *Lachine Canal, Montreal*, 1910, oil on panel, 18.4 x 23.5 cm (7¼ x 9¼ in.), signed lower right, signed, dated, and title verso. The Ontario Heritage Foundation Firestone Art Collection.
36. *Figure against the Sky*, 1913, oil on panel, 26.7 x 21.6 cm (10½ x 8½ in.), The McMichael Canadian Collection.
37. *Spring Freshet, Buckingham, Que.*, April 1967, oil on panel, 26.7 x 34.3 cm (10½ x 13½ in.), signed lower left. Mrs. Elizabeth Kirk, Buckingham, Quebec.
38. *Notre Dame de la Salette*, 1968-1971, oil on canvas, 40.6 x 50.8 cm (16 x 20 in.), signed lower left. Mrs. Elizabeth Kirk, Buckingham, Quebec.

39. *Canadian Flag*, ca. 1959, water colour on cardboard, 20.3 x 27.9 cm (8 x 11 in.), signed and dated lower right. The Ontario Heritage Foundation Firestone Art Collection.*

40. *Père Raquette*, 1921, tempera on board, 78.7 x 63.5 cm (31 x 25 in.), signed lower right. The McMichael Canadian Collection.

41. *Frobisher, Baffin Island*, 1965, oil on panel, 26.7 x 34.3 cm (10½ x 13½ in.), signed lower right, dated and title verso. The Ontario Heritage Foundation Firestone Art Collection.

42. *Frobisher*, 1965, pencil drawing on paper, 30.5 x 22.9 cm (12 x 9 in.), signed lower middle, dated and title lower left. The Ontario Heritage Foundation Firestone Art Collection.

43. *Frobisher*, 1965, pencil drawing on paper, 22.9 x 30.5 cm (9 x 12 in.), signed, dated, and title lower right. The Ontario Heritage Foundation Firestone Art Collection.

44. *Baffin Island*, 1965, ink drawing on paper, 22 x 22.9 cm (8⅝ x 11¾ in.), signed and dated lower right, title lower left. The Ontario Heritage Foundation Firestone Art Collection.

45. *The Entrance to Halifax Harbour*, 1919, oil on canvas, 64.8 x 80.7 cm (25½ x 31¾ in.), signed and dated lower right. The Tate Gallery, London, England.

46. *The Red Barn*, 1930, oil on canvas, 64.1 x 81.3 cm (25¼ x 32 in.), signed lower right. Sold by dealer Watson to a private party.

47. *Northland* [title changed to *Terre Sauvage*], 1913, oil on canvas, 127.0 x 152.4 cm (50 x 60 in.), signed and dated lower right. The National Gallery of Canada.

48. *Pangnirtung*, 1930, pencil drawing on paper, 21.5 x 30.3 cm (8½ x 11 15/16 in.), signed lower left, dated and title lower right. The National Gallery of Canada.

49. *Great Bear Lake*, 1938, pencil drawing on paper, 22.5 x 30.3 cm (8⅞ x 11 15/16 in.), signed, dated, and title lower left. The National Gallery of Canada.

50. *Ashcroft, B.C.*, 1945, pencil drawing on paper, 22.7 x 30.3 cm (8 15/16 x 11 15/16 in.), signed, dated, and title lower right. The National Gallery of Canada.

51. *Barns, Sugarbush, Brownsburg, Quebec*, April 1965, oil on panel, 26.7 x 34.3 cm (10½ x 13½ in.), signed lower right. Embassy of the Union of Soviet Socialist Republics, Ottawa.

52. *Lake Rouvière*, 1961, oil on canvas, 81.3 x 101.6 cm (32 x 40 in.), signed and dated lower right, dated and title verso. The Ontario Heritage Foundation Firestone Art Collection.*

53. *Autumn Scene*, 1961, oil on canvas, 63.5 x 81.3 cm (25 x 32 in.), signed lower left. Sold at Sotheby's auction, 8 April 1970.

54. *Bear River Camp, N.W.T.*, September 1950, oil on panel, 26.7 x 34.3 cm (10½ x 13½ in.), signed lower right. Sold at Sotheby's auction, 8 April 1970.

55. *St. Hilarion, Philips Corners*, pencil drawing on paper, 22.2 x 27.6 cm (8¾ x 10⅞ in.), signed lower left, title lower right. Sold at Sotheby's auction, 8 April 1970.

56. *Morning, Baffin Island*, 1928, oil on canvas, 63.5 x 81.3 cm (25 x 32 in.), signed, dated, and title on the stretcher. Sold at Sotheby's auction, 20 October 1975.

57. *Madawaska River in April*, ca. 1945, oil on canvas, 54.8 x 81.9 cm (25½ x 32¼ in.), signed and title verso. Sold at Sotheby's auction, 20 October 1975.

58. *Spring at Calabogie, Ont.*, April 1960, oil on panel, 26.7 x 34.3 cm (10½ x 13½ in.), signed lower right, dated and title verso. Sold at Sotheby's auction, 20 October 1975.
59. *Pincher Station, Alberta*, ca. 1946, oil on panel, 26.7 x 34.3 cm (10½ x 13½ in.), signed lower right, title lower left. Sold at Sotheby's auction, 20 October 1975.
60. *Water's Edge, Duhamel, Que.*, 1968, oil on panel, 26.7 x 34.3 cm (10½ x 13½ in.), signed verso. The Ontario Heritage Foundation Firestone Art Collection.

NOTES

Preface

1. Ballantyne, "A Fascinating Record."
2. Jackson and Hannon, "From Rebel Dauber to Renowned Painter," p. 62; Jackson, *A Painter's Country*, p. 26.
3. Groves, "A Profile of A.Y. Jackson," p. 16.
4. Harris, *Catalogue* [Vancouver exhibition, Group of Seven], p. 10.
5. Jackson and Hannon, "From Rebel Dauber to Renowned Painter," p. 64; Jackson, *A Painter's Country*, p. 31.

Chapter 1

6. Jackson and Hannon, "From Rebel Dauber to Renowned Painter," 27ff.
7. Jackson, "Recollections on my Seventieth Birthday."
8. Jackson, *A Painter's Country*, p. 60.

Chapter 2

9. Duval, *A.J. Casson*, p. 20; Housser, *A Canadian Art Movement*, p. 104.
10. Housser, *A Canadian Art Movement*, p. 53.
11. Jackson, *A Painter's Country*, p. 8.
12. Housser, *A Canadian Art Movement*, p. 56.
13. Jackson, *A Painter's Country*, p. 19.
14. Robson, *A.Y. Jackson*, p. 8.
15. Jackson, *A Painter's Country*, p. 24.
16. Ibid., p. 77.
17. Ibid.
18. Jackson, Notes.

19. "Art Gallery Gets Sketch by Jackson."
20. McDougall, *Anne Savage*, p. 43.
21. Ketchum, "A.Y. Jackson at 84."
22. Jackson, *A Painter's Country*, p. 80.
23. Reid, *The Group of Seven*, p. 198.
24. Housser, *A Canadian Art Movement*.
25. *Canada Year Book, 1927-28*, p. 773.
26. *Canada Year Book, 1926*, p. 720.
27. Jackson, *A Painter's Country*, p. 80.
28. Reid, *The Group of Seven*, p. 134.
29. Robson, *Canadian Landscape Painters*, p. 156.
30. Ibid.
31. "A.Y. Jackson Gives Exhibit of Work."
32. "Sage of Alaskan Highway."
33. Buchanan, "A.Y. Jackson," pp. 284-85.
34. Jackson, "Recollections on my Seventieth Birthday."
35. Foley, "A.Y. Jackson."
36. Haycock, "A Northern Tribute."
37. "Veteran Painter Vigorous at 77."
38. Magner, "A.Y. Jackson."
39. Jackson, *A Painter's Country*, p. xi.

Chapter 3

40. Jackson, *A Painter's Country*, p. 156.
41. McDougall, *Anne Savage*, p. 144.
42. Carrol, "Last of the Seven Says Farewell."

43. Magner, "A.Y. Jackson."
44. Smith, "A Sketch of A.Y. Jackson."
45. McDougall, *Anne Savage*, p. 197.
46. Ketchum, "A.Y. Jackson at 80."

Chapter 4
47. Groves, "A Profile of A.Y. Jackson," p. 18.
48. Haycock, "A Northern Tribute to A.Y. Jackson," pp. 38-41.
49. Moss, "A.Y. Jackson: Portrait of an Artist," p. 4.

Chapter 5
50. Charlesworth, "Canadian Painting for Tate Gallery."

Chapter 6
51. Jackson and Hannon, "From Rebel Dauber to Renowned Painter," p. 61.
52. "Veteran Painter Vigorous at 77."
53. Charlesworth, "Canadian Painting for Tate Gallery."
54. Smith, "A Sketch of A.Y. Jackson."
55. Harris, "The Story of the Group of Seven," p. 11.
56. *A.Y. Jackson, Paintings, 1902-1953.*
57. Addendum to the A.Y. Jackson Exhibition.
58. "A.Y. Jackson — A Retrospective Exhibition."
59. Jackson and Hannon, "From Rebel Dauber to Renowned Painter," p. 58.
60. Jackson and Hannon, "From Rebel Dauber to Renowned Painter," p. 63.

Chapter 8
61. Ketchum, "A.Y. Jackson at 80."
62. Jackson, *A Painter's Country*, p. 148.
63. Ibid., p. 83.
64. Duval, *Four Decades*, p. 39.
65. Jackson, *A Painter's Country*, p. 117.

66. Ibid., p. 149.
67. Ibid., p. 83.
68. Ibid., p. 36.
69. Carr, *Growing Pains*, p. 321.
70. Jackson, *A Painter's Country*, p. 118.
71. Ibid., p. 119.
72. Duval, *Four Decades*, p. 40.
73. Jackson, *A Painter's Country*, p. 117.
74. Ibid., p. 82.
75. Ibid.
76. Duval, *Four Decades*, p. 42.
77. McDougall, *Anne Savage*, p. 43.
78. Ibid., p. 45.
79. Ibid., p. 99.
80. Ibid., pp. 95-96.
81. Ibid., p. 96.
82. Ibid., pp. 111, 116.
83. Ibid., p. 117.
84. Ibid.
85. Ibid., p. 119.
86. Ibid.
87. Ibid., pp. 174-75.
88. Smith, "Unknown Letters."
89. McDougall, *Anne Savage*, p. 208.
90. Ibid., p. 79.
91. Ibid., p. 119.
92. Dobbs, "A.Y. Jackson at 89 — Beautifully Alive," p. 7.

Chapter 9
93. "Group of Seven Artist Has Flag Design."
94. Munro and Inglis, *Mike*, III, p. 273.
95. Walker, "Test Flight for Flag on Parliament Hill."
96. "Say A.Y. Jackson's Flag Pick of Design Committee."
97. "A.Y. Jackson Would Make Bars Horizontal, Wavy."
98. Ibid.
99. Walker, "Test Flight for Flag on Parliament Hill."

Chapter 10
100. Jackson, *A Painter's Country*, p. 30.
101. Groves, "A Profile of A.Y. Jackson," p. 17.
102. Jackson, *A Painter's Country*, p. 63.

103. Jackson and Hannon, "From Rebel Dauber to Renowned Artist," p. 67.
104. Barbeau, *The Kingdom of Saguenay*, pp. 74-76; Barbeau, "Père Raquette."
105. Jackson, *A Painter's Country*, p. 60.
106. Ibid., p. 59.
107. Baird, "A.Y. Jackson, A Portfolio of Arctic Sketches," p. 6.
108. Groves, "A Profile of A.Y. Jackson," p. 19.

Chapter 11
109. Jackson, *A Painter's Country*, p. 67.

Chapter 12
110. Art Museum of Toronto, *Catalogue*, 1920.
111. Ibid.
112. Reid, *Group of Seven*, p. 203.
113. Canada, *British Empire Exhibition*, Canadian Section of Fine Arts.
114. Reid, *Group of Seven*, p. 166.
115. Canada, *British Empire Exhibition*, Canadian Section of Fine Arts.
116. "Empire Art at Wembley."
117. Hind, "Life and I."
118. "New School of Landscape Painting."
119. "Canadian Landscape Painters at Wembley."
120. Jackson, *A Painter's Country*, pp. 77-78.
121. "The 'Seven' and the 'Star,'" pp. 358-59.
122. Canada, *British Empire Exhibition*, Canadian Section of Fine Arts.
123. "Art at Wembley: Fine British and Imperial Exhibition."
124. Konody, "The Palace of Arts at Wembley."
125. "Remarkable Exhibition of Canadian Productions."
126. Greenaway, "Jackson Says Montreal Most Bigoted City."
127. "Who Bit Mr. Jackson?"
128. Art Gallery of Toronto, *Catalogue*, 1930, p. 3.
129. Hubbard, *Catalogue of Paintings and Sculpture*, III, p. 128.
130. Reid, *Edwin Holgate*, p. 10.
131. Art Gallery of Toronto, *Catalogue*, 1930, pp. 3-10.
132. Ibid., p. 3.
133. Powell, "The School of Seven."
134. "Group of Seven Showing Works."
135. Myers, "In the Domain of Art."
136. Ibid.
137. Jackson, *A Painter's Country*, p. 44.
138. Ibid., p. xiii.
139. Ibid., p. 51.
140. Art Museum of Toronto, *Catalogue*, 1920, foreword.
141. Quoted in Jackson, *A Painter's Country*, p. 53.
142. Huxley, *Essays of a Humanist*, p. 98.

Chapter 13
143. Magner, "A.Y. Jackson."
144. McDougall, *Anne Savage*, p. 42.
145. Duval, *A.J. Casson*, p. 24.
146. Ibid.
147. Ibid., p. 37.
148. Jackson, *A Painter's Country*, p. 114.
149. Duval, *A.J. Casson*, p. 151.
150. Jackson, *A Painter's Country*, pp. 135-36.
151. Harper, *Painting in Canada*, p. 336.
152. Jackson, *A Painter's Country*, p. 137.
153. Ibid., p. 131.
154. Ibid., p. 117.
155. Ibid., p. 88.
156. Jackson, "Arthur Lismer," pp. 16-17.
157. Jackson, *A Painter's Country*, p. 144.
158. Harper, *Painting in Canada*, p. 336.
159. Irving, "What Canada Lost in A.Y. Jackson."
160. "Veteran Painter Vigorous at 77."
161. Jackson, *A Painter's Country*, p. 115.
162. Jackson and Hannon, "From

Rebel Dauber to Renowned Painter," p. 67.
163. Foley, "A.Y. Jackson: He's Too Busy to Feel Old."
164. Ketchum, "A.Y. Jackson at 80."
165. Maggs, "Project Mural Leaves A.Y. Jackson Puzzled."
166. Town and Silcox, *Tom Thomson.*
167. Foley, "A.Y. Jackson: He's Too Busy to Feel Old."
168. McDougall, *Anne Savage*, p. 198.
169. Town, "Tom Thomson, the Pathfinder," p. 110.
170. Harris, "Modern Art and Aesthetic Reactions," pp. 240-41.
171. Irving, "What Canada Lost in A.Y. Jackson."

Chapter 14
172. Hubbard, *Catalogue of Paintings and Sculpture*, III, *Canadian School.*
173. National Gallery of Canada, *Annual Report*, 1963-64, p. 24.
174. Ketchum, "A.Y. Jackson at 84."
175. Royal Commission on National Development in the Arts, Letters and Sciences, *Report*, p. 80.
176. Ibid., p. 314.
177. Ibid., pp. 314-18.
178. Cross, "Canada Had Its Chance to Buy Good Paintings."
179. House of Commons, *Debates*, May 4, 1966, p. 4682.
180. House of Commons, *Debates*, May 16, 1966, p. 5168.
181. House of Commons, *Debates*, May 4, 1966, p. 4681.
182. Jackson, *A Painter's Country*, p. 81.
183. Ibid., p. 27.
184. Ibid., p. 81.
185. Ibid., p. 139.
186. House of Commons, *Debates*, May 4. 1966, p. 4681.
187. Ketchum, "A.Y. Jackson at 84."
188. "LaMarsh Idea: Wants $6 Million Painting."

189. House of Commons, *Debates*, May 31, 1966, p. 5782.
190. Ibid.
191. Ibid.
192. Hubbard and Ostiguy, *Catalogue.*

Chapter 15
193. Jackson, *A Painter's Country*, p. 157.
194. Ibid., p. 115.
195. Ibid.
196. "Candid Critic Talks of Art."
197. McDougall, *Anne Savage*, p. 87.
198. Ibid., p. 206.
199. Brown, "The Story of a Fight for a Heritage."
200. Jackson, *A Painter's Country*, p. 32.
201. Lismer, "A.Y. Jackson," pp. 7-8.
202. Jackson and Hannon, "From Rebel Dauber to Renowned Painter," p. 67.
203. Ibid.
204. "New Goals for Canadian Art Urged by Dr. Arthur Lismer."

Chapter 17
205. Foley, "A.Y. Jackson: He's Too Busy to Feel Old."
206. Haycock, "A Northern Tribute."
207. "Veteran Painter Vigorous at 77."
208. Foley, "A.Y. Jackson: He's Too Busy to Feel Old."
209. "Famed Artist Donates Works."
210. "A.Y. Jackson Recalls."
211. "Appreciation of Art 'Improved' in Canada."
212. *A Catalogue of Selected Canadian Paintings*, pp. 39, 41; see also Appendix.
213. Ibid., p. 43.
214. *A Catalogue of Important Canadian Paintings*, p. 37.
215. Ibid., p. 17.
216. Ibid., p. 68.
217. Ibid., p. 12.

218. Jackson and Hannon, "From Rebel Dauber to Renowned Painter," p. 62.
219. Jackson, *A Painter's Country*, p. 3.
220. Moss, "A.Y. Jackson: Portrait of an Artist."

Chapter 18
221. Allen, "Introduction," p. 5.
222. *André Biéler: 50 Years*, item 66.
223. Ibid., items 38 and 44.
224. Ibid., items 16 and 33.
225. Ibid., items 2, 6, 8, 20, 21, 31, and 66.
226. Jackson, *A Painter's Country*, p. 3.
227. Jackson and Hannon, "From Rebel Dauber to Renowned Painter," p. 61.
228. Lismer, letter to Eric Brown, 21 March, 1920, National Gallery of Canada.

Chapter 19
229. Smith, "A Sketch of A.Y. Jackson."
230. McDougall, *Anne Savage*, p. 98.

231. Jackson and Hannon, "From Rebel Dauber to Renowned Painter," p. 58.
232. Jackson and Groves, *A.Y.'s Canada*, p. i.
233. McDougall, *Anne Savage*, p. 84.
234. Ibid., p. 206.
235. Ibid., p. 79.
236. Jackson, *A Painter's Country*, p. 59.
237. McDougall, *Anne Savage*, p. 92.
238. Jackson, *A Painter's Country*, p. 161.
239. Ibid., p. 162.
240. Fulford, "A.Y. Jackson: A Heroic Age Ends."
241. McDougall, *Anne Savage*, p. 119.
242. Ibid., p. 92.

Chapter 21
243. Foley, "A.Y. Jackson: He's Too Busy to Feel Old."
244. Duval, Introduction, *Canadian Art: Vital Decades*.
245. *Group of Seven, Kanadische Landschaft-Maler*, p. 24.

BIBLIOGRAPHY

"A.Y. Jackson — A Retrospective Exhibition." *Canadian Art* 11 (1953): 4-5.

"A.Y. Jackson Gives Exhibit of Work." *Mail and Empire* (Toronto) 27 Feb. 1934.

"A.Y. Jackson Recalls Wandering at Unveiling of Paintings Here." *Kingston Whig-Standard* 3 Dec. 1964.

"A.Y. Jackson Would Make Bars Horizontal, Wavy." *Ottawa Journal* 26 June 1964.

"Addendum to the A.Y. Jackson Exhibition, Winnipeg, March 14 – April 4, 1954." In Art Gallery of Toronto, *A.Y. Jackson Paintings, 1902-1953.* N.p., n.d. [March, 1954].

Agnes Etherington Art Centre. *André Biéler, 50 Years: A Retrospective Exhibition, 1920-1950* [catalogue]. Kingston: 1970.

Allen, Ralph. "Introduction." In Agnes Etherington Art Centre, *André Biéler, 50 Years: A Retrospective Exhibition, 1920-1950.* Kingston: 1970.

"Appreciation of Art 'Improved' in Canada." *Ottawa Citizen* 3 Dec. 1958.

"Art at Wembley: Fine British and Imperial Exhibition." *Nottingham Guardian* 9 May 1925.

"Art Gallery Gets Sketch by Jackson." *Kitchener-Waterloo Record* 11 Feb. 1959.

Art Gallery of Toronto. *A.Y. Jackson Paintings, 1902-1953* [catalogue of a joint National Gallery of Canada-Art Gallery of Toronto exhibition]. N.P., n.d. [October, 1953].

——, *Catalogue of an exhibition of the Group of Seven, Canadian Society of Painters in Water Colour, Society of Canadian Painter-Etchers [and] the Toronto Camera Club April, nineteen hundred and thirty [at] the Art Gallery of Toronto.* [Toronto: 1930.]

Art Museum of Toronto. *Catalogue* [of an exhibition at the Art Museum of Toronto, May, 1920]. [Toronto: 1920.]

Ballantyne, Michael. "A Fascinating Record, A.Y. Jackson's Canada." *Montreal Star* 23 Nov. 1968.

Barbeau, Charles Marius. *The Kingdom of Saguenay.* Illus. by A.Y. Jackson, George Pepper, Kathleen Daly, and others. Toronto: Macmillan, 1936.

——, *Painters of Quebec.* Toronto: Ryerson, 1946.

——, "Père Raquette." *La Presse* 27 April 1935.

Beston, Henry. *The St. Lawrence.* Illus. by A.Y. Jackson. [Rivers of America Series.] New York and Toronto: Farrar and Rinehart, 1942.

Brown, Florence Maud. "The Story of a Fight for a Heritage." *Ottawa Journal* 19 June 1970.

Buchanan, Donald W. *The Growth of Canadian Painting.* Toronto: Collins, 1950.

——, "A.Y. Jackson, the Development of Nationalism in Canadian Painting." *Canadian Geographical Journal* 32 (1946): 284-85.

Canada, Bureau of Statistics. *Canada Year Book*, 1926. Ottawa: 1927.

———, *Canada Year Book*, 1927-28. Ottawa: 1928.

Canada, Canadian Government Exhibition Commission. *The British Empire Exhibition, Wembley Park, London, England, April to October, 1924*. Canadian Section of Fine Arts. Ottawa 1924.

Canada, House of Commons. *Parliamentary Debates*, 1964, 1966.

Canada, Senate. *Parliamentary Debates*, 1964.

"Canadian Landscape Painters at Wembley." *International Interpreter* (New York) 24 May 1924.

"Candid Critic Talks of Art; Percy M. Turner Has Made Survey of Canadian Field, Praises Group of Seven." *Globe* (Toronto) 9 Nov. 1922.

"Capsule History of the Flag Debate." *Ottawa Citizen* 14 Dec. 1964.

Carr, Emily. *Growing Pains*. Toronto: Oxford University Press, 1946.

Carrol, Jock. "Last of the Seven Says Farewell." *Weekend Magazine*, 3 June 1955 8ff.

Charlesworth, Hector. "Canadian Painting for Tate Gallery." *Saturday Night* 1 Nov. 1924.

Colgate, William. *Canadian Art, Its Origin and Development*. Toronto: Ryerson, 1943.

Cross, Austin F. "Canada Had Its Chance to Buy Good Paintings." *Ottawa Citizen* 20 Feb. 1959.

Dobbs, Kildare. "A.Y. Jackson at 89 — Beautifully Alive." *Star Week* for Oct. 16 to 23, 1971: 2ff.

Duval, Paul. *A.J. Casson*. Toronto: Roberts Gallery, 1975.

———, *Four Decades: The Canadian Group of Painters and Their Contemporaries, 1930-1970*. Toronto: Clarke, Irwin, 1972.

———, "Introduction." In *Canadian Art, Vital Decades: The McMichael Conservation Collection*. Toronto: Clarke, Irwin, 1970.

"Empire Art at Wembley, Dominion Contrasts." *The Times* 28 May 1924.

"Famed Artist Donates Works to Gallery." *Victoria Times* 19 Dec. 1962.

Foley, Dennis. "A.Y. Jackson: He's Too Busy to Feel Old." *Ottawa Citizen* 19 Feb. 1966.

Fulford, Robert. "A.Y. Jackson: A Heroic Age Ends." *Toronto Star* 6 April 1974.

Greenaway, C.R. "Jackson Says Montreal Most Bigoted City." *Toronto Star* 10 Sept. 1927.

"Group of Seven Artist Has Flag Design." *Ottawa Citizen* 26 June 1964.

Group of Seven, Kanadische Landschafts-Maler [catalogue of travelling exhibition of McMichael Canadian Collection, Munich, Hamburg, Berlin]. 1977.

"Group of Seven Showing Works; Oils, Watercolours and Drawings Occupy Two Rooms at Art Gallery." *Gazette* (Montreal) 9 May 1930.

Groves, Dr. Naomi Jackson. "A Profile of A.Y. Jackson." *Beaver* 297 (1967): 15-19.

———, *A.Y.'s Canada*. Pencil drawings by A.Y. Jackson. Toronto: Clarke, Irwin, 1968.

Harper, John Russell. *Painting in Canada, A History*. Toronto: University of Toronto Press, 1966.

Harris, Lawren. "Modern Art and Aesthetic Reactions." *Canadian Forum* May 1927: 240-41.

——, "The Story of the Group of Seven." In Vancouver Museum and Art Gallery, *Group of Seven* [catalogue]. Vancouver, 1954.

Haycock, Maurice. "A Northern Tribute to A.Y. Jackson." *North* 17 (1970): 38-41.

Hind, C. Lewis. "Life and I." *Daily Chronicle* (London) 30 April 1924.

Housser, Frederick B. *A Canadian Art Movement: The Story of the Group of Seven*. Toronto: Macmillan, 1926.

Hubbard, R.H., ed. *Catalogue of Paintings and Sculpture*, vol. 3, *Canadian School*. Toronto: University of Toronto Press for the Trustees, National Gallery of Canada, 1960.

—— and Ostiguy, J.R. *Three Hundred Years of Canadian Art. Trois cents ans d'art canadien. An Exhibition Arranged in Celebration of the Centenary of Confederation*. Ottawa: National Gallery of Canada, 1967.

Huxley, Julian. *Essays of a Humanist*. Harmondsworth, England: Penguin Books, 1964.

Irving, Kit. "What Canada Lost in A.Y. Jackson." *Ottawa Journal* 6 April 1974.

Jackson, A.Y. Notes prepared in response to an inquiry by Marius Barbeau, Toronto, June 1933 [manuscript]. Ottawa, National Gallery of Canada.

——, *A Painter's Country: The Autobiography of A.Y. Jackson* [foreword by Rt. Hon. Vincent Massey]. Toronto: Clarke, Irwin, 1958.

——, "A Portfolio of Arctic Sketches." *Beaver* 297 (1967): 7-14.

——, "Arthur Lismer." *Educational Record of the Province of Quebec* 81 (1955): 16-17.

——, *Banting As an Artist*. Toronto: Ryerson, 1943.

——, *The Far North. A book of drawings by A.Y. Jackson, with an introduction by Dr. F.G. Banting and descriptive notes by the artist*. Toronto: Rous and Mann, 1927.

——, "Recollections on my Seventieth Birthday." *Canadian Art* 10 (1953): 94-99.

—— and Hannon, Leslie F. "From Rebel Dauber to Renowned Painter: A Self-Portrait of A.Y. Jackson." *Mayfair* Sept. 1954: pp. 27-29, 58, 61-64, 67.

Ketchum, W.Q. "A.Y. Jackson at 80: 'The World's a Bloody Awful Mess but with Still a Glimmer of Hope.'" *Ottawa Journal* 29 Sept. 1962.

——, "A.Y. Jackson at 84: War Wounds a 'Lucky Break.'" *Ottawa Journal* 1 Oct. 1966.

Konody, P.G. "The Palace of Arts at Wembly." *Observer* (London) 24 May 1925.

"LaMarsh Idea: Wants $6 Million Painting." *Globe and Mail* (Toronto) 16 May 1966.

Lismer, Arthur. "A.Y. Jackson." In Art Gallery of Toronto, *A.Y. Jackson: Paintings, 1902-1953* [catalogue]. [Toronto: 1953.]

Maggs, Heather. "Project Mural Leaves A.Y. Jackson Puzzled." *Cornwall Standard-Free Holder* 21 Nov. 1958.

Magner, Brian. "A.Y. Jackson." *Globe Magazine* 27 Aug. and 3 Sept. 1960.

McDougall, Anne. *Anne Savage: The Story of a Canadian Painter*. Montreal: Harvest House, 1977.

McInnes, Graham. *Canadian Art*. Toronto: Macmillan, 1950.

Moss, Bruce. "A.Y. Jackson: Portrait of an Artist" [photostory]. *Weekend Magazine* no. 18 (1966): 2-5.

Munro, John A., and Inglis, Alexis I. *Mike, the Memoirs of the Right Honourable Lester B. Pearson*, vol. 3, 1957-68. Toronto University of Toronto Press, 1975.

Myers, Reta W. "In the Domain of Art." *Vancouver Sun* 25 Oct. 1930.

National Gallery of Canada. *Annual Report, 1963-64*. Ottawa, 1964.

"New Goals for Canadian Art Urged by Dr. Arthur Lismer." *Ottawa Citizen* 18 May 1950.

"New School of Landscape Painting." *Morning Post* (London) 28 May 1924.

Powell, S. Morgan. "The School of Seven." *Montreal Star* 7 May 1930.

Press Comments on the Canadian Section of Fine Arts, British Empire Exhibition, 1924 [pamphlet]. Ottawa: National Gallery of Canada, 1924.

Press Comments on the Canadian Section of Fine Arts, British Empire Exhibition, 1924-25 [pamphlet]. Ottawa: National Gallery of Canada, 1925.

Radford, J.A. "Artists' Sketches." *Vancouver Sun* 10 Dec. 1932.

Reid, Dennis. *Edwin Holgate* [Canadian Artists Series, no. 4]. Ottawa: National Gallery of Canada, 1976.

————, *The Group of Seven. Catalogue Prepared for an Exhibition to be Held at the National Gallery of Canada, Ottawa, June 19 – September 8, 1970*. Ottawa: National Gallery of Canada, 1970.

————, *The MacCallum Bequest of paintings by Tom Thomson and other Canadian painters and the Mr. and Mrs. H.R. Jackman Gift of the murals from the late Dr. MacCallum's cottage painted by some of the members of the Group of Seven*. Ottawa: National Gallery of Canada, 1969.

"Remarkable Exhibition of Canadian Productions." *Yorkshire Herald* 26 Jan. 1926.

Robson, A.H. *A.Y. Jackson*. Toronto: Ryerson, 1938.

————, *Canadian Landscape Painters*. Toronto: Ryerson, 1932.

Royal Commission on National Development in the Arts, Letters and Sciences [the Massey Commission]. *Report*. Ottawa: King's Printer, 1951.

"Saga of Alaskan Highway Told in Jackson Paintings." *Toronto Telegram* 20 May 1944.

"Say A.Y. Jackson's Flag Pick of Design Committee." *Ottawa Journal* 20 Oct. 1964.

"The 'Seven' and the 'Star.' " *Canadian Forum* 4 (1924): pp. 358-59.

Smith, I Norman. "A Sketch of A.Y. Jackson." *Ottawa Journal* 23 Nov. 1959.

Smith, I. Norman. "Unknown Letters . . . Revealing the Artists' Empathy. . . . Correspondence of A.Y. and Anne." *Ottawa Journal* 14 Jan. 1978.

Sotheby & Co. *A Catalogue of Important Canadian Paintings, Drawings, Watercolours, Prints and Books of the 19th and 20th Centuries*. Toronto: Sotheby & Co. (Canada), October 20 and 21, 1975.

 A Catalogue of Selected Canadian Paintings, Drawings, Watercolours, Prints and Sculptures of the 19th and 20th Centuries. Toronto: Sotheby & Co. (Canada), April 8, 1970.

Town, Harold. "Tom Thomson, the Pathfinder." In *Great Canadians: A Century of Achievement, selected by the Rt. Hon. Vincent Massey, George Ferguson, Maurice Lebel, W. Kaye Lamb, Hilda Neatby*. Illustrated by Franklin Arbuckle. Introduction by Pierre Berton, editor-in-chief. Toronto: Canadian Centennial Publ. Co., 1965, pp. 107-110.

——— and Silcox, David P. *Tom Thomson: The Silence and the Storm*. Toronto: McClelland and Stewart, 1977.

"Veteran Painter Vigorous at 77." *Quebec Chronicle-Telegraph* 24 Nov. 1959.

Walker, J.R. "Test Flight for Flag on Parliament Hill." *Winnipeg Tribune* 5 June 1964.

"Who Bit Mr. Jackson?" *Montreal Standard* 24 Sept. 1927.

ACKNOWLEDGEMENTS

We are grateful for the co-operation of the following individuals in allowing the reproduction of copyrighted materials.

P.37 Courtesy Lawren P. Harris. Reproduction by John Evans Photography Limited, 519 Sussex Drive, Ottawa

P.39 National Film Board, No. 89173

P. 43 Courtesy Mrs. Betty Kirk

P. 66 Courtesy Mrs. Betty Kirk

P. 96 Courtesy Mrs. E. M. Leslie

P. 106 Courtesy Mrs. Betty Kirk

P. 127 Courtesy Henri Masson

P. 151 Courtesy Mr. Jack Nutter

P. 176 Reproduction by John Evans Photography

P. 181 Courtesy Mrs. Marjory Lismer Bridges

P. 187 Courtesy Mrs. Marjory Lismer Bridges

The works of A. Y. Jackson and quotations from his letters to Anne Savage (taken from Ann McDougall, *Anne Savage: The Story of a Canadian Painter*) courtesy Dr. Naomi Jackson Groves

and, of course,

The Ontario Heritage Foundation, owners of the Firestone Art Collection, who allowed complete access to the Collection while the book was in preparation.